I'M PEI

All Original Conten

All Rights Reserved. No part of this book may be used or reproduced in any manner whatsoever without appropriate written permission, except where permitted by law.

This book is a remembrance of law enforcement in Collier County in the 60's, 70's, or thereabouts. It's a collection of cop war stories, history, and outrageous events and is true and accurate to the best of the author's recollection and/or what research allows. Although the incidents depicted in these tales are true, some of the people's names have been changed to protect the easily embarrassed. Or the true names have been lost to history. In some cases composite characters were used.

Except for cops. Most of their names are genuine, except where noted as otherwise.

Cover Illustration by the author, G.D.Young

I'M PEDDLIN' AS FAST AS I CAN

THANK YOU

No one writes a book on their own. The contributions by others are many. I wish to thank the following folks for their efforts in this project.

First, my wife Sandy, who acted as my proofreader, editor, and memory in many cases.
Then, our children
Wayde, Lori, Sean and Kenny,
who encouraged me to write down the yarns I would tell them.
And, for the appreciable contributions of Dave Dampier, Chief Ben Caruthers, Mike Grimm, Chester Keene, Dave Johnson, Gail Addison, Mike Gideon, Tom Smith & Bill Gonsalves.
And any others that I may have overlooked.
Thanks again.

POLICING THE ELEPHANT'S GRAVEYARD

I'M PEDDLIN' AS FAST AS I CAN

or
Never Love a Pachyderm
They're So Hard to Kiss GoodBye

By

G.D. YOUNG
Former Chief
Naples Police Department

I'M PEDDLIN' AS FAST AS I CAN

To my brothers and sisters
The Cops
*Whose stories aren't always
so much fun*

1st PRECINCT

I'M PEDDLIN' AS FAST AS I CAN

Once, in the 70's when I was Chief of the NPD, I was attending a budget hearing. The subject was cutting costs. One councilman, who we'll call Erhard Gerbil, noted for his nasty disposition and hair-brain ideas, suggested we cut costs by converting cars to bicycles. This was greeted by muffled snickers in the august chambers. But he persisted, saying he'd read this had been done in some cities.

I explained that those were *big* cities, and the bicycle patrols supplemented radio car patrols in very dense population areas. In no case were they used in the suburbs.

But Erhard plowed on, grumbling, I just can't see why we can't try it here.

Exasperated, I said, "Well, let's suppose we receive a call from your terrified wife who is home alone and says a rapist has broken into your home.

Do you want us to say: "*Just hold on, I'm peddling as fast as I can.*"

Four "Wheel-gunners" at the Range

Ken Kitchell, Ed Hellenek, Chief Ben Caruthers, Bob Alexander

Photo from early '60 at a training session with revolvers. Semi-automatics were not in use, as the *wheel guns*--named because of the cylinder--were considered safer. These cops were all experts, unlike the next group.

GOOFY GUNSLINGERS

Most gun owners are responsible people. Except for a few buffoons you run into that remind you of an old joke. A gun nut, dressed in full cowboy attire--fur chaps, fringe shirt, ten-gallon hat, two .45's, boots and spurs--jangles up to the Dairy Queen window. " I want a sundae," he says. The waitress asks, "Want your nuts crushed?" Whereby our hero draws his .45's, points them at the waitress and growls: "You want your az shot off?"

Such a clown came to our Range, at the City Dump beside the Airport, on one of the days we allowed civilians to shoot. Done up like Sunset Carson, and packing a S&W .44

I'M PEDDLIN' AS FAST AS I CAN

Magnum, he had his lady in tow. When he got to the firing line, he pointed for the girl to stand to the rear and, with a flourish worthy of Roy Rogers, pulled his six-gun. You must keep in mind this weapon, at the time, was called by none other than Dirty Harry, Clint Eastwood, *the world's most powerful handgun*. And Mr. Eastwood does not exaggerate.

When we noticed the goofy gunslinger had no ear protection and was holding the cannon straight out with a single-hand grip, we knew we were in for a show.

After posing a while, he pulled the trigger, the air split with thunder, and the recoil slammed the pistol backwards, hitting him right between the eyes. Sleepy time for Sunset. The barrel split his forehead open, causing it to gush blood. Fortunately, with this doofus, there was no danger of any brains leaking out. When he returned to the world of the reasonably sane, realizing what an ass he'd made of himself, he wrapped his head in a bandanna and headed for the ranch. We had to remind him that he'd left his magnum and lady, with a wry smile on her face, at the firing line.

GOOFY GUNSLINGERS, TOO

When I was involved with the hiring for local law enforcement agencies, the ratio was about 1 out of 100. That's one applicant selected out of one-hundred applicants. Most cops are some of the brightest folks in the work force. The 10% rule, however, does apply. That being said, no matter how diligently you test, screen, or investigate applicants in the hiring process, when they are hired 10% will prove to be idiots. And, 10% will be superior. The old bell curve thing. An officer who we'll call Herbert Brawley was in the bottom ten.

Herbert was wacky about firearms. His duty weapon was a Colt Python, the most expensive revolver Colt made. Most cops couldn't afford one. A beautifully crafted weapon, its precision craftsmanship made it a high failure weapon on the range. We all practiced and qualified with reloaded ammunition. Reloads sometimes don't have the primer fully seated, causing the cylinder to lock in a precision made gun. The Python suffered from this problem.

I'M PEDDLIN' AS FAST AS I CAN

It was beautiful and Herbert liked to show his off. A cop is never supposed to unholster their gun unless they may have to use it. Herbert had trouble with this concept, liking to take it out and fondle it or show it to the public. Repeatedly warned about this, he continued to do it until other cops derisively mocked his Southern drawl and frequent comment: *Do you wanna to see my Piiiithon?*

Herbert became an ex-member of the NPD on the sad day he whipped it out, in the old *W.T. Grants* store in the Naples Shopping Center, to show to a customer. He accidentally discharged a round into the terrazzo floor, sending chips flying. Two customers received minor cuts and Herbert got a map back to Arkansas.

The Sheriff once had a Deputy from Immokalee, that we'll call Big 'Un, who was a crack shot on the street, but couldn't qualify on the range. His worst problem was at the 60 yard line. There, you were required to drop to your knees, draw your weapon, fall forward on your elbows and fire from the prone position. His ample belly may have been the problem. Whatever it was, he just couldn't do it and most cops didn't want to be anywhere near him when he tried.

Everyone had a blanket laid out at their feet to keep them out of the dirt. Big 'Un regularly dropped to his knees, drew his weapon, and shot a hole in his blanket. Once, the hot slug even set the blanket on fire. God only knows what would've happened if we'd had semi-automatics back then.

HARD TO KILL

When most of us are stabbed, or shot several times, we're in serious trouble. Some folks come to mind for which these rules didn't apply.

Cops at the NPD were stunned when in walked a customer wanting an arrest made. He said he'd been drinking in *Rabbit's* and someone started *signifyin'* on him.

This was a sure preamble to trouble. *Rabbit's* was a juke in the infamous McDonald Quarters, a ghetto where most of Naples black folks lived then. It was a bloody bucket, a knife and gun club. The term signifyin' meant bad mouthing. He went on.

I'M PEDDLIN' AS FAST AS I CAN

The signifyin' led to shoving and then our complainant, being a peaceful man, turned to leave. That's when he was hit in the back. And it hurt, too. Hurt so bad he went to his car to go home, but it was so painful to lean back in the seat, he'd walked to the PD.

It was probably a mile or so from The Quarters, which was in the River Park area, to the old PD on 8th and 8th South. This man must be serious.

He then began to try to reach around to his back, twisting and turning. Damn back itches, he complained. When he turned around, you could see why. Between his shoulder blades, next to his spine was a knife. A knife buried up to the hilt. It was a Texas Toothpick, a single-blade folder with a 5" blade. He was quickly eased into a chair and told not to move. And not to lean back.

EMS responded and he was whisked off to the hospital. After x-rays, the knife was carefully removed. With stabbing wounds, where the blade is still embedded, you should always let trained medical personnel remove the blade. Frequently, more damage is caused taking the knife out than the initial stab made.

Incredibly, except for the skin puncture, there was no damage. Doctors said the blade came within millimeters of his heart. Essentially it hit a hole in his carcass. That same night, he walked out of the hospital with nothing more than a small patch on his back.

The Angels of Mercy must've been working overtime that night.

HARD TO KILL Part 2

We responded to a shooting in McDonald Quarters. The victim, who we'll call Dew Drop Rhodes, had been shot with a .38 caliber pistol. He'd been taken to the hospital, before we arrived, by friends.

At the hospital, emergency workers said it looked like Dew Drop had been hit five times in the torso. Four slugs were still in him, one having worked its way out while he lay on the gurney.

A detective returned to The Quarters, to work the case. An arrest was made, statements taken, crime scene work done.

I'M PEDDLIN' AS FAST AS I CAN

We'd been there about two hours, when up walks Dew Drop. Said did we need anything? If not, he was tired and wanted to go to bed. We were stunned. This is a man who just a few hours before had been shot five times. Dew Drop said the hospital wanted to keep him overnight, but he'd raised so much hell, they'd let him go home.

"I'm okay," he said, taking off his shirt to show us, just a few bandages.

And it was so. He had a few patches here and there, but that was all. I'd seen more damage after a kindergarten rumble.

The ER doc said Dew Drop's wounds had barely penetrated his skin, evidenced by the one that fell out on the gurney on its own. Explanation? Who knows. Might've been old ammo. Defective ammo. It was the same stuff cops were all using: .38 Special, 158 grain, round-nose lead slug. We hated it. At it's best, this stuff wouldn't stop a peed-off gerbil.

This was all the evidence I needed that we were underpowered. Although it was strictly against regulations, I upgraded to a custom, hotter load shortly thereafter. Gradually, everyone else did, too. As the old cop saying goes: *Better to be judged by twelve than carried by six.*

SKEETERVILLE

An old joke is that when the Army had a base at the Naples Airport in WWII something landed on the runway and a mechanic put 30 gallons in it before he realized it was a swamp mosquito. When the swamps were up close and personal, this story could've been true. Almost.

Except for Everglades City and in other remote areas, mosquitoes today are a mere inconvenience. In the days before the swamps were drained they were intolerable.

To try and fight them, spray planes and the bug trucks were used. A bug truck was a pickup fitted with a device that mixed diesel fuel and bug spray together, converted it to smoke, and blew it out the back. Find a bug truck and you'd see a mob of kids running in the cloud of toxins behind the sprayer. Strangely, I can't recall anyone getting sick from this insanity.

I'M PEDDLIN' AS FAST AS I CAN

Mike Gideon, a longtime friend and retired CCSO Deputy, recalled that, as a child living in Everglades City, he had to suit up to go out to play. The gear included a long sleeve shirt, long trousers, hat, and a bandanna worn bandit style over the mouth. Properly attired, he could bear the onslaught of the vicious swamp skeeters. Not much fun in the oppressive sub-tropical heat.

Marco Island was infected with, not only skeeters, but sand gnats, or no-see-ems--billions of them. They flew in any open mouth, nested in your ears, and gnawed on your body. Called No-see-ems, they were hard to find. . . until they bit you.

Working as a cop wasn't a lotta fun. The cars had no AC, so you patrolled with the windows down. Once you got out of the car it was worse. I recall making traffic stops and wiping the skeeters off my arms, leaving them covered in blood from the squashed critters. Many a ticket was abandoned and the driver told to move on because you just couldn't take it any longer.

There was some law enforcement benefit. Escaped prisoners were regularly found by the roadway after a short spell in the swamps. They begged to go back to jail--or, on occasion, the hospital for a transfusion.

Another buddy, and retired NPD cop Dave Dampier, reminds me that nobody begged to go back to the Paw Paw Patch. The Paw Paw Patch was the original city jail. It was located between The Cove and the Old Naples Hotel. With no glass in the windows, prisoners could be heard slapping and cursing the little vampires all night long, yelling, "Cale, let me out of here. These damn skeeters are killin' me."

(Cale Jones was Chief at the time)

BED, BREAKFAST, AND BARS

Was a time you didn't have to be arrested to get in jail. Had a friend, a reputable businessman, who was an alcoholic. He was a good member of AA and would go for months, maybe a year or two, without backsliding. But, when the urges got too strong, and he feared he was going to cave in, he'd go to Immokalee and check himself into the jail. Might stay there two weeks or more. Eventually, he'd check himself out and go back to his business until the next bout with his devils.

Back then, that happened. Wasn't even considered that unusual. There were several rounders who used to lock themselves up to stay out of trouble. If no guard was in attendance, they'd get the keys, lock themselves in, and toss the keys over on the desk. And you thought *The Andy Griffith Show* was over the top! (Wait'll I tell you about some of the Barney Fifes we had)

At the City, we had a very high ranking politician who would get drunk and rowdy. And when he did, he was a load. We'd lock him up until he sobered up, all the while listening to his threats of firing us when he got out. And, he could've. But he didn't. He'd thank us in the morning.

Never happen today. And, there's a real good reason why some of the humane things we used to let happen were curtailed. Like the friendly jail policy. It went on for years. Until, in one of the jails, a drunk locked himself in a cell with a woman and raped her.

NINE ONE WHAT?

First off, did you know that 9-1-1 was initially advertised widely as nine eleven? *Call nine eleven for all your emergencies.* You might remember that and wonder why they changed it to nine one one. You're not going to believe the answer. Had to change it because too many people complained that there wasn't an eleven on their telephone. If I'm lyin', I'm dyin'.

Before even that happened, in the fifties, Naples and Collier County had their own systems. Naples lone indoor theater, on Third Street South, was owned and operated by Mr. Arnold Haines. He also owned the popular sundries shop, *The Beach Store*, next door. And, Arnold was a City Councilman, the one selected to be Police Commissioner. That required Arnold to keep track of the cops.

So, a plan was put in place that when things got slow, the cop on duty would go into the movie theater, grab some popcorn, and enjoy the latest black and white Bogart epic. If

I'M PEDDLIN' AS FAST AS I CAN

trouble reared it's infrequent head, just call ol' Arnold and he'd send the usher to get the cop.

Collier County had even a stranger system. In Immokalee there was a light on a pole near the Sheriff's Office. Course the Sheriff's Substation was closed after dark. It was only occupied when the lone deputy assigned duty there would drop by to use the restroom or maybe even put someone in jail.

If you needed a deputy, you'd flick on the light on the pole. When the deputy, in the course of his rounds, saw the light flashing he'd know someone needed his services and start looking. The customer usually waited nearby.

Not as sophisticated as today's electronic communications but, at the time, a grand way of doing business.

THE POOL CAGE CAPER

Responding to a construction accident call in Coquina Sands, I found a backyard pool cage collapsed and three workers checking themselves for damage. All were wet, having landed in the pool. Asked if anyone was injured. The consensus was they were okay. Called the PD and advised that no ambulance was need, then asked who was in charge.

A hefty middle-aged guy stepped forward and said he was senior on the job. Said his name was Lamar. Asked him what'd happened.

Lamar cleared his throat, scratched, blinked, and generally looked like that Governor that got caught with the hooker.

I told him I wasn't leaving until I got a story so he might as well cough it up. He thought about that a bit, shrugged, then said this:

"We had the frame up and were startin' with the screen. LeRoy was on top, I was feeding him the fabric. Then, all of a sudden LeRoy stops, whispers be quiet, and waves me up. He's lookin' across the fence in the neighbor's backyard. I figures he's seen somethin' good so I heads up. Sure enough the lady next door is out there sunbathin' in nuthin' but 'er good intentions. An' she's a looker, I wanna tell ya."

"How many you reckon were up there?" I asked.

I'M PEDDLIN' AS FAST AS I CAN

He started counting on his fingers, then said, "Hard to tell. Soon as it give in, most of 'em skedaddled. We must've had eight or ten of ours."

"Of yours? There were others?" I said.

"Oh, sure. There was the guy from next door, and ,uh, the mailman, and, oh, yeah, that Jehovah's Witness feller, pool's full of his flyer things. . ."

"Got it," I said, "anything else?"

"Yeah, there is," Lamar said. "You know when that cage come down and we headed for the drink I swear I could hear that woman over there laughing."

Sometimes you find out more than you need to know. I told Lamar to never mind, no one was hurt, no need for a report. He breathed a sigh of relief. I went back on patrol.

Had I known they were going to be on the cage that day I could've warned them. The lady next door was famous for her nude sunbathing and, like the man said she was a hottie. I answered a bogus call at her residence once and she answered the door in a towel that, like our budget, was experiencing a shortfall.

Cops see these teasers a lot. And over the years you get used to them. Almost.

LEGEND OF THE LOVE APPLES

In the 60's the intersection of Goodlette Road and Pine Ridge Road was out in the sticks. The N/E corner, in particular, was a barren field bordered by railroad track. Luscious red tomatoes, however, grew there. And, until the tourists came down each year and picked them, there was a bountiful supply. Why? Because the locals wouldn't touch them.

Back then most folks had some kind of septic system. Septic tanks eventually have to be pumped and this was done by what we called the honey dippers. The honey dipper would pump the sludge into the giant tank on his truck and, when it was full, take it to a remote area and dump it. Not all those environmental regulations to worry about then. Just find a remote spot and turn on the empty valve. They did rotate spots, giving one a chance to dry up before they reused it.

That corner on Pine Ridge and Goodlette was such a place. But why did they dump it in a tomato field? They didn't. It was just the opposite. Seems a tomato seed will survive the rigors of passing through the human disposal system. So the honey dippers, in effect, were planting tomato seeds in very rich fertilizer. And a bumper crop always ensued.

Locals never let out the secret about the tomatoes because it was too much fun to watch the tourists going after those dung patch love apples.

Naples was a sleepy little town then, but you have to admit it was a front runner in recycling and organic gardening. And that wasn't the only example of early recycling. The Moorings/Coquina Sands area was once the City Dump. At the time, the city cops found a body there that was never identified. So, must've been a graveyard, too.

BIG JOHN AND THE WALLABY WRANGLERS

Big John, a self-made millionaire, lived beachfront on Gordon Drive. A rebel, he reminded many of a sane Howard Hughes. John liked to drink but not at exclusive clubs that pandered to the rich. John was a common man, and gravitated to *The Anchor*, a downtown dive since replaced by, what else, a Walgreen's.

Because of his earthy leanings, Big John wasn't a favorite with some of his snobbish Gordon Drive and Port Royal neighbors. And there was another small thing that ticked them off; his menagerie. He'd converted his estate into a zoo, off sorts. He had saltwater pools with dolphins, sea turtles, and seals. Among his collection was a galapagos tortoise, a dwarf burro, and a kangaroo type critter called a wallaby.

A lover of children, he opened his estate to families each Wednesday. This alone caused some neighbors to despise him. Allowing the great unwashed masses to encroach on their *sanctum sanctorum*. These were the crybabies who called us incessantly about people on their beach, or a suspicious vehicle--anything that wasn't a Rolls, Caddy, or Lincoln.

I'M PEDDLIN' AS FAST AS I CAN

Then there were the seals that barked all night long, prompting enraged calls to the PD, which caused Big John to laugh and throw the noisy critters another fish.

We, the cops, loved him. There were many good folks in Port Royal that supported PAL and the police. But there were a lotta politically powerful dicks, too, and John stuck it to them, when we couldn't always do it ourselves.

Big John's animals had a bad habit of escaping. His swans would magically leave the zoo confines during mating season and uproot the neighbor's elegant flower beds, while making a nest. His burro liked to walk down the beach to the City Pier, munching landscaping on the way. Finally, his neighbors complained to sympathetic puppets on the City Council and pressure was put on John to get rid of the zoo. Bad move!

Shortly thereafter, John went to *The Anchor* about midnight and announced that his wallaby had escaped in Port Royal and he was offering a $100 reward for its return. In five minutes every stumbling drunk was weaving down Gordon Drive. Some stopped off to call their buddies to join the search party. In short order there were more than 100.

Soon, our switchboard was flooded with calls from outraged aristocrats claiming there were drunks in their yard yelling "Here wallaby." And some climbing trees, thinking perhaps the Wallaby was a roosting animal. Or searching their cabin cruisers, looking for a nautical species.

It was a very busy evening for the NPD in Port Royal. But we loved it.

Big John kept his zoo until his untimely death. Rest in peace, my hero.

HUMPHREY AND POCAHONTAS

I've always had a soft spot for the mentally ill, perhaps recognizing kindred spirits. Nowadays, these poor souls receive professional help with dispatch. Wasn't always that way. Before, when you slipped a gear you'd be slapped in jail. When a psychiatrist showed up, you were loaded down with Thorazine, and sat there for up to two weeks waiting for the commitment hearing, and a reservation for a hospital. By the

I'M PEDDLIN' AS FAST AS I CAN

time you were ready to be shipped out, the stay in jail with little professional care had driven someone with minor eccentricities goofier than a politician with taxpayer's dollars.

Most returned from the institution as sane as the rest of us.--admittedly, a poor standard. There was however, a flaw in the system. These folks were heavily medicated. The drugs had aggravating side effects like malaise, insomnia, or diarrhea. Soon the patient would rationalize that since they were sane there was no need to take these drugs that made them feel awful. So they'd quit taking them and go nuts again, now not capable of recognizing the medicine kept them sane. It happened repeatedly.

One poor soul who rode this cycle we'll call Humphrey Bogart. A local business man, he'd morph into Bogart when he slipped over the edge. The signs were obvious. First a slight lisp, and talking out the side of his mouth. Then the snap-brim Fedora. In a few more days, the trench coat. And finally, the Colt .45 semi-auto tucked in his belt along with an urge to waste Nazis and bad guys. We'd sack him up, he'd go through the drill, and in a year or so, he'd come home to stay for a while. But he always backslid. As did many others.

Another problem was transporting them to the care facility. Our two resources were the G. Pierce Wood facility in Arcadia and Jackson Memorial Hospital in Miami. No ambulance. No straight jacket*. Just a police car and a prayer the Thorazine would do its job. That didn't always happen.

A beautiful black woman, who we came to call Pocahontas, arrived in Naples fresh out of college. She'd received a touchy-feely grant to teach family values in the ghetto. (It was the sixties) To do this, she'd taken up residence in the Quarters. We'd warned the gentle, sophisticated lady that she'd be entering a foreign world. A dangerous world for which she wasn't prepared. She would have none of it, saying if she didn't live with her clients she wouldn' t be respected. She lasted a week before she was beaten and raped. Then she turned into Pocahontas.

The shrink explained that she couldn't reconcile someone of her race doing this to her so she'd abandoned her race and

I'M PEDDLIN' AS FAST AS I CAN

become an American Indian. In her cell she liked to strip naked and dance, chanting around a fire only she could see. So she was drugged, leaving her seldom awake. Eventually, they had an opening at Jackson Memorial.

On the hundred mile ride to Miami, Pocahontas was more alert than usual, but quiet and morose. Her cop chauffeur, J.A. Foyt, was relieved things were going so well. And she remained sedate until they reached downtown Miami. Then she abruptly stripped off her clothes, began chanting, and doing a frantic dance in the back seat. This was an instant hit with most spectators--she was quite beautiful. But Foyt was horrified. He weighed his options. If he stopped and tried to control her, he'd sure as hell be on the evening news, a cop wrestling a naked indian princess. Nope, not this ol' hoss. Flipping on the siren and lights, he decided to get to Jackson Memorial on the double.

Emergency lights don't give you much of an edge in Miami traffic. Besides, the show was drawing a crowd. Cars following, honking horns, pedestrians trying to keep pace, some now in the street, running around the car for a better look. Disaster would've been eminent if a higher power hadn't interceded. Out of nowhere, a South Florida frog-strangler materialized. Torrents of rain, lightening, the works. It's hard to be a soggy voyeur so the crowd disappeared. Foyt proceeded on to the hospital unencumbered.

Parking the cruiser, Foyt looked back at his charge, who had dressed and was calm. That dance you were doing, he asked. That couldn't have been a rain dance could it?

Pocahontas didn't say a word. Just looked at him and gave him something he hadn't seen before. Something quite beautiful. A smile.

*Trivia note: *Since we had no straight jacket at the jail, when someone became violent we'd wrap them up in a wet sheet. Works great!*

WHEN ONLY ONE WORD WILL DO

There are times when only a certain word will do. It's usually an expletive. Here are three examples.

I'M PEDDLIN' AS FAST AS I CAN

Portnoy the painter, although big and burly, was the victim of spouse abuse. And from a wife who was as petite as Minnie Mouse. She did, however, have a broom and a swing like DiMaggio. She also knew the sweet spot on the broom-- where the straws all come together tight and hard at the handle. If Portnoy got too drunk the beating would begin. And the neighbors, hearing Portnoy's screams, would call us.

When you answered these calls, you had to feel sorry for Portnoy. He'd be lumped up, where the sweet spot had connected, and humiliated by having been thrashed again by the tiny Tyson. He'd never consider filing a complaint against his wife--he loved her dearly--so we'd take him to a shelter. In his case a fishing shack he owned off Kelly Road. *(Since we got snooty, this is now Bayshore Drive)*

Driving down 41, Portnoy was in the passenger's seat. There weren't any cages then, so you put someone you needed to watch in the front seat with you and kept one eye on him and one on the road. To my horror, as we approached The Anchor bar, Portnoy muttered, "Gotta have one more," opened the door and stepped out while we were going about 45 MPH. In the rear view mirror I could see him doing a series of backflips, like a gymnast doing a floor exercise, culminating in a double high loop that ended with him splattered face down on the asphalt. I decided to mail my badge in to avoid the Chief's rage, but did go back to try to keep the traffic off his corpse.

Waste of time. Portnoy, the benefactor of that magical cloak of protection that shrouds drunks, picked himself up, brushed himself off, and said the word: *DAMN!*

Then there's Hot Roddy and his Dodge Challenger. Roddy's beast had a 440 with a 6 Pack that could outrun anything we had. This night he'd picked up a caravan of NPD and CCSO cars, that were fading fast as he raced up U.S.41. But, just South of Bonita, he lost control, crossed the highway and smashed into a power pole, ripping the car in half behind the front seat. We expected to see a gory mess. Not so. Again the drunkard's patron Saint had wrapped her arms around her sodden child.

Still sitting in the driver's seat, his hands on the wheel, he looked at his dissected vehicle, then us, and said: *DAMN!*

I'M PEDDLIN' AS FAST AS I CAN

Trivia alert. I was so impressed by the power of this engine I later bought it from the junkyard and installed it in my racing swamp buggy, *Super Fuzz*.

Now for the grand finale. Mary Jane Hemp was stoned on her favorite herb when she lost control of her Datsun convertible, crossed the divided highway, and drove under the trailer of a long-haul rig going the other way. When we arrived, we could see parts of the windshield and steering wheel which had been sliced off by the trailer. With trepidation, we looked for the driver's head. The car had traveled another 200 yards and was bogged down in the underbrush beside the highway. We approached, again dreading what we'd probably find.

Nope. Mary Jane stumbled out of her squashed chariot, tried to focus her eyes on us, and said one word: *DAMN!*

The drunkard's Saint also watches out for druggies. Mary Jane'd nodded off on the highway, fallen over in the seat, and was below the windshield level when her car went under the trailer.

Having witnessed all these strange events I can close with only one word: *Need I say it?*

CASE OF THE UNTRUSTWORTHY TRUSTEES

Trustees do many worthwhile jobs in the jail. They cook, cleanup, do the laundry, wash cars. Usually it's a good deal, both for the cops and the inmates--who hate sitting in a cell. But, it doesn't always work out that way.

A good example is Larry, who was making six months with us at NPD. He'd done six before. And before that, like many, booze turned his brain into silly putty, winning him vacations in the lockup. Sober, he was smart and a quick study.

He became interested in fingerprints so we showed him how to take them. Having mastered that, he started learning how to classify prints. Soon, he was doing all the fingerprinting and, I expect, there are several hundred fingerprint cards at the FBI in DC bearing his signature as ID Officer.

I'M PEDDLIN' AS FAST AS I CAN

We had our own darkroom and a few trustees were taught how to develop and print film. This was a big help because detectives, at the time, had to do this work themselves, plus keep up with their caseload.

Too bad they didn't all turn out like that. The County decided that to save money the trustees should reload the practice ammo. Bad move. No matter how trustworthy they seem, some are just working the system and have deep antisocial problems. One such A-wipe hot-loaded several rounds. (*Put in way more power than is needed*). This resulted in a Deputy's gun exploding on the range and damn near taking off his thumb. So much for saving money,

The worst example has to be Cruikshank the Cook. At the Sheriff's Office there was dining room off the kitchen where Deputies and other cops ate. It was also used by civilian County workers, including Commissioners and Judges. Cruikshank decided that to get back at the system he would urinate in the huge coffee urn. So he did. And did. And did. When he was finally caught, he was in the tenth month of a one year sentence. When asked how long he'd been doing it, he just smiled. Those of you who wonder why we didn't notice the coffee didn't taste right have never sampled jailhouse Coffee. Tasted normal to me.

FAST TALKIN' WILLIE WALKEN

Fast Talkin' Willie Walken was a minister of the gospel. Or a missionary. Or a deacon. Faith? Baptist, Mormon, Jehovah's Witness, Catholic. You name it, he had the papers to prove it. Problem was the credentials, like Will, were bogus. Will, you see, was a con man.

We first had the pleasure of his company, when we received a call that there was a suspicious minister, trying to cash a check at *Gene's Fifth Avenue Florist*. He'd bought a bouquet and was asking to write a check for over the amount of the purchase so he'd get cash back. A common scam. By the time we arrived, Will had everyone in the store chuckling, with his warm manner, good looks, and charm. All except the sharp-eyed clerk, who'd noticed that Will's

I'M PEDDLIN' AS FAST AS I CAN

wallet was bulging with ID cards. We took Will aside for a chat.

Will explained that he was a roving minister and made his living by being a guest speaker at local churches. He said it was a nice touch to gift the prospective church with a bouquet. He got a lot more jobs that way. He, reluctantly, showed us the wallet with all the IDs. He said they were *honorary* credentials, granted by a grateful flock. Uh-huh. That made us want to look further.

We asked Will where his car was parked. He pointed outside where a baby blue 60 Chevy was at the curb. From inside the store, we could see that the back seat was full of bouquets. Looking back, Will rolled his eyes, laughed, and said, "Looks like the next place I'm gonna be preachin' is at the jail, huh?"

When Will's car was inventoried, besides the flowers there were boxes full of diplomas, ID cards, certificates, and check books attesting that Will was in the religion business.

After he'd been bagged, Will was affable, even helpful. He said those certificates were available anywhere. Said he'd made his living being a fake minister for years. Except for periods of jail time. He'd come from Utah, where he admitted he was wanted for parole violation.

He did leave out one small detail. Will had been traveling with a woman. He had dropped her off at a beauty shop, with instructions to *Give her the works*. After he was arrested, he just wrote her off. She was stuck with no money until the local aid society came to her aid.

Will waived extradition, and the folks in Utah said they'd be down *post haste* to reclaim the wily William. It took about a week, while Will relaxed in our jail. During that time, he won most of us over. We found a buyer for his car--after verifying it was legit. One cop loaned him money until he was paid for the car. Truth be told, he was so damn funny we hated to see him go.

Just before he boarded the gray Chevy with the Utah Dept of Prisons lettering, Will said, "You folks've been real decent to me and I appreciate it. I expect some day I'll see you

I'M PEDDLIN' AS FAST AS I CAN

again." We said that wasn't necessary. We'd probably be better off if he stayed away. He laughed and they were gone.

Six months later, Dave Dampier came into my office, grinning and shaking his head. You're not going to believe this, he said. Parked outside the station was a gray Chevy with Utah Prison lettering on the doors. The ignition had been hot wired. A quick call verified what we suspected. Will had worked his was up to trustee, stolen the prison's vehicle, and driven it across the country to Naples, Florida. And left it where we couldn't miss it, proof that he'd kept his word.

Never got to see Fast Talkin' Willie Walken again. But, for a long time, every now and then I was sure I could hear him laughing.

SGT. C.H.DASHER

Sgt. C.H. Dasher was one of the nicest people you'd hope to meet. And maybe the strongest. Not a shaved, oiled, puffed-up 'roid monster from the gyms. The sloping bear-like shoulders, fence post wrist, wide body type that are born that way.

C.H. was a teacher. Taught me that simple solutions are usually best. And, the power of menacing sound.

Once, in the sixties, an angry crowd formed in the Quarters. Upset over some issue that was important at the time, it was a volatile situation: One spark could set off a riot. While we were standing around deciding how to disburse the crowd without making the situation worse, up pulls C.H.. He gets out of his car, turns on the car's P.A. system and takes out his shotgun. Placing the shotgun next to the mike, he racks the slide one time. There is no other sound like this. It says *SHOTGUN*. And that means *Wide, Indiscriminate Shot Pattern*. In ten seconds the street was empty.

He also had great healing powers. Bozo, a big-mouthed contractor, thought he was above the law. One evening he was D&D; Drunk and Disgusting. He wasn't going to jail, or get in the damn car, or do anything the f-ing cop wanted. Unfortunately for Bozo, the cop he as baiting was C.H. That was his first mistake. His second was taking a swing at said officer. C.H.'s counter uppercut couldn't have traveled four

I'M PEDDLIN' AS FAST AS I CAN

inches. But it was bedtime for Bozo. You might say the punch was therapeutic. He enjoyed a restful sleep for several hours and, upon waking, the A-hole was instantly cured. We never had another problem with him.

C.H. led by example. We had a dispatcher, Betty Jo, who was popular and, therefore, fair game for cop's pranks. One favorite was to lift the front of her VW over the curb, so she couldn't drive home after work. Course, after a suitable period of aggravation, two or three cops would lift it over the curb and back in place. C.H. thought enough was enough.

One evening, at shift change C.H. announced that Betty Jo's car needed to be lifted over the curb. The officers gave him questioning looks as they hadn't touched it that night. C.H. led them outside and there was the car and it was over the curb all right. But not the light front end. It was the heavy rear end, where the motor was housed, that was straddling the curb. C.H. pointed to the car and said, *Get busy.*

The cops whined. "We can't lift that. That's where the motor is. We'll need a wrecker or something."

C.H. smiled, walked to the rear of the VW, bent and lifted it over the curb. Audible gasps could be heard.

"Next time Betty Jo's car gets put over the curb, that's the way to do it, rear-end first. I see it parked any other way, I'm gonna be real upset." Betty Jo's car was never lifted again.

Though long gone, in his own way C.H. is still contributing to local law enforcement. His son, like his father, is an excellent local cop.

DEADLY HUMOR

Medical Examiners have tough jobs. I asked one how he could spend his days cutting up human bodies. He told me the work was interesting, challenging, and important, but if he ever stopped to consider that he was slicing and dicing the remains of real people, he'd go nuts. He also said that, like cops, he'd developed a dark sense of humor.

I first encountered Medical Examiner Fun and Games 101 in Ft. Lauderdale. While attending the police academy with

I'M PEDDLIN' AS FAST AS I CAN

Dave Dampier, part of the training required us to view an autopsy.

As soon as we entered the autopsy room we knew we were in trouble. On one wall was a giant photo mural showing three medical examiners dissecting burn victims. These *crispy critters*, as they're called, are charred black, except for the pink where the examiners had opened the chest cavity. Bad enough. Then you notice the examiners are wearing chef's hats, and holding barbecue tools. And, oh yeah, the caption; *Steak or Ribs?*

There is nothing a medical examiner loves more than torturing rookie cops. If they can't get at least one to pass out, or puke his guts out, the day's been a bust. They don't have many unhappy days.

If cutting off the top of a head doesn't do it, opening the stomach will. The odor is horrendous, especially if the corpse is over-ripe. The examiner makes it worse by probing the contents, and critiquing what he finds. *I see our victim had corn for supper,* or *Oh, my favorite, clams.* Then, stopping, thinking, announcing, *That reminds me, it's snack time.* Producing a sandwich, he'd munch away, while returning to the ghoulish work. I can still hear giant cop's skulls bouncing off the floor as they keeled over.

Finally, there's the soup pot. One rookie is directed to a stainless steel pressure-cooker-looking pot. The pot is boiling. He's told to lift up the ladle and see if the soup's ready. The ladle is actually a device that holds a human head, being boiled to remove the flesh so skull fractures can be examined. Usually, just about the time the cook realizes what he's pulled up, it's barf bag time in *Sick Humor City*.

Over the years, after you've seen all the horrors cops see, you get used to this stuff. Kinda.

OUR BUDDY SAM

When the NPD was on the corner of 8th and 8th South, we had a neighbor who loved to visit. His name was Sam. He was an English Bulldog, the one's that are pictured in Marine Corps ads. Sam would drop by and spend hours at the PD, bumming snacks, getting scratched, and just socializing.

His favorite game was tug-of-war. We'd get an old pair of uniform trousers out, toss him one leg and a cop would take the other. We never won. English Bulldogs have huge heads, muscular shoulders, and short legs. Once that jaw clamps on something and those legs start churning, forget it.

Except for two small social problems, he was the perfect companion. He was a constant drooler, sometimes requiring a bib. And, he had a gas problem. To be fair, it was probably from all the junk we fed him. But, when he erupted, it would wilt the leaves on a philodendron.

Sometimes Sam would volunteer for patrol duty. His head was a perfect fit for a uniform hat. And you could put a ladies police shirt on him, an unlit cigar butt in his mouth, and he was ready to make the streets of Naples safe.

We'd lean him up in the passenger's seat just like a human, put on his lap belt, and he'd ride for hours, never moving except to stare out the side window. Seemed to love it. And he never spit out the cigar butt. It was a sight, prompting many a double take. I've seen some damn ugly cops, but that guy wins the blue ribbon.

The only trouble we ever had with Sam, was patrolling McDonald's Quarters. As soon as you made the turn into that filthy hell-hole, Sam would go nuts, growling, barking, struggling with the seat belt, trying to get out of the car. It was the only time he wasn't just *Good Ol' Sam*.

We don't think Sam was a bigot. We like to think he was a visionary, protesting the abhorrent living conditions in the Quarters.

Miss you, buddy.

THE HOBO EXPRESS

The City of Naples has always been particular about its image. Anything ugly's taboo. Back then, this included humans--unless they had money. Vagrants had to go. So, we had to develop systems to rid *Paradise In The Elephant's Graveyard* of this blight.

The vagrant law was still on the books. If you had no money and could show no visible means of support you were a bum. And, you got the rush. Since the city didn't want to keep bums in jail and feed them, we'd get them on the road to elsewhere as soon as possible. This usually involved sneaking over the Lee Co line and dumping them, or hauling them out US 41 past Everglades City.

Sometimes, when the bum population started to bloom, we'd send them a message. Knowing they had a communications network, we'd deliver a reminder to stay away.

(*Today, we find "The Homeless" with information packets on how to get to Collier County, where to go when they get here, what charities give free pots and pans, where to get free meals, where to flop; an entire vacation program*)

To send the message, we'd crank up the Hobo Express. It worked like this. Grab a couple of bums, call Dade County and ask if there was a car available for the Hobo Express. This was usually about 4 in the morning, when calls were slow. That established, we'd drive to the Dade county line, transfer our cargo to their car. That car'd take them to Broward County, then into another up to Palm Beach. By sunrise the cargo had been delivered to Ft Pierce, who didn't seem to notice the new citizens. Having been to Ft Pierce, I can understand why.

Cruel? Insensitive? Probably. But we never had burglaries or thefts perpetrated by the *homeless*. And, they didn't mug innocent citizens. Didn't murder each other in our city. Most importantly, we never did it to anyone that was legitimately, down on their luck and trying to pull themselves out of a hole. It's real easy to tell the difference.

I'M PEDDLIN' AS FAST AS I CAN

The Usual Suspects

Administration in the 1970's

From left, Lt JD Spohn, Chief John Woodruff, Asnt Chief GD Young, Capt Dave Dampier

These gents are sporting the new blazers, the patches with golden threads.

2nd PRECINCT

YOU'RE NOT LISTENING

Chief Samuel Ben Caruthers was the first Chief to bring modern methods to the NPD. A graduate of the FBI Academy, he instituted a comprehensive report form system, used standardized tests to select applicants, and provided training to us, superior to what is available today. If the subject was Counterfeiting, Ben arranged for the Secret Service to do the instructing. Narcotics:the Bureau of Narcotics. And on down the line. This was at no cost to the agency. Out-of-town Feds loved to relax in Naples. And the FBI, who provided training, photographic supplies, and training ammo, viewed their help as a pay-back for using our firearms range.

Ben had worked hard to nurture these relationships and we all benefited from it. You have to remember this was a time when, under state law, it was not even necessary to send recruits to a police academy. And most agencies didn't. We went to the Broward County Police Academy, recognized as a premier one in the state.

Anyway, having so much federal training under my belt, and respecting their offices, I always took advantage of an opportunity to learn, when working with them. Once, a US Postal Inspector from Miami, who knew our family--my father was the Postmaster--dropped by and said he had a problem to take care of. Would I like to go along? Certainly.

The problem was a family we'll call the Burrs, who were a constant problem to us, as well. They lived in a filthy hovel in the boondocks and socially were two steps below *white trash*. If anything was stolen in their neighbor, you need look no further than The Burr's: father or one of his gaggle of children. The immediate problem involved a violation of Federal Law.

The Inspector, let's use Jake Wayne, was a big man, confident in his authority and ability. He was easy talking and I'd never seen him get the least bit upset. I was anxious to see how he'd handle the Burr's, who could've given Buddha apoplexy.

We arrived at the Burr's nest and knocked on the door. Ma Burrs asked: "What is it now?"

Wayne ID'd himself, then, "I'm afraid we have a problem, Mrs. Burrs. It seems your children have been stealing US Mail, and destroying mail boxes." (*Mail was stolen for the money people sometimes foolishly enclosed*)

She put her hands on her hips. "Say's who?"

"Says our mail carrier, who saw them, tried to intercede, and was rocked for his trouble."

"Huh, that's his tale," she said, "I'm sittin' on mine."

The conversation with the sullen bitch went on a few more minutes before Wayne, seeing he was getting no where said, "Could I see Mr Burrs, please?"

A nasty dirtbag, who'd obviously been listening around the corner, appeared in the doorway. "What the hell's this all about?" he demanded.

I'M PEDDLIN' AS FAST AS I CAN

Wayne looked at me, shrugged, grabbed Burrs by the throat and lifted him outside. Not letting him down, he said. "Listen to me, you inbred idiot, if you don't stop this thievery, I'm going to come back, beat you till you blubber like a baby, kill your dog, rape your wife, burn down your house, and anyone that happens to be left, put them UNDER the federal prison. Understand?"

After several gulps, "*Yessssss, Sir, Surrrrre do.*" And he did. No more mail was ever violated in his neighborhood.

And I learned a valuable lesson from a smooth operating fed. *Sometimes it's not just what you say, but how you say it.*

THE PERILS OF PAULINE?

Best I can tell, Naples first woman cop was hired in the late 60's. Average size and fit, she had some experience with the Pennsylvania State Police. We had a Secretary and Dispatcher, June Holzhausen, who was designated a Matron when one was needed for female searches and the like, but the one we'll call Pauline was the first full-time, sworn female officer.

At the time, lady cops were a novelty, particularly in the South. The predominate feeling was that women were just not built, physically or psychologically, to handle the sometimes grim work. This was a time when there was a height requirement of about 5' 9" and the heftier a specimen you were, the better. After Pauline was hired, those feelings manifested in a protective attitude among her fellow officers.

When she was assigned a call, another car or two in the area just happened to cruise by, to assure she was okay. This bubble of security followed her for several months. Until she got the call from the Emergency Room.

An ER sometimes encounters patients who are violent. They can be folks with an adverse drug reaction, drunks, or, more logically, those presented with their bill. Many reasons. When that happens, they call us.

One night a call came in that there was some druggie tearing the place up and the ER people needed help quickly. Pauline immediately radioed that she was just around the corner and was on it. This caused concern, as there weren't any other units in service near her.

It took about five minutes--a long time when someone is beating you about the head and shoulders--for help to arrive. The two responding officers could hear screaming and cursing coming from the ER area. Fearing the worst, they moved even more quickly to the scene.

On arriving, they witnessed mayhem, alright. But Pauline was on the delivery end. The wild man was on the floor, on his belly, screaming his lungs out. That was because Pauline had him in a bar hammerlock, with her knees in his back. When she saw her backup arrive, she looked up and said, calmly, "You wanna get my cuffs outta my case for me so I can secure this A-hole?"

The officers looked at each other, laughed and said, "Yes Ma'am. Anything you want."

All good cops watch out for each other. There's a whole lotta *them* and not many of *us*. But, Pauline's *extra* security shield went away. Wasn't needed. In fact, some cops, when they got in a crack, secretly hoped she was right around the corner.

AN ALTERNATIVE LIFE STYLE

One day, when working for the CCSO, my friend Joe and I were walking from the Headquarters Building to the CID Building. A short stroll, or exercise fiends that we weren't, we would've driven. We were behind two young Investigators. One was snorting and fuming. You couldn't help but overhear his rant. I asked Joe to listen.

This feller was railing about queers, and faggots, and crotch cowboys, and rump rangers and all things homosexual. I elbowed Joe and said, "Let's have some fun." Joe, wary of my twisted sense of humor, gave me a look, but nodded okay.

Approaching my boisterous fellow travelers, I said, "Excuse me, but I couldn't help but overhear your comments. Just wanted to mention that sayin' those things can be very hurtful to someone who enjoys an alternative lifestyle. Like myself."

I'M PEDDLIN' AS FAST AS I CAN

After eye popping stares, one took off at double time. The other jumped backwards at a height and distance that could have qualified for some Olympic events. Then, he too, cut a choagy. Joe was about to bust a gut but held it in until they were out of sight, then roared laughing. "You don't have brain one," he said.

"Ain't it true," I agreed. "Now, promise me you won't say anything to spoil this. I want 'em to stew for a few days." It turned out to be so much fun, it lasted much longer.

I could encounter either of my marks on a sidewalk and they would leave said pavement, circumscribing a wide circle around me like I was *Typhoid Gary*. Or cross the street. Or in a closed meeting room, they'd find the furthest chairs from yours truly. And there was no eye contact, like I might possess some deadly Liberace Laser vision that would put them, instantly, in tutus and instill a compulsion to watch *The View* and sing show tunes.

Finally, their Captain told them I was yankin' their chain, and ruined the fun. Then, there was a complete switch of attitudes. Couldn't get enough of me. *We knew it was all BS.* Sure. *Didn't fool me.* Of course, not. *Anyone can tell what a real sissy boy looks like.* You bet. And, *You sure are funny, Mr. Young.*

Sure hope so. Some days are mighty long, otherwise.

PERKY'S PROBLEM

In the 60's, south CR 951, now Collier Blvd, was in the woods. The roadside canal was a favorite spot for snake hunting. Hunter's would stand on the 951 bank and shoot rattlers and moccasins on the other side. Or, since both are great swimmers, pop them cruising in the canal.

One avid hunter was Earl Perkins. Tall, handsome, and good humored, Perky was a popular member of the Naples Police force. A lover of the outdoors and hunting, whenever

I'M PEDDLIN' AS FAST AS I CAN

he had time off, you'd find him at the canal. He and his family picnicking on the bank, making a day of it.

On one outing, Earl's .22 snake killer misfired, wounding him in the forearm. Ironically, the bullet targeted a snake tattoo he had on his arm. Rushed to the NCH emergency room by his family, he was admitted, quickly, into surgery. (*It wasn't like today. People didn't use the ER as a free family doctor*)

Of course, when we heard Earl had been shot, and not knowing the severity of his injury, we gathered in the ER waiting room. The surgery seemed to take forever.

Finally, the nurse ushered a few of us into his room.

Earl was propped up in his bed, making jokes with the nurses. Oddly, he had his hand shielding his mouth like he had bad breath. We asked how he was doing.

"Well, the Doc says he has good news and bad news," Earl said with a chuckle. "Says the bullet barely penetrated my arm and I'll be good as new. He wiggled a bandaged forearm. The bad is, while they were takin' the bullet out, the surgeon dropped his scalpel in my mouth and knocked my front tooth out."

Whereupon, he took down his hand, revealing a significant space where a front tooth had been.

He what? we wondered aloud.

"Dropped the scalpel, took out my tooth," Earl said, "which I swallowed. But it ain't all bad. First, the surgery is on the house. Second, they're gonna pay to have my tooth replaced. And, third, and best, I'm just glad the tooth was there to stop that scalpel. Can you imagine swallowin' that damn thing?"

Today, we wouldn't have been able to get into the room for the gaggle of personal injury vultures smelling a fat settlement. Earl could have owned NCH. But, I don't think the thought ever crossed his mind.

Just indicative of an older, more honorable, time.

SLICK'S MAGICAL MYSTERY TOURS

I'M PEDDLIN' AS FAST

With his thinking hair, past forty paunch, and average Joe looks Harold Slick was a lady killer. What? Sure. Cause he had what some women find irresistible: a smooth line of BS.

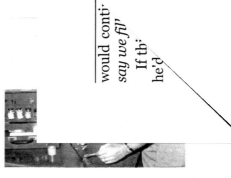

Det. Ray Barnett was in the room next door to Slick, at the Golfing Buccaneer Hotel, then on Mooringline Drive and US 41. Ray was working a stakeout that had fizzled out. He was about to call it a night when he noticed an attractive lady enter Slick's room. That caused him to recall that he'd seen several ladies enter that room. His cop's intuition got his mind to working.

Maybe the guy he'd seen in there was a male prostitute. Or the women were ho's. But who could handle that much exercise? Maybe he was running hookers for other guests, Whatever it was, Ray decided he was going to find out.

Grabbing a recorder, with a sensitive pinhole mike, from his car, Ray returned to his room and fired it up. The walls were thin, so he could hear what was going on next door. And what he heard blew his mind. When he finally had it all sorted out, this was the caper.

Slick, had been holed up at the *Buccaneer* for two weeks, camped out in the bar looking for worthy marks. Finding one, all single ladies, he'd buy her a few drinks then go into his spiel:

I work for a very wealthy man. He loves to go to exotic places and enjoys the company of an attractive companion. They travel all over the world, at no cost, on his yacht, plus he gives them a handsome allowance. My boss is also the friend of many famous people who sometimes travel with him. Movies stars, you name it. I wonder if you might be interested?

That would scare some off. Other's would ask more questions, then leave. But, a surprising number stayed. Slick

...ue, I have the applications in my room. What'...one out.

...s didn't drive them away, they'd go to his room where...close the deal.

I'm sure you realize, he'd say, *my boss would require sexual favors. Nothing kinky, but he is vigorous. And he trusts my judgment to audition, so to speak, candidates. So...*

Unbelievably, that was it. Short, simple, sweet. Even more astounding, was the number that agreed to the audition. Within minutes, the sound of squeaking bed springs could be heard.

Before we could figure out how to handle him, Slick was gone like a cool breeze. We were left with the tape that some cops wore out trying to memorize his lines. Remembering the number of times he'd audition in a night, some of us just wondered what Slick had been eating.

BAD, BAD, BERTIE AND THE BATTERED BURGLAR

We'll call her Bertie. On this night, though, she earned a more glorious handle.

Bertie was a widow, lived alone on Gordon Drive. A small, mature lady, she looked like a favorite aunt. When the burglar, Wet Willie, first saw her--sitting there in a rocker, with the latest best seller--he had the same impression. That is, after his initial shock of finding someone in a house he thought was unoccupied. They saw each other simultaneously. She, having heard the sliding glass door open. He, hearing her soft, *Who's there?* Both stared at each other, their mental computers sorting the data. Bertie's had a faster processor. She sensed danger and that produced rage.

Bertie opened up a can of *Whoop-ass*. First she threw her book at him. Then she charged him, hammering him with anything she could use as a bludgeon. This included her foot stool, a floor lamp, and a putter she used for a walking stick. She continued the onslaught until Willie, battered and bleeding, staggered from the house and jumped over the rear seawall. Then, having taken out the trash herself, Mizz Bertie called us.

I'M PEDDLIN' AS FAST AS I CAN

After we grabbed Willie, we asked Bertie why she'd done such a reckless thing.

"I don't know," she said. "I can't imagine me doing that. But, when I looked up and saw him in my home, uninvited, I just lost control. . .him trying to take advantage of a defenseless woman." (Yep, Bertie, defenseless. You and the 5th Marines)

We'd found Wet Willie on the beach, his hands shielding his head, sobbing. When we turned him over he seemed relieved it was just the cops. All we'd do is put him in jail. A better alternative than *more Bertie*. All the way to the jail he muttered, "*What's wrong with that woman? I was gonna leave, I was gonna run.*"

Could be, but tucked in Wet Willie's belt, we found a Ruger Single-Six .22 revolver. Just happened to have it along in case he broke into an empty house and found out it wasn't. A great plan. . .unless you happen to cross paths with a Bad, Bad, Bertie.

THE BUBBLE BUTT BLUES

Creeping Clarence was a burglar. Not a very good one, but he was diligent. When he got out of jail, for one attempt, he'd be back in for another before they'd changed the sheets in his cell. Clarence was stupid. He always confessed. He had no imagination.

For starters, he liked to break into the same buildings, especially those within walking distance of his flop. His favorite was *Hartley's Variety Store*, then just a few blocks north of 4 Corners. Another problem, his MO never varied-- pry open the bathroom window and slither in. When you found these two constants, you knew Creeping Clarence was at work again.

What befuddled us was how in hell Clarence squeezed through those little windows. They were half-size at best and Clarence was no small man. An easy six feet, he was slim and muscular. But the butt was a problem. It was disproportionally large. He was bubble-butted.

I once asked him how he did it--crammed that rear end through the window. He said, "Any thang you can gets yo

I'M PEDDLIN' AS FAST AS I CAN

head and one arm through, be big enough for yo whole body."

I told him, "Could be, but one of these days you're gonna eat an extra hush puppy and you're gonna get stuck."

He just laughed, and waved me off.

On night, I got a call from a patrol cop asking me to meet him behind Hartley's. There, I found a smiling uniform officer, pointing to the store's bathroom window, on the alley. There was Clarence, wedged, his head and one arm locked in place. He was squirming and grumbling like a budgie bird.

I couldn't resist. "Clarence," I said, "I warned you about that bubble butt one day gettin' you stuck tryin' to break in a building."

To which my man Clarence snorted, "Lot you knows. I's already brokes *IN*. I's tryin' to breaks *OUT.*"

Did I mention that Clarence was stupid?

GATOR TALES

One of my favorite cops, who shall remain nameless for fear a bunny hugger will burn a lumberjack on his front lawn, was the rarest of all things in Southwest Florida: A native Floridian. Born and raised here.

In his youth, times were hard and his family did what had to be done to get by. That included taking an occasional gator for it's tail, meat, and hide. When the EPA decided the gators were becoming extinct, we were glad he, with his unique experience, was around.

This was in the 60's and it's still a mystery as to how they came to that goofy conclusion. Anyone who went to the woods (swamps) knew you couldn't take a step without tripping over a gator. They may have been extinct in Washington, D.C.. Here, we were flush with them.

But, gators were put on the endangered list, hunting them was prohibited, and they proliferated, crawling all over the city. The *Depot* area was *Gator Central*. The canal behind 6th Lane North, and others, were full of them. And, the abutting yards were full of small children. This caused so

I'M PEDDLIN' AS FAST AS I CAN

many gator calls the wildlife folks were overwhelmed. So, the NPD had to improvise. Enter my associate.

He knew just how to lasso them, secure their killer jaws, and tie them up for portage. We'd hold on to the critters until it was obvious the wildlife folks weren't gonna show. Then, he'd put them in his trunk, take them home, and flop 'em in his bathtub. There they rested until he got off duty. Soon they were transformed into prime eatin's, and, the hides were going for $21 a foot.

The same EPA nonsense was applied to eagles, a first cousin of a vulture. When we were supposed to be in dire danger of losing them, the folks at the dump had to run flocks of them off so the garbage trucks could get in.

Your tax dollars at work!

FIDDLE FUDDER'S FOOD FOIBLES

There was an NPD cop who was about 6' 5" and weighed over 300 lbs. Let's call him Fiddle Fudder. He did play the fiddle, but his real talent was eating. Fudder couldn't get through the night without hitting the Burger Palace for three or four burgers, a plate of fries, and a few Cokes.

A wide body needs a lotta grub and Fudder was always on the prowl for munchies. One night, he was at 4 Corners, trying to keep awake, when a loaded watermelon truck rumbled by. Fudder's food radar alerted with a loud stomach growl. Firing up his cruiser, he was on the truck like Cryin' Jimmy on a hooker, and pulled him over. The driver, innocent of any offense he knew of, asked Fudder why.

"Your truck is overloaded. Looks to me about two melons heavy."

The driver nodded, knowingly, climbing up into the bed. Selecting two, prime melons, he showed them to Fudder, who smiled and nodded. The driver then hurled the melons off the truck, smashing them on U.S. 41.

"That about right?" he said.

He got no answer. Fudder was still standing there, with his mouth open, when the truck drove off.

I'M PEDDLIN' AS FAST AS I CAN

Fudder had a German Shepard, Bubba, who was his constant companion. Stopping by the PD to gab one evening, he left Bubba in the car. Big mistake. Fudder never went anywhere without emergency rations and he'd just bought a dozen tasty donuts. They were in the car with Bubba.

Need I say more? Fudder stayed in the station, talking longer than he'd planned. Finally returning to his car, he found the donut box empty and Bubba lying on the seat, groaning but with a strange satisfied look on his face. Bubba, you see, didn't know the donuts rule; not even a cop should eat a whole dozen. Doing so will make your bowels loosey-goosey and your pucker string unreliable.

Fudder was so upset he gave Bubba a punch. Bubba responded by, uh, spray painting the interior of the car with liquid donuts. This upset Fudder more, and he poked Bubba again. More unmentionable squirting. And so it went.

Over time, Fudder and Bubba forgave each other. And, after Fiddle Fudder's vigorous scrubbing, the car cleaned up and looked presentable. It always had, however, a strange *Krispy Kreme*/outhouse aroma about it.

LET SLEEPING COPS LIE

In olden times, when the bars had closed and all the drunks tucked in, Naples was a mighty quiet town. Moribund. Usually by 3:30 you were slapping your face, trying to keep awake until the *Bus Station Restaurant* opened and Liz and Bert could cook you a decent breakfast.

I never could sleep on duty. Marine Corps had ruined me. I'd seen what they did to Marines who slept on duty and it'd scared me straight. Think of having your thumb placed in the receiver of an M-1 rifle, and the spring-loaded bolt slammed shut on it. Or worse. Some guys could snooze though, and they just found a quiet spot and cribbed.

In fairness, most cops worked at least two jobs and were always tired. Yet, those who couldn't sleep still begrudged those that could. So we messed with them. One favorite prank was to collect a few garbage cans, and tie them to the bumper of the dozing defender's car. Then we'd get on the radio and make a emergency call to sleeping beauty: *Seven-*

I'M PEDDLIN' AS FAST AS I CAN

five, 10-19, 10-18. Cop talk for Officer 75, return to the PD quickly.

Sleeping cops can be comatose behind the wheel and still awaken instantly when their number is called. Without exception, they'd roar outta their hidey hole, dragging all the cans behind them. That would usually cure them for a couple of weeks.

Some cases were harder. Ft. Myers had a cop that couldn't make it past midnight, even when activity was hot and he was needed. When the clock struck twelve, this bozo grabbed his security blanket and hit the sheets. His favorite spot was by a remote railroad crossing.

One early morning, cops arranged for the slow-moving morning train to creep up there and stop. Then, they shoved this Rip Van Dinkle's cruiser up on the crossing, directly in front of the engine. On signal, the engineer hit the locomotive's air horn. Van Dinkle was a notoriously sound sleeper, but when that air horn blasted he reared upright in his seat, saw the train and . . . Witnesses say his laundry required some extra scrubbing that week.

Another dumbo in dream land, Shuteye Sullivan, liked to sleep on a dock. It was sturdy, and just wide enough for the car. Making it custom made for his cure. An emergency call ruined his catnap: *Sullivan, Sullivan, your car's on fire! Get out, get out!* As planned, Shuteye promptly opened the door and took one giant step into the drink.

And some of you must've wondered how the cops stay awake all night.

LET SLEEPING COPS LIE Part 2

Some cops like to get comfy when they crib. Chittlins Brown was one. He'd remove his gun belt and accessories and lay them on the dash. Thus unencumbered, he could saw some serious logs. Sleeping on duty, making yourself a target, was stupid enough. Taking off your weapon? Great Jumpin' Jessie Jackson! Chittlins obviously needed to be taught a lesson. Sgt. J.D. Spohn was just the man to do it.

Early one morning, J.D. found Chittlins snoring on the front seat of his cruiser, in the bushes off 5th Ave North.

I'M PEDDLIN' AS FAST AS I CAN

Approaching with rhino-like stealth, J.D. removed the gun belt and the car keys that were still in the ignition.

When Chittlins finally made it to the NPD several hours later, he had a lot of explaining to do. Must've had a helluva story, cause he continued to work there for a while. Our next miscreant, who we'll call Beau Dumell, needed a real good story, too.

Beau, a young Deputy with the CCSO, was a legendary lady killer--in his own mind. And shrewd in his philandering. Or so he thought. In fact, the residents at the *School for the Deaf and Blind* could've told you who Beau's latest conquest was and where it happened. Beau had a big mouth!

Attracting women wasn't a problem. A few ladies have a thing for cops and let them know. They would get in front of a cruiser and alternately blink their tail lights, left, right, left, right. That meant pull over, and lets talk about the weather. I can't vouch for this personally, you understand, but I'm told that would happened. Howsumever, I digress.

Beau's M.O. was to arrange for a sweetie to meet him at a remote location, usually after midnight. Then he'd show up and it was belly rub time!

Beau, a spiffy dresser, didn't want to crumple his uniform, so he'd take it off and spread it on the hood of his patrol car. Along with his drawers, socks, shoes, and gun belt. No problem. He was in the woods and who knew?

Who knew?

Every Deputy on the CCSO and half the City cops.

It was time for some fun. One evening, when Beau was busy in the back seat of his cruiser, a Deputy crept up and stole everything off the hood. Including the car keys. To make matters worse, this time Beau had brought his paramour to the love nest. There was no other car.

Not without compassion, the Deputies allowed Beau to suffer for only three of four hours before they returned his gear.

THE THREE FOOT CARROT

I'M PEDDLIN' AS FAST AS I CAN

Miami was having a crime problem. A rash of home invasion robberies had disrupted the regular menu of murder, rape, and illicit drugs. These robberies had the added horror of victim torture and they were getting more frequent and violent. One of the latest outrages involved a wheelchair bound victim being beaten senseless, then rolled into his pool.

To get the responsible scumbags, a special squad was formed. Their mandate was to use any means to bag them. Since regular police work wasn't getting it done, the more innovative the better. And innovative they were.

The A-holes who shoved the cripple in the pool were caught immediately. They'd brought so much heat down on the usual criminals, the regulars ratted them out. But, there were many others. Some were 100% suspects but nothing could be proven. These were treated to a night at the golf course. Snatched up, they were taken to the Doral golf course, roughed up, urinated upon, and told to leave Miami and never come back. And, terrified, they did.

Worse suspects got to meet the big rabbit. One of the squad members was a giant, *Hulk Hogan* type. Somewhere a rabbit suit to fit him was located and a giant carrot was fabricated with a baseball bat inside. Picture this. A perp is in the interrogation room and demands his lawyer. The interrogator yells, *Lawyer*. The door bursts open and in comes the rabbit, with his carrot that is applied with vigor to the perp's body. Then the cops says, "*Okay there's your lawyer, do you want your priest?*"

The huge cop had another costume: a gorilla mask and a jock strap. Thus, attired, he would respond to the Lawyer call and do what he did best. Few returned to the interrogation room and the northbound lane of the Florida Turnpike was gridlocked with criminals headed for Orlando. Of course, if a weasel did go to court and complain he was beaten by a six foot rabbit with a big carrot, or a gorilla in a jock strap, he was laughed out of the building.

This good work went on for some time. Robbery/torture was eliminated and other crime rates took a nosedive. But all good things must end. Finally, the special squad was disbanded when a judge said that he knew how criminals were wont to be liars, but if he heard one more story about being brutalized by a big rabbit with a three-foot carrot somebody was going to be in trouble.

SILLY SALESMEN

Mike Grimm and I were sitting in the Detective's office, trying to write reports. Our office was a converted 6'x9' closet. We each had a small desk against one wall. When the guy in back wanted out, the guy by the door had to get up and go out in the hall. But, since *there is no cheese, I won't whine.*

In Sam Bass, the Chief's, office next door, a salesman, Wilson Weasel, was jabbering so loud we couldn't work. I instinctively got up because I knew Mike was gonna do something about it. We wandered into Sam's office, who rolled his eyes, pleading for some relief. Sam was a true southern gentleman and he'd put up with a lot before he was rude to someone, no matter how obnoxious.

The Weasel was touting a revolutionary new raincoat, miracle fabric, lets the air through and keeps the rain out, you name it. He handed one to Mike to inspect. Mike looked at it and inquired, "There's no stitching around the sleeves. How's the sleeve gonna stay on during rough wear?"

"Glad you noticed, that," Weasel yammered, "that was my next point." He turned the raincoat inside out, showing the arm-to-coat seam. "This, my friend, is another unique feature of this coat. The sleeve is welded to the body with a laser gun. They're melted together. No amount of force can pull them apart."

Mike's a big guy with a grand sense of humor. And he loves to let the air out of the overinflated. "Welded, huh?" he said.

"Certainly," Wilson said, "give it your best shot."

Mike clenched his big hands around the coat, gave a vicious jerk and the sleeve tore away from the body. He tossed it to the salesman,. "*You musta brought the wrong sample."*

Wilson Weasel murmured something about having a pressing call he must make, then beat a hasty retreat. Mike winked at Sam and we went back to more mundane duties.

I'M PEDDLIN' AS FAST AS I CAN

Another time, Shirley, my secretary came into my office and said, "There's a guy out there wants you to shoot him."

"Look like he needs it?" I said.

"Probably," Shirley said, "he's a salesman."

Turned out it was the inventor of the *Second Chance* bullet resistant vest. His gimmick was to go to cop shops and demonstrate his product my having a cop shoot him in the chest. I declined this foolishness, so he offered to shoot himself as he had done at several other agencies. He showed us a purple chest to prove his point. We passed on that, too.

The vest was a new product, much lighter than those previous. It became police standard issue in many agencies. His unique advertising campaign read: *Shoot the man who shot you and win a .44 magnum*, or something along those lines. The idea being if you were wearing the vest the assailant's bullet wouldn't kill you so you'd have a chance to kill him. And the company did give you a reward if that happened.

There were some odd cats selling police equipment.

BIG'UN AND THE MAN IN BLACK

Big'un was Fred's German Shepard watchdog at the body shop. Fred was a NPD cop who, like most cops, had something going on the side so he could afford the little extras in life: food, and shelter. He was a talented mechanic and auto body repairman. I sometimes worked for him in the evenings and on weekends.

Fred was a fantastic dude himself who we'll feature later on. This one is about Big'un, whose picture should've been on the *Warning Bad Dog* posters. Big, with bear-like fur, he was scarred from his encounters with just about anything that moved. He looked at you like a dieter eyes a *Krispy Kreme*. He was malevolent, too. Most watchdogs start barking when they hear someone trying to break into the property they're guarding. Not Big'un. He'd be deadly silent, wait for the culprit to get inside, then attack. A Big'un attack wasn't like when Granny's spoiled Schnauzer nips your ankle. Big'un could put you in the hospital.

I'M PEDDLIN' AS FAST AS I CAN

So, I'm working alone in the repair shop one evening and Big'un is locked up in the office for my protection. This is not without great trepidation on my part. Especially, after Fred says when I leave to just unlock the office door and leave it shut. If Big'un hears an intruder later, he'll just bust the door down and get them.

I'm keeping one eye on that door, not confident that the ten-cent lock is gonna keep Big'un in there if he really wants out. Then I remember that Fred said Big'un was a music lover. And mounted on the wall is one of those 8-Track players of old, two large speakers, with a tape already inserted. What the hell, couldn't hurt. I could use a few tunes myself.

Turning it on, it's Johnny Cash. John starts rumbling his *I Walk The Line*. One of my favorites. *I keep a close watch on this heart of mine. . .*then there's this *Hummmmm.* What's that? That's not on the recording. *I keep my eyes wide open all the. . .Hummmmm.* There it was again. And it's coming from the office. And the only one in the office is Big'un.

The humming continues through the entire song, in perfect tune, and in just the right places. When the song ends, the *backup singer* quits, too. I'm dumbfounded. *Must be over-tired. Didn't really hear that. Better go home, get some sleep.*

The next day, I make an anxious special trip to see Fred. He's behind his desk, shuffling some papers. I can't wait to ask him: *Does Big'un sing?*

Fred looks up. "Sing? Nah," he says. "He does hum a little. But he only knows one song, '*I Walk The Line*'."

I know. I know what you're saying: He's been into that cheap booze again. But, it's all true. Think about it. Who could've made up a story this wild? Bottom line, Big'un was a baritone.

THE WATER PISTOL SALESMAN

One day my partner, Dave Dampier, smiling, came in my office and said, *There's something out here you need to see.* Since Dave knew me better than most, I knew it must be a treat. It was. Out in front of the PD was a parked car with a

I'M PEDDLIN' AS FAST AS I CAN

plastic gun on a chain tied to the rear bumper. I looked at Dave, said *What the. . . ?* Dave nodded to an exuberant fella near by.

"Hi," he said, "I'm Harold Huckster and I'm gonna show you the most revolutionary handgun ever made." I looked at the black plastic water pistol-looking thing again. "Our work generally requires we use real guns," I said.

"Oh, it's real enough," Harold said. And it was. It was the 9mm Glock 17 semi-auto, now a police standard, then something from outer space. Glock, knowing that the S&W or Colt revolvers were *the* police guns, figured they were going to have to come up with some innovative marketing to interest cops in this new, funny-looking semi-automatic.

Harold's act worked like this. He'd drive into a PD's parking lot with the Glock on a chain, dragging behind. He claimed it'd been there since he left Miami but who knows. The gun was scruffed up but still in one piece.

Then came his spiel. "This gun is made in Austria from the finest steel and a new, miracle nylon polymer. It's virtually indestructible. Won't rust. And to prove that, I want you to put this one in a bucket of salt water. I'll be back in about three weeks. If that Glock doesn't fire I'll give you nine free ones."

The saltwater soaked air in South Florida is hard enough on firearms. Blue steel rusts easily without constant attention. Total immersion in salt water, for that long, would turn most weapons, even stainless steel, into a corrosive green lump. We laughed but took him up on it, mostly to get rid of him. Our range officer, Jim Spohn, duly took the gun and drowned it in a five-gallon bucket of briny liquid.

When Harold returned, we quit laughing. Taken out of the bucket, wiped off, loaded, it fired an entire seventeen-round magazine. And, there was no rust. That day began the evolution from the old *wheel guns* (revolvers) to semi-automatics. It has been so total that when I retired from the SO I was the only cop that still carried a revolver.

Still do. To me, whenever I see a Glock I expect to see a stream of water squirting out of the barrel. Besides, Dirty

Harry wouldn't be caught dead with something as ugly as that.

STOP GAP MEASURES

When folks consume enough *liquid stupid*, or narcotics, they do some dumb things. Especially with sharp objects.

In McDonald Quarters there were two prescribed ways to fight with a knife. First, go for any slash or stab that will put your opponent away. The second, is meant to punish, but not necessarily kill. The blade of the knife is held with about a half-inch exposed beyond the fingers. The adversary is stuck, or *jooged*, with the knife and a slight, shallow wound results. After one has had enough, the fight is ended.

Problems can arise. We worked one homicide in which the deceased had been jooged over a 100 times. The cuts had been made with a 3" Case pocket knife. But the multitude of cuts had allowed the *stickee* to bleed out. He had, in fact, gone back in the *Juke,* and had a couple beers before he fell over. When he did fall over, he was dead.

That was one. An alert girlfriend prevented another. Willie Wazzup, after being stabbed, had fallen to the ground, dripping blood from each hole. His paramour, Florence Nightenhen, knew he'd never make it to the hospital. So she improvised. Finding a newspaper, she tore off little pieces and stuffed them into the cuts with a Popsicle stick. When Willie was suitably patched, she rushed him to the ER.

The ER doctor was impressed. He said, "I'm an MD, supposed to know it all, but faced with the same situation, and without my tape and bandages, I wouldn't have thought of this. That woman saved his life." And so she did.

Another case involved a half-dozen college kids, in a house near Royal Harbor, who took bad trips on LSD. All in attendance were stoned into another dimension. One, Timothy Bleary, was having terrifying visions. There was some horrible beast in his stomach trying to rip itself out. No, problem, another of the buzzed ones allowed. He'd operate and remove the monster. And operate he did, with a hunting knife, while Bleary lay squirming on the living room floor. Satisfied the beast must have escaped, and noting a

I'M PEDDLIN' AS FAST AS I CAN

copious amount of blood, the *doctor* removed his T-shirt, stuffed it in the six-inch slice in Bleary's belly and left the operating room.

The least stoned, a girl who remained naked though the whole affair, thinking her clothes were feathers and it was molting season, had enough sanity remaining to call EMS. We arrived before EMS, and noted Bleary, strangely serene on the floor, content that the monster had been released. He felt no pain and didn't remember the *operation.*

The *surgeon* was still so stoned he didn't realize what he'd done, but, in reparation he had, by plugging the wound with the T-shirt, probably saved Bleary's life. Another victory for the Angel who protects the stoned and stupid.

STUPID SNAKE LOVERS

Recently, pythons in the Everglades proliferated until they're a menace to other wildlife. The rangers are now hunting them. Pythons? How'd they get there? By dumb-az pet owners turning them loose after they got tired of them. Same thing with piranhas. They're not indigenous. Stupid pet owners have dumped them there after they bit off their finger tip and swallowed their pet guppy. Cops have to deal with these idiots. Two come to mind.

The first Bozo lived in Royal Harbor. We got a call that his python had disappeared. On entering the house, you had to walk by homemade screen cages full of snakes, his *pets.* Several of the doors were unlocked or ajar. Some of the ajar ones were empty. "These supposed to be empty?" I asked.

"No, but they're not poison snakes. They're around here somewhere."

No comfort there. What snake lovers don't realize is that to the rest of us all snakes are repulsive and poisonous. We don't want to be in the same state with one. He moved to one of the cages that was unlocked, "Probably ought to latch this. Copperhead."

His problem, aside from being stupid, was that he'd just fed his seven-foot python and he couldn't find him. Said the thing would hole up for weeks now since it'd had a big meal.

I'M PEDDLIN' AS FAST AS I CAN

I didn't ask what that meal was but hoped it was one of his off-spring who were snake nuts, too.

So we're crawling around looking for this critter and I'm as jumpy as Jessie Jackson at a grand jury investigation, thinking there's a snake under every tea cup. I get tired and sit on the couch. Something under me moves. I jump up.

"Oh," Bozo says, "why didn't I think of that?" He tips the couch back and part of the ticking has been pulled loose. And here's this nasty damn thing interwoven among the springs. Bozo was ecstatic and profuse in his thanks for my help. I got the hell outta there.

About six months later I returned to his snake's den. "Missing a snake?" I asked.

He got a sheepish look on his face and said, "I was just getting ready to call you..."

"Car just ran over one, about six-feet long, two streets over. Thought it might be yours."

"Oh, no," he whimpered, "my new boa. He wandered off and..."

We'd contacted the animal and wildlife people before about this clown but they could do nothing. Finally, he got tired of the things and got rid of them. I suspect by dumping them in the Everglades.

Another dope, used to carry his seven-foot python around in public. We were always getting calls from terrified folks he'd encountered. "*It's perfectly safe,*" he'd say, all the while wrestling the thing to keep it from coiling around his neck. One day he brought the snake into the Sheriff's Office lobby causing me to have a meaningful dialogue with him, explaining how he could avoid incarceration and his snake an untimely demise. He was duly terrified and we had no calls about him for almost a year. Then he stepped on his carrot again.

He'd taken the thing to the mall. There, he was showing it to a frightened mother and her two-year-old baby. Without warning, the beast unhinged its jaws and clamped them over the head of the child. It took some effort to pry the monster loose. The baby suffered bites on the top of her head and chin from the snake's teeth. And long-term psychological damage.

The turd went to jail for a time but wonderful retribution came a few years later when a civil jury wiped him out financially.

THE ROPED ROMEO

Enforcing homosexual laws was low priority. But, sometimes, we'd get so many complaints about aggressive male homosexual activity we'd have to do something about it. One location was the *Men's Restroom* at the *City Pier*.

The City tried, since the Pier was its crown jewel, to keep it in good repair. One problem was homosexuals liked to bore holes in the divider partitions like woodpeckers, woodpeckers being a propitious term as you will see. The holes were bored at waist level adjacent to a urinal. This allowed a latrine Lothario sitting on the toilet to place his eye up against the partition and check out the equipment of someone taking a leak.

Might not sound like a fun way to pass an afternoon, but it was popular. Soon as the holes were patched, they'd be re-bored.

The other type of hole was bored in the thin divider between two stalls. This allowed two folks to engaged in oral sex by one placing his, uh, *serious intentions* through the hole so the other fella could. . .well, you get the point. Hence the term, woodpeckers.

Had these gents been particular and kept their games to those who appreciated them, there wouldn't have been much cause for our grief. But, they didn't. We'd have reports of someone enjoying a relaxed sit-down, in one of the stalls, when suddenly a one-eyed worm would wiggle through the wall. Or through the eyeball hole by a urinal.

As mentioned, we didn't have a lotta time to waste on this foolishness and thank Heaven, American ingenuity solved the problem. Some good citizen, evidently a victim of probing penis syndrome, decided to take matters into his own hands: literally.

I'M PEDDLIN' AS FAST AS I CAN

One night, we received an anonymous call referencing a *something suspicious in the men's restroom at the pier*. At first we though it was a joke because the caller was laughing. We did, however, in due time respond. Our officer, on entering the restroom heard a muffled *"Please help me"* coming from one of the stalls. Opening the door, he saw a man with his belly flush up against the partition. The man gasped, *"The other side, the other side."* Opening the door, the cop saw what caused him to roar with laughter. This in turn making our toilet tryst seeker yell, *"It's not funny!"*

Someone had tied a slip-noose in a piece of rawhide, which in turn, was tied to one of those green concrete sprinkler donuts. It seems that when the wandering wang poked through the hole, our hero slipped the noose over it and snugged it and the donut up tight, thereby trapping the prober.

We called an ambulance for the roped Romeo--none of us were about to undo that thing. He was taken, with his now blue Magoo, to the ER where he was treated and release. We didn't have any charges we cared to press, figuring nothing worse could happen to this guy. And we never found the problem solver.

Nor did we look very hard. There was a rumor that it was an off-duty cop but we discounted that as totally ridiculous.

IT AIN'T THE MAYO CLINIC

Naples once contracted the job of City Doctor. The duties included giving physicals, treating injured workers, and attending to the Jail's medical needs. Usually it was a young doctor, just starting their practice. Since the contract was essential income, some were too protective of the City's interests.

One sawbones, who we'll call Dr. Cash R. Check, sometimes went overboard. When I was in the Marines, if you got scruffed up in a bar or barracks fight, an officer might inquire as to what happened to you. *"Tripped on a locker box, Sir,"* was the correct answer. No one, officially, really wanted to know so that answer served the purpose.

I'M PEDDLIN' AS FAST AS I CAN

Dr. Check was probably a former Marine. Whenever a prisoner had been battered in the course of effecting an arrest, the medical report read: *Tripped on stairs in Jail.* To anyone who really cared, this answer might've been suspect. There were no stairs in the Jail.

We once jailed a huge brute, a Bluto, who'd fought our own huge brute, Ed Jones, when Ed tried to arrest him. During the fight, he wrestled Ed's .41 revolver from its holster and Ed had a helluva time staying alive. Finally, Ed twisted the arm holding the revolver up in a hammer lock, got his finger on the trigger, and squeezed off two rounds into the A-Hole's back. Shoulda killed him. But, as with many primitive life forms, the bullets did little damage and Bluto was put in jail.

In retaliation, he'd rip the bandages off, and gouge the wound until it started bleeding, requiring us to call the City Doctor. After Dr. Check had made his third visit to tend to this turd, he asked Bluto why he was doing it. Bluto said: *Because I like pain.*

"Oh?" said Dr Check. "Then this should tickle you to death," thereby forcing his index finger into one of the gunshot wounds, and giving it a few spirited twists.

Turns out Bluto was a liar. He didn't really like pain, so indicated, by giving a soprano-like scream and passing out. And Dr. Check's innovative procedure cured Bluto of self-abuse. He never pulled the dressings off again.

Another time our City Doctor was working the ER room. In came an unruly arrestee who'd been in a knife fight in McDonald Quarters. The victim, dripping blood, was so combative that two of our cops had to hold him on the ER table.

Dr. Splint told the dumb-az to hold still as he was going to need many stitches. Still no surcease. So the good doctor started to work anyway, and without a drop of pain killer, sewed in over 300 stitches. Some required sub-surface, deep stitches and, after the first few, the curses turned to screams. Then to groans and moans. He was thereafter, however, a righteous patient.

Not exactly the Mayo Clinic but an excellent example of *government provided, free medical care.*

3rd PRECINCT

DETECTIVE TRAINING

Det Jack Bliss was a big help to my career. Early on, he told me that some day soon the NPD was going to need two detectives and that job would go to the person who had some experience doing the work. He said that if I was interested he'd show me how to work cases and do the reports. I'd have to do this off-duty, but I jumped at the chance. I never was real big on writing traffic citations  unless some A-hole really deserved one: drunk driving, reckless driving, something like that.

One early morning, Jack called me and said he had a gunshot suicide and could use me. I was just getting off the 11 to 7 shift, so I responded immediately. When I arrived I saw the most gruesome site I'd seen up to that time. The

I'M PEDDLIN' AS FAST AS I CAN

deceased had sat down on the floor, with his back to a corner, put a shotgun under his chin, and pulled the trigger with his toe. His entire head, in gory chunks, had been blown up the corner walls, ricocheted off the ceiling and splattered the room.

Glad I hadn't eaten breakfast yet, I helped Jack photograph the scene, do the evidence collection, and write notes for the report. When we'd completed, Jack told me to photograph the outside of the house. I complied.

When I returned, Jack, excited, said, "There's a rare creature over there. Go take its picture."

I looked at him, questioning his request.

He pointed to the headless body, still sitting in the corner. *Cyclops*, he said.

On closer inspection I could see that there was a single eyeball, balanced on the remaining spinal stalk. Jack busted out laughing, grabbed the camera and started taking photographs. This work of art had required him to fish around in the goop until he'd found an eyeball, then delicately balance it on the spinal stem.

The resulting photo bounced around the PD for years and caused many a rookie gastric distress.

Another time we were at the funeral home and Jack was showing me how to fingerprint a corpse. This can be quite a trick, especially if it's during a period of rigor. This one, a mature, heavy, man required that we break loose several of his fingers. There was a device called a spoon, to help you obtain the print, but it didn't work too well. You got a better print if you just cracked the finger loose from it's curled position, and rolled it on a regular pad and card.

I was thankful that this wasn't a floater. The water so shriveled their skin, that you had to cut off the fingertip skin, flatten it in saline solution for a while, then place it over your own finger and roll out the print.

Howsumever, our gruesome work was interrupted by a thunderous fart, obviously from Bliss. But he wasn't going to take credit. Cradling the deceased's chin in his big hand, he tilted the head and looked into its half-open eyes. "If you're that damn lively, you can fingerprint yourself."

By that time, I'd been around awhile and discovered that dark humor could keep you reasonably sane. I joined Jack in healthy laughter.

RIDING THE RAILS

We've talked before about how tough it is to stay awake on slow nights. Everyone has their own tricks. One Sgt was a stargazer. He'd sit for hours staring at the heavens. Trouble was, he stared so long he became convinced he was seeing flying saucers and became a nut on the subject.

Sleepers have been mentioned. Others rigged up portable reading lamps in their cars. Some ate till they earned nicknames like Roundy and Bucket Butt. A few came to work prepared for a healthful rest. Ray Barnett said the first time he worked the Midnight shift with Jimmy Spohn, Jimmy showed up carrying a blanket and pillow. Then there were the one's who were truly inventive. Sam Bass was the Tom Edison here.

Sam, then a Sgt, later the Chief, gave me a call one dreary night. "How 'bout you 56 (meet) me over at 5th Ave North and the tracks." I complied. (*The railroad tracks then followed, generally, Goodlette Road, to the north, until the road ended at Pine Ridge Road*)

Sam motioned me to park my cruiser off the road. He had his car turned sideways, sitting on the asphalt crossing, aimed up the railroad track. "Ever ride the rails?" he said, flashing that wonderful Sam Bass grin.

"Nope," I said, wondering what he had in mind.

"I found out if you line these Chevies up just right the tires hang over the rails, keeping the thing in place and you can ride it like it was a train."

"Huh?"

"No stuff," Sam said. "Wanna try?"

If this worked as Sam said, there was little danger. The train only ran once a day, in the afternoon. And it just crept along, since we'd given it a ticket for speeding. No kiddin', we did. Had to. Couldn't keep the engineer from speeding through the uncontrolled crossings.

I'M PEDDLIN' AS FAST AS I CAN

Anyway, I helped Sam line up the car just right, got in, and away we went. It was the best automobile ride I've ever taken.

Never had a smoother one. And, it took very little engine power to propel the car along, so there was no noise. Sam, of course, didn't have to steer. We cruised at about 15 MPH-- didn't want to get a ticket--up to the Pine Ridge crossing, and got off. After that night, when the city was dead asleep, we took many rides, sometimes going as far as Bonita. I even learned how to do it by myself.

What a waste of time, you say. Jackasses at play! Maybe, but there was benefit from the training. We'd received a call one morning that a burglar had just been routed in a North Naples home, and was running away up the railroad right-of-way. Since there was no parallel road beyond Pine Ridge, officers were trying to find a motorcycle or something to give chase. My partner, Ken Mulling, and I heard the call and radioed to never mind. We'd ride the rails.

We put our car on the tracks at Pine Ridge, and began the chase. No one could've been more surprised than our desperado when, some miles up the tracks, he looked back and saw an unmarked police car, blue light flashing, closing on him. So surprised was he to see the unique method of transportation, that he just stood there, stupid and staring, until we put him under arrest.

Always wondered what he told his fellow convicts in prison about how he got caught. *Guess you might say I got caught by Detectives in a loco-mobile.*

SATURDAY NITE FIGHTS

The *Anchor Lounge* was another favorite venue for the Saturday Night Fights. Their constant barmaid, Inez figured in a lot of them.

Inez was middle-aged and stout with beautiful white hair, that she had professionally set every day. It was her trademark. That and her *Don't Mess With Inez* reputation. She could handle most unruly customers herself and when she had to call us, we knew it we were going to earn our money.

Sometimes the customers called us on her. Once a responding cop found a drunk standing outside the entrance, with the rear end of his trousers soaked in blood. The cop inquired and got this;

"I wuz leaving and was gonna take two for the road. They wuz outta plastic cups so I just got two drinks in regular glasses. Knowin' you ain't supposed to leave with their glasses, I snuck 'em in my back pocket. Was almost out the door when Inez stops me."

There was a quiver of terror in his voice when he mentioned her name. He went on.

"She spins me around, pushes me up against the wall and says 'No glasses out of the building'. I say I'd don't have any. So she says, *'Then this won't hurt,'* and puts her hands on my hips and shoves me into the wall, bustin' the glasses and doin' this." He pointed to his ragged arse.

"So what you want me to do?" the cop said, "You want to press charges?"

"Holy Christ, no," the drunk babbled. "And get her REALLY pissed off?"

At about 3 AM, one Saturday night, an officer was cruising by the closed Anchor when he heard muffled screams. On closer inspection he could tell they were coming from the lounge area, someone screaming *"Oh God, help me, I'm blind."* The cop radioed in to have dispatch notify Bill, the owner. Shortly, he arrived on the scene.

"What the hell?" Bill said, unlocking the door. Inside the screams were ear-splitting, *"I'm blind, I'm blind."* Bill turned on the lounge lights. Under a corner-booth table they found the screamer, Six-Pack Slocum. He was in the fetal position, and drunker than Hogan's goat.

"Open your eyes," the cop ordered.

Slocum eased open his eyes, looked around, and weeping, said, "I'm healed. Thank you, Jesus. I'll never drink again."

Two miracles? The blind healed? More impressive, Slocum giving up the booze? Hardly. He was drunk again before noon. And the healing miracle was short-lived, too.

I'M PEDDLIN' AS FAST AS I CAN

Turns out Slocum had decided he was gonna do some az-kickin' that night, just before closing time. This is a common side-effect of drinking too much liquid stupid. Staggering out on the dance floor, he made a terrible choice of opponents. It was NPD cop, Jack Bliss, who was big, strong, and ex-Airborne. One punch and Slocum went skidding on his back, across the slick dance floor and up under the booth's table. There he remained, passed out and overlooked when the bar closed. He'd awakened in the dark lounge and, in his stupor, thought he was blind.

Others who'd been KO'd by Jack Bliss could attest that he could sure do that to you.

MO HO, HO, HO'S

An old cop joke was that there was no prostitution in Naples because hookers couldn't compete with free enterprise. Truth was, we did have a few then. No escort or massage services, like today, but prostitution is always ubiquitous.

Lulu Loosey, a real sweetie, was operating out of The Cove Inn. We, the cops, hadn't received any complaints on her and, if a hooker was running a legit game, she was low priority. She must've, however, tread on somebody's carrot cause we got word from above to shut her down. Wasn't gonna be easy.

Lulu had tricks to entice customers and detect cops. Ever hear the one about catching monkeys by filling hollow coconuts with rice, and cutting a hole just big enough for the monkey's hand to get through. Once it grabbed the rice it wouldn't let go and the closed fist was too big to come back out. Lulu must've heard that yarn.

Soon as the John entered her room, she'd hit that button hooker's have on their costume that makes it fall away, instantly. Then she'd yank down the customer's fly, insert her hand, grab ahold, and not let go. This, all the while rubbing her bountiful boobies in their face. Legit customers, of course, loved it. Cops, it put in an awkward position. Some forgot why they were there. Or would have a hard time testifying in court. Defense attorney: *And just how long did*

I'M PEDDLIN' AS FAST AS I CAN

you stand there, with the defendant, allegedly, holding your, uh, credentials, officer?

See what I mean? We needed a plan and just the right officer.

We selected one of small stature who didn't look like cop. Since we knew that Lulu was too smart to talk about money until she had you in her grasp, we told him to stand with his back to the door, try to ward her off until she set the price, then, kick with his heel on the door. We'd be right outside and bust in. We were Det Ray Barnett and yours truly.

Our cop, who we'll call Donnie Dumplin, was reluctant. "Don't know if I can do it," he said. "Woman get's her hand on me like that, I might cave in."

We talked it over and Donnie was the only guy we had that didn't look or talk like a Joe Friday. So, he agreed, with great reluctance, and the assurance we'd be right outside the door.

That evening everything was going like clockwork. Donnie took a seat in the bar, and before he had one sip of his ginger ale, Lulu was beside him. Twenty minutes later they were headed for her room. Ray and I followed, discretely, and when they went inside we positioned ourselves, as promised, just outside the door. In less than a minute, there was woodpecker-like hammering on the door.

Then that unexplainable quirky cop's sense of humor kicked in. Ray looked at me, I looked at him, and we both went and had a beer.

Later, we told Donnie we'd received a 10-18 and had to leave. Donnie, who didn't ride in on a rutabaga truck, said nothing happened. Lulu was suspicious and wouldn't say the right words to allow an arrest. Uh-huh.

Still under pressure, we had a meeting with Lulu and explained the facts of life to her. She said it was getting warm up north anyway, so she'd venture back to New York. And all was well. Crime was quelled in the big city, and the gentle citizens of Naples were safe once more.

Donnie Dumplin never mentioned the incident again. But, he always smiled when he drove by The Cove Inn.

PROSTITUTES IN PARADISE

Prostitutes in Paradise? Trollops in the Elephant's Graveyard. Say it isn't so.

My first encounter with ho's while on the job happened when I was a rank rookie in 1963. The newest cop, I hadn't even been to the academy yet and was acting as Duty Officer/Dispatcher. About 11 p.m. two lovely young ladies, in revealing dresses and showgirl makeup, sashayed up to my desk.

"Help you?" I asked.

One was Barbie blond, the other had long, dark hair like Cher. Barbie answered. "We just wanted to let you know what a lame-ass town you live in—if you don't know already."

"It ain't New Orleans," I said.

"Tell me about it," Cher said, "and we just wasted an evening's wages findin' that out."

"How's that?"

"Case ya didn't know, we're workin' girls from Miami. We read about the Pet Milk convention over at the Beach Club and decided, havin' heard so much about Naples, to come over and have a nice little vacation and turn a few tricks."

I'm sure my eyes lit up at this blatant admission.

"Didn't work out that way. We lost our ass, so to speak. If one of those old codgers had ever had a bone, some dog had carried it off and buried it."

"Yeah," said a pouting Barbie, "We could've gotten more action with a bowl of wet noodles."

I laughed.

"So, we already have our room rented for the night, and we decided to drop by to see if maybe we could perform some public service. Unless the cops over here are all relics, too. Prices slashed, and maybe. . . if you show us a good time. . ."

Being a rookie, I was stunned. Having served a hitch in the Marines, I was conversant with the concept of prostitution. And I knew that in big cities the cops had special arrangements with hookers. Maybe Miami was like that and that's why the girls were so open about their proposition. But

I'M PEDDLIN' AS FAST AS I CAN

it was supposed to be illegal and I probably should be doing something about it.

I said "Excuse me a minute," and went to the back room to consult with the Sergeant who was in the office preparing for shift change at eleven. I told him about what was going on and that I wasn't sure how to proceed. He peeked around the door frame, to check out the two ladies, and said. "These vice things are tricky. Better let me handle it. Send 'em back."

After a few minutes I could hear the girls high pitched laughter. Then the room was filled with cops going off duty and cops coming on. Really loud laughter, now, male and female. Soon the Sergeant and two off-duty cops in civies came strolling by the duty desk. The girls smiled and Barbie blew me a kiss. The sergeant turned, and winked as they left the building.

The next evening, before his shift started, the Sergeant came up to me. "Appreciate that deal last night, You done good, real good."

"I'm just glad you were able to get those girls straightened out, didn't have to put 'em in jail."

The Sergeant looked at me a few seconds, then roared with laughter. "You've got a helluva sense of humor, kid," he said.

After a few months, when I'd seen how the real world worked, I realized just what he'd thought was so damn funny.

MORE DOG TAILS

We enjoyed a rover in Naples whose name was Bonaparte, Napoleon, or the Little General, depending on who you asked. He was a kinda Basset, and belonged to Naples icon, Jack Breeden. *(Jack's a guy you could see around town driving his Model T Ford)* Napoleon roamed the city at will, collecting treats, greeting old friends, seemingly taking in the sights. Much like Jack.

One day we were in Cambier Park, doing our P/E program. I was the leader that day. Standing in front of the reluctant group, I was surprised when everyone began laughing. Looking down, I could see why. Bonaparte had expressed his opinion of exercise programs by peeing on my sweatpants clad leg.

Then there was the lady who walked her Poodle each day down to the PD at 8th and 8th South. This was her dog's favorite toilet area--again probably expressing an opinion. For such a small beast, it left prodigious piles of um pah. On day we mentioned to her that she should do something about the messy operation. She did. From then on, after the daily dump, she wiped the dog's rear end with a Kleenex.

Jack Bliss, then a Captain, had a large German Shepard named Prince. Prince had a game, each day, of racing Jack to work. Jack lived near the hospital, and it took him but a few minutes to get to the PD. But, Prince, who knew all the shortcuts, would leave at the same time and beat Jack to work. Evidently he could tell time, too, as he'd appear after work to race Jack home.

One day we noticed that Prince's jaws were puffed up. He was holding something gently in his mouth. We wondered what until he lowered his head and spit out a baby duck, a little fuzzball that he'd come upon. Prince would stand guard while the little feller foraged or did what little ducks do. But if a perceived threat presented, the baby would run to Prince's open jaws. Prince brought the duckling to work with him until it was just too large to carry.

Detective Ken Mulling had a big Shepard, too. Ken stopped by his house one afternoon to check on a birthday cake his wife Donna had baked. He placed the masterpiece on the kitchen table. Then he remembered they needed ice cream. On returning from the store, Ken could hear groans from inside the house even before he opened the door. There he found his trusted friend, lying on his side with a huge distended belly, moaning. And on the kitchen table, was a cake plate licked dishwasher clean.

(*Ken recently left us. He'll be missed. God rest his soul*)

SMOOTH OPERATOR -Part 1

When I was a rookie, a veteran Sgt. Robert Dennis, became my tutor. At the time you could work months before you went to the academy, so someone had to show you the ropes.

I'M PEDDLIN' AS FAST AS I CAN

When Chief Ben Caruthers hired me, he gave me a gun and a city map, showed me where the law books were, and said *"go get 'em, hoss."*

Sgt Dennis was a smooth operator. Slow-talking, even-tempered, and a treat for the ladies. One evening he was showing a rookie how to handle people who were drunk and disorderly.

"Never hit a drunk. It is not an opportunity to play catchup for having a bad day. Don't know about you, but I've been drunk myself and done some dumb things. I appreciated when people overlooked and didn't take advantage. If you handle yourself properly there is never any reason to hit one. I have no respect for cops that do." It was good advice.

"Now," he said, "the Cardinal rule; never, never, ever, hit a woman. Never. No way you can win. She can be as big as King Kong, and twice as smelly, but you lay one finger on her, in the eyes of the public you're wrong. You understand?"

The rookie nodded yes.

"That's never," he said, making eye contact for emphasis.

Just happened they were dealing with a woman. A respected member of the community, an architect's wife. We'll call here June. Well liked, respected, she was into charities, lived in the right neighborhood, and knew the best people. She was also a binge drunk, who'd been picked up stoned in her Caddy. And when she was drowning in liquid stupid she wasn't worth a damn. Filthy-mouthed, demeaning, unruly.

That night, they'd taken June into the front office and were trying to contact her husband to come get her. She wouldn't sit still, finally jumping to her feet, crashing through the front door, and falling off the porch with a grand thud. Fearing she'd hurt herself, they rushed to her and lifted her up. The angel of drunken mercy had saved her--no damage. And her mouth was working perfectly. "Like to touch me, huh? I knew it. I saw you staring at 'em. Well, here," she said, ripping off her blouse and pulling down her bra, "have a good look."

I'M PEDDLIN' AS FAST AS I CAN

Sgt. Dennis tried to pull up her bra, or get her blouse back around her, but that wasn't working. The rookie was frozen stupid, not knowing what to do. Wrestling June, Dennis lost balance and fell into a chair. June mounted him, smothering his face with her, uh, accouterments, and humming what, to the rookie, sounded like the kid's tub tune, *Rubber Ducky*.

Dennis pushed her off, but she charged again, this time landing a healthy haymaker on his honker. He muttered an oath, and delivered a short karate kinda chop to June's neck that put her to sleep. Instantly.

It turned out, June wasn't hurt. She didn't even remember what'd happened. Her husband arrived, took her home, and they were done with her until the next time. That left just the sergeant and rookie. The rookie looked at him.

Dennis shrugged, said, *"What?????"*

"The never, never thing..."

Sgt Robert Dennis smiled. "That's never, never...unless they start actin' like a man. Then, it's the Bap, Zoom thing," imitating Jackie Gleason's famous *To The moon, Alice* gesture.

"And, the last rule, one I forgot to tell you," he concluded, "don't let anybody see ya do it."

SATURDAY NIGHT FIGHTS Part 2

Each weekend, what we called the Saturday Night Fights took place. These impromptu fisticuffs were held at the Anchor Lounge or more often, at the Burger Palace, a 24-hour joint in the wedge formed by Davis Blvd and US 41. One of the frequent gladiators was a maggot we'll call BO Splatt.

When BO got enough booze guts he had to pick a fight. An expert at the sucker punch, he was so obnoxious he didn't need to use it to work up a good punch-out. His problem was, he wasn't much of a fighter. Oh, sometimes he'd win if his opponent was drunker than he, or crippled, or a woman. But generally he was awarded a much deserved az-whoopin.

Sam Bass, who was once Chief, taught me how to work a BO Splatt type fight. If BO happened to be winning, you'd plow right in, grab BO and do as much damage as possible

I'M PEDDLIN' AS FAST AS I CAN

placing him under arrest. If he was losing, you'd just stand there and say in a relaxed voice, "Come on boys, let's break it up," until BO's face was beaten into blueberry cobbler.

One night BO got in a shoving match inside the Burger--we called it *Burglar*--Palace. During the scuffle he was shoved into one of our giant retired cops, Fred Scott, who was at the counter enjoying a dozen or so tasty burgers. You didn't interrupt Fred when he was eating. He responded by grabbing BO by the neck and grinding his facing into the plate of food. Fred then told the waitress, "Give me some fresh burgers and give this A-hole the check."

One night BO had taken his act to the *Anchor*. Drunk and wild, he'd backed up to a wall, taken out his knife and was slashing at the air, shouting, "*Don't touch me, I'm crazy, I'm crazy.*"

Det Jack Bliss, who'd slipped up beside him, took out his revolver, screwed it in BO's ear and said "Bet you're sane now." And miracle of miracles, cured he was, being calmly led away in cuffs to the derisive laughter of the bar's patrons.

Finally BO became so *persona non grata* at his regular haunts, he moved on to new ground, The Royal Castle, on 41 at about 12th Ave No. Maybe there was someone up there he could whip. Didn't take long to spy a likely opponent--The One-Armed Man. *Hell, one arm how tough can he be?* It was a choice that probably gave BO nightmares in the future during his long prison nights. (*His regular occupation was sneak thief and burglar. He was also a rat for the Sheriff's Office.*)

Anyway, The One-Armed-Man had, well, one arm. He was medium height, stocky, of pleasant disposition, and seemed to have no special physical talents. But, Lord-A-Mighty could he fight. He used a technique that nowadays is called the spinning back fist, where he spun on one foot, his lone arm extended. The attached fist, propelled by centrifugal force, cracked into skulls like a sledge hammer. One of those skulls, of course, belonged to BO Splatt.

Byron Tomlinson, a cop who witnessed the carnage, said BO was knocked cross-eyed, literally, from the punch, and for several hours couldn't remember his name, number, or nomenclature.

It's these ironic little moments of justice that can make life so sweet.

TRAVELS IN STUPIDVILLE

Ever think back on stupid things you've done and wonder why you did them. Answer's easy: *Seemed like a real good idea at the time.*

After work, I was headed home up Goodlette Road. Had the weekend off, kinda, and was as happy as a fat kid with a chocolate bunny. Kinda, because being one of only two Detectives I was on call-out. But it was the summer and business was slow so maybe I'd skate.

Up ahead a young, red-headed W/M, in a green shirt, bolts across Goodlette and heads into the auxiliary City Dump, south of where the PD now stands. I was wondering what was chasing him when a BOLO came over the radio. For a young red-headed W/M, in a green shirt, who'd just robbed a merchant on 10th Street South. Caution was advised as the perp had brandished a revolver.

So I said to myself, *Self, that sounds like the dude that just ran in front of you.* Maybe you better check this out. (An example of my keen perceptive powers, and relentless pursuit, causing criminals to jump in my lap) I accelerated and notified dispatch of the situation.

Pulling into the small dump, I could see the man struggling to climb over a pile of trash. He'd take two steps, lose footing, and fall back three. I stopped the unmarked Chevy and reached for my duty weapon, a Colt Detective Special. Whoops, since I was off for the weekend, I'd locked it in my desk. No problem, there was an extra revolver, for just such occasions, in the glove compartment. Keeping an eye on the suspect, I fished around blindly in the glove compartment. Nothing there. I looked to be sure. Nope, no gun. Turns out my partner's pistol was at the gunsmith's and he'd borrowed that one.

Now what?

Just then, the perp turned and I could see his face. I'd arrested him before. Knew him. And he knew me. I couldn't see a gun in his hands. Not having many options except getting the hell outta there, I decided to try and bluff him. Opening the door, I stooped down behind it, and pointed my finger at him like kids do when they play cops and robbers. And hoped, at this distance, he thought it looked like a gun.

"*Okay, Roho,*" I yelled, "*you know the drill. Toss the gun, on your belly, hands behind your head.*"

Roho looked at me for what seemed an hour, then lifted his shirt, and reached toward his trouser's waistband.

I was sweating now. *Don't be stupid Roho. Don't make me shoot you. Take out that gun, with two fingers on the grip, and drop it.*

He responded with, "*I'm doin' it, I'm doin' it*" and did just that. And, like a good dog, he flopped down on his belly. I moved on him quickly and picked up his gun. It was just an old Saturday Nite Special but, at that moment, it felt very welcome. Pointing it at him, I got him up, and walked him back to the car where there was a set of handcuffs hanging on the emergency brake lever.

On the way to the station, Roho got religion and started confessing. "Knew it was a bad idea but did it anyway. Before I leave the house, my wife says, 'don't do anything stupid.' She knows me. Shoulda listened. But, no, put the gun in my pocket and start walkin' around, no place in particular. Come on the store, some reason it looks good. Then, I start to think maybe not. Come an ace of not goin' in. But I did."

"Yep," I muttered, not wanting to slow him down. *(We didn't use Miranda back then or other asinine warnings that slow confessions. Ignorant us, we thought cops were supposed to get confessions.)*

Roho went on, "Things had been different, not an assed up deal to begin with, I might not've been so easy to bring in. The gun, it's empty. I forgot to load it. If I had . . ."

Long as it was confession time, I probably should've told Roho the truth. But I didn't. Truth was, it was a day for dumb plays. A dumb robber. And a dumb-lucky cop, arresting thugs with a .38 caliber finger.

I'M PEDDLIN' AS FAST AS I CAN

But it did seem like a good idea at the time.

A REALLY BIG SHOPLIFTER, REALLY!

Maxine Gluteus was a big shoplifter. In every way. She made big hauls. She carried out big items--so large they appeared impossible to hide. And, she was a big woman. At five-ten, Maxine weighed in at an enormous 400+ lbs.

Maxine's methods were unique. She covered her mountainous brown bod with a Hawaiian muu'muu, that hid everything but her feet. In that flowery tent she looked like Mt. Kilauea decorated for a luau.

She'd modified the dress by sewing fishing weights in the front hem. She could jerk up the front, hide her loot, and drop it in an instant. Under her dress she wore a giant pocket made from a butcher's apron. The pocket had a wire-reinforced top to keep it partly open. And, for large items, the choice spot. In between those garbage can thighs. That's why she moved with a slow shuffle, her feet just scuffing the ground.

Maxine was rarely caught. We had her in jail only because a store clerk, on her way to work at the *Kwik-Chek*, saw her surreptitiously unloading her haul into her car. The clerk first though she was watching a magic act. One of those where the magician keeps making stuff appear from their bare hands. Except Maxine's act was far more impressive. From under that robe-thing, she was hauling out six-packs of beer, canned goods, bread, and, from between her legs, a twenty-two pound turkey. (Why not? She'd been doing her Thanksgiving shopping)

Hell, that was nothing. Once, in a jewelry store, she absorbed five Rolex watches, ten jeweled bracelets, sixteen rings, and a box of silver service for eight. In clothing stores she could steal enough threads to clothe Diana Ross and the Supremes--and their band. Probably a VW dealer wouldn't have been safe.

Once in jail she was a model prisoner, her only problem not getting enough to eat. But, she did pose a different problem one night when a guard, walking by her cell, heard a

I'M PEDDLIN' AS FAST AS I CAN

baby crying. Looking closer, there it was, balanced on Maxine's belly, wet, gooey and still attached to its mama.

"What the . . .?" the incredulous guard said.

"Don't as' me," Maxine said, as befuddled as the guard. "*It jus' come.*"

Fact of the matter was, Maxine was so fat and so ignorant she didn't know she'd been pregnant. And, when she started getting cramps she thought it was because of those belly robbers in the jail kitchen starving her.

Much later, a hearing was held to try to figure out what to do with her. By that time the jail diet had slimmed her down to a svelte 300 lbs. When asked by the judge who the father was, Maxine broke up the court by saying, "I don't be knowin'. yo' honor. Then giggling and saying, They wuz always three or fo' of 'em at me."

ORDER IN THE COURT? Part One

When the County seat of Collier was Everglades City, our County Judge was the ornery SS Jolley. There's some dispute over whether he was an actual lawyer, but that made little difference at the time. If you lived in a small county, anyone could run for the job. Or, you could be a Justice of the Peace without being a lawyer. The bottom line was SS Jolley may not've been a lawyer but he was damn sure a judge.

He was an expert at using innovative methods to get the job done. If the court had a full docket for the day, he'd use his *Right-Left* justice system. It went like this. The Judge would say, "*All you folks who want to plead Guilty get up and go stand on the right side of the courtroom. All you that want to plead Not Guiltily, go stand on the left.*" The cases could include any misdemeanor: petty larceny, DWI, drunk and disorderly, the full gamut.

"Now," he'd continue, "all you folks on the right are fined $25.00. Pay the Clerk. Let's hear the first Not Guilty case." And so it went.

He also didn't let the lack of one of his laws being on the books deter his rulings. Once a scalawag from Miami brought his lawyer with him to insure he'd beat the rap in the *Cracker Court*. At the end of the proceeding, when it was

I'M PEDDLIN' AS FAST AS I CAN

time to rule, Judge Jolley found the rascal guilty of Vitamin Deficiency or something. The lawyer was aghast. "Your honor," he said, "there's no law like that on the books that I'm familiar with."

"It's one of the *Ochopee Statutes*," the judge responded. "Next case."

The Ochopee Statutes were what the Judge called justice tailored to the crime. When the written law didn't cover the circumstances, he'd make something up that did. And he got away with it for years.

Yep, he's the one they named the Marco Bridge after.

ORDER IN THE COURT? Part Two

Judge Richard Stanley wasn't anyone to mess with. A WW II paratrooper, he had a gravel voice and a icy stare that could turn a big-mouth lawyer into a stuttering wimp. And, he carried a .45 Colt under his robe. He could be so tough and mean, in some quarters he was known as *Wretched* Stanley. (*The Judge knew this and loved it*) He held Juvenile Court for many years. The juvenile justice system back then was not well defined. Judges could do just about what they pleased. And they did.

If a juvenile denied the charges in court, they were immediately given a lie detector test by the examiner assigned to court that day. I know, I was one of them. The terrified delinquents usually cracked when they just looked at the polygraph.

Sentences? The judge regularly put them on a diet of Gerber's baby food and water. And, he liked to lock them in a cell that had no light. Total darkness. They normally lasted about two hours before they were born again on a righteous path.

Those who had traffic accidents got off fairly easy. Before sentencing, they only had to look at a series of 8x10 photos showing the most gory wrecks ever seen, with the judge doing the play-by-play. *See that Son? That's where the driver's head used to be.* They keeled over like French soldiers confronting the enemy.

I'M PEDDLIN' AS FAST AS I CAN

This was a time of abundant hirsute adornment. The judge hated long hair on males. One of our cops, Mike Grimm was also a barber. The judge would have Mike use his shears to turn long-haired hippies into Parris Island recruits.

Have a child you couldn't control? Judge Stanley would command one of the cops in attendance to give the incorrigible turd ten good ones with that *special piece of equipment*. That equipment being the 3" leather gun belt we all wore. The juvenile would be bent over the defense table and justice would be applied.

I know, I know. Barbaric. Inhuman. Maybe, but it was a rare juvenile that ever returned to Judge Wretched Stanley's court. Makes you wonder, if we'd done things that way longer how society would be today.

When the Judge moved to Misdemeanor Court, he was still a tough customer. Once a gang of shoplifters out of Miami, had been bagged and were on trial, defended by their Miami attorney. The gang would raid a store en masse, divide up so they were impossible to monitor, and go to work. They could steal merchandise worth thousands in one store.

After the prosecution presented its case, Judge Stanley, enraged, broke in and said, "It's obvious what's going on here. You think you can come over from the big city and rob us yokels. Well that's damn sure not the case. I find each of you guilty and sentence you to the maximum in the County Jail." (*One year, at the time*)

Astounded, the defense attorney jumped to his feet. "Your honor don't I even get the opportunity to present the defense's side of the case?"

Judge Stanley gave him that stare and said, "Can if you want, but I don't think it's gonna do any good." And it didn't.

Oh, for the good ol' days.

JIM PEACOCK, FHP

At one time the Florida Highway Patrol had no station around Naples. We let them use a desk at the NPD and worked closely with them. One of my favorites was Trooper Jim Peacock--his real name. Jim, a Clint Eastwood type, had a soft voice and an infectious grin. He'd grin all the time he

I'M PEDDLIN' AS FAST AS I CAN

was being berated by an irate motorists. Grin and just keep writing that citation. And, if you bowed up at him, grin all the time he was kicking your keester. I can only recall one occasion when the grin faded.

The NPD, CCSO, and FHP were all out in force looking for an escaped prisoner. As I recall, he'd cut a prison guard's throat and escaped from a work party. The search had gone on for hours and we were about tapped out. The fugitive seemed to have evaded us. Peacock was particularly tired, having been on duty most of the day, and now all night. The sun was just coming up and Jim, far east on US 41, decided it was time to grab a coffee and some breakfast before he resumed the search. And he needed to make a long due rest room stop.

Jim found a side road through the palmettos, pulled in, and parked the cruiser. Selecting a likely clump of bushes, he headed that way, unzipping his fly. At just that moment, up jumped the murderer from behind the bush, screaming, "*Oh God, don't shoot. Don't shoot.*" It so shocked Jim, he almost wet himself.

Peacock later reflected that, considering where he had his hand then, he wonder just what the convict figured he was going to shoot him with. Anyway Jim quickly grabbed his real gun, and took the A-hole into custody.

Jim never gave anything but a factual account of how he'd bagged his game. Having a keen sense of humor, he reveled in its irony. The press, however, is always on the lookout for heroes and Peacock fit the bill. He made every rag in the South. This eventually culminated in a story in the men's adventure magazine, *Saga. Jim Peacock, Law of the Everglades.* It was a romantic accounting of Jim's relentless pursuit of the criminal using all his police tracking skills.

When we ribbed him about it, he'd just say the more he read it, the more he believed that maybe that's how it really did happen. And then he'd grin.

IS THAT THE WHISKEY TALKIN'?

Once we did a study to find out what caused folks to call the police. Over 80% of the time there was booze or drugs involved. Mostly, alcohol. Here are some examples of just what liquid stupid, in excess, can do for you.

A frequent flyer was pulled over for driving on both sides of the road. We all knew him. He was hump-backed from getting in and out of police cars. The kind of numb-nuts who'd fail the *oral* DUI test we sometimes used: *Was Mickey Mouse a cat or a dog?*

At the driver's window, I asked for his DL. He looked at me, rolled his eyes, and said indignantly, "You got a helluva nerve. You took it away from me the last time you arrested me."

The man had a point.

Wasted Wally was particular about what he drank. It had to have alcohol in it. Paint thinner, mouthwash, wood alcohol, any number of cleaners and disinfectants. You name it. He was so addicted his wife made him use Brylcreem cause it was the only hair tonic he couldn't drink.

Wasted Wally forgot that you can't have this much fun and not rot your brain. The booze was getting to him. He spent more time in jail than the cockroaches and every time he was locked up he was more frail and feeble. Then, when he'd start to dry out, he'd get the DT's. With his pickled brain and delusions, there was no predicting what he was likely to do.

Once Assistant Chief Dave Dampier was making the rounds in the jail and noticed that Wasted Wally had ripped up his mattress and was stuffing the cotton up his nose. Prodigious amounts of cotton. Some prisoners do rip up their mattress. None pack their snout with it. This peaked Dave's interest.

"What're you doin' Wally?" he asked.

Never missing a beat, Wally snorted a nasal, "Eatin' tater salad." And, in his poor demented mind it must've been tasty as he went right back to it in earnest.

Then there was Little Alph. Alph was a politician's son who we'd watch grow up. Though intelligent when sober, drunk he had the brains of a hemorrhoid. He'd go on binges and violate his probation. Or drive on a suspended license. Or collect a nice DWI.

I'M PEDDLIN' AS FAST AS I CAN

During one stay in the jail, he was selected to be the benefactor of a new scheme being tried to cut down the jail population. This is an ongoing activity as the jails usually fill faster than you can build them.

The judge explained the deal to Alph. "You have thirty days left on your sentence and your conduct has been commendable. I'll let you out of jail today if you agree to reimburse the County $75 a day for each day you were incarcerated. That's what it costs to feed and house you."

Alph stared at the judge as though he'd morphed into an articulate jackass, then said, "Seventy-five dollar a day? That's robbery. Hell, Judge, $75 a day I could lay up in the Holiday Inn with a case a Bud and a hooker."

The courtroom exploded with laughter. Except for the judge. He decided that, on second thought, Alph probably should make that next 30 days. Plus an extra 10 for his keen observations.

HAPPY HOMEMAKER'S HINT

We dreaded getting calls like this: *We haven't see 'ol so and so in a day or two. Wonder if you'd check to see if they're okay.* We especially hated to get these calls in hot weather. Why? Many times ol' so and so had come to an untimely demise and was rotting on the premises.

The worse place to answer these calls was McDonald's Quarters, Naples' shameful ghetto. The shacks, no better than a tool shed, had no air conditioning and on hot days were an oven, hastening the decay. On such a day we responded to a call. Big Bertha, it seems, hadn't been seen by her neighbors in about a week. Bertha would sometimes hole up in her shack for a few days, drunk as a rock star, but never for a week.

Checking out the shack, the window glass seemed to be moving. A terrible sign. That was a thousand flies trying to get in so they could contribute to the putrefaction chain. When we opened the door, a vile eruption that can't be described assailed our noses. It was the kind of instant retching, eye-watering, knee-buckling, foulness that permeates your clothes and can't be washed out. We would've paid a thousand bucks for an oxygen mast but the City didn't see fit to buy them at the time.

Bertha was on her back on the floor, swarming with maggots, and bloated and ruptured around the stomach. We slammed the door and called *Mr. Sears*. Mr. Sears was the black undertaker in Ft. Myers that all blacks used. He was quick to respond.

He parked his hearse, opened the back door and took out a coffee can and a frying pan. He greeted us, walked by and set the pan on the stove, turned it on, and poured in about a cup of ground coffee. He came back outside, passed the time of day with us for about fifteen-minutes, then opened the door and sniffed. *Ah,* he said, *that'll do.* We, reluctantly, followed him back inside. Miraculously, the toasted coffee smell had made the air now, at least, bearable. We were able to do our work. A grisly trick of the trade I've always remembered.

So our Helpful Household Hint. Left those steaks in the fridge a week too long? Toilet back up on you? Got a fat dog that leaks more methane than the city dump? Or maybe it's just your fat dog husband, vegetating in front of the TV, starting to smell like a warthog.

Fear not. Get out that ol' fryin' pan, dump in some ground coffee, heat it up and shortly *Juan Valdez* will've saved the day.

CHRIS-TAL CAPER

At about midnight, Det Jerry Weinbrenner was going off duty. Passing the *Chris-Tal Market* on the corner of 10th Ave So and US 41, he thought he saw movement in the closed store. He pulled over to investigate, causing two burglars to flee out the back door. One weasel ran up 10th, the other toward a green Buick in the rear lot of the market. Jerry took off, on foot, after the one heading north.

Jerry was about 50 feet behind his man when the thief turned and fired over his shoulder, still running at full speed. Jerry felt something hit him in the shoulder. He stopped to inspect. He'd been shot. This really wasn't what he needed after a long days work. He pulled his .38 Chief's Special and fired all five shots. The perp went down like he'd been hit by a truck. Jerry cautiously moved froward. To his surprise, the perp jumped to his feet and took off running again.

Other cars were on the scene, one being Sgt J.D.Spohn. Spohn pursued the Buick, now heading for the Cove area. He fired two shots at the speeding car. The bullets hit the rear window and glanced off, not even breaking the glass. The car sped to the water's edge, the perp jumped out, dove in the bay and began swimming with a frenzied arm thrashing movement.

Spohn, took out his pistol again and waited on the shore. When the swimmer tired, Spohn fired a round close in the water to the slimeball's head, then shouted, "Come back or I'll kill you."

This caused the swimmer to pound the water once more, trying to get away. Soon out of gas, he stopped again. Spohn fried another close-in round. "I'm better at this than you are," he taunted. "Come on back."

This went on for a while until finally the perp yelled, "Okay, I'm comin' out." And he did.

Meanwhile, Weinbrenner had gone to the hospital and the CCSO trackers had been called in. The filth that had shot Weinbrenner had circled around and run into a vacant field beside the Atlantic station, next to Chris-Tal.

The old bloodhound, Belle, was an excellent tracker but refused to let her handler's know when she'd found her quarry. She'd stop, but make no other indication. They were tracking along, when something on the ground said, *Ouch!* At their feet was the shooter, lying on his belly in the weeds. He'd said "*Ouch*" because Belle had stepped on his back, in which he had two of Weinbrenner's bullets.

He was cuffed and turned over, and under his body we found his weapon: a miniature .25 revolver, maybe three-inches long. This turd had made the shot of all time, running at full speed, shooting over his shoulder, not even looking, and hitting Weinbrenner.

Jerry recovered, but the slug was left in his shoulder, causing him pain when the weather changed. His two slugs in the back of the burglar, who got up and ran around for

I'M PEDDLIN' AS FAST AS I CAN

another fifteen-minutes, were more evidence of our underpowered ammo of the time.

The two Ass-Wipes had just been released from prison, upstate, stolen a car, and were after booze, cigarettes, and money in the Chris-Tal. They were soon returned where they belonged.

Later, back at the station, Sgt J.D.Spohn was cleaning his . 357 Magnum and in excellent spirits. "Damn," he said, "haven't had so much fun since that hillbilly back in Hazard, Kentucky took a pot shot at me. Ever time I'm back up there, I stop by and piss on his grave."

KEYSTONE COPS REDUX

One day there was a revival of *Max Sennett's Keystone Kops* on the streets of Naples. It was inadvertent, but anyone who saw it would swear Fatty Arbuckle and his gang were at work. It happened like this.

A recipe for disaster was present. The Trail had recently been repaved and it was summer. And, it hadn't rained for weeks. This allowed the sun to boil oil from the asphalt up to the surface. Then, when it does rain, the water/oil mixture is as slick as the proverbial cat's back door. Traffic accidents quadruple. Although all streets become slicker, some locations are worse than others. I recall that crossing the Gordon River Bridge from the east was particularly treacherous. Try to turn onto Goodlette Road and you probably were gonna end up doing a helicopter spin, with no control over your car. Another bad spot, evidently, was in front of the Holiday Inn, then at about 12th Street No and US 41.

We received a call, during a welcome thunderstorm, that there was a Signal-4 (traffic accident) there. Patrol officers then heard a call that now' there were two Signal-4's, the responding ambulance having slid into the car who had rear-ended another. The first police car arrived and promptly slid into the ambulance. Same with the second police car. Finally, the Sergeant went to see what in hell was going on and he slid into the second police car, making a daisy chain of the original two wrecked cars, one ambulance, and three police cars.

The Florida Highway Patrol, who did the accident investigation, could've used the same report for all: *Hit the brakes and nothing happened.* Ironically and thankfully, no one was injured. The ambulance had been called by a passerby and wasn't really even needed. Except, maybe, to make the daisy-chain longer.

Yep, no one was hurt, but three cops suffered several days of wise-ass remarks from their associates. And there where some painfully bruised egos.

THE MAGIC SAFE

We all know that a proven way to protect your valuables from theft, fire and destruction is to put them in a safe. The average random burglar can't pry one open. It will withstand the ravages of fire, and is a stronghold during a hurricane. Once, however, we found a safe that would do more than that; it would make money.

A market was a victim of B&E one night. An alert cop saw flashlight beams moving in the closed and dark store, investigated and rousted three scumbags who fled the scene but were soon captured. Since they were interrupted, the thieves only had time to steal two garbage bags full of cigarettes. Or so it appeared. Detectives were called in to work the scene.

During the flight the culprits had dumped their booty along the way so the weight wouldn't slow them down. We called the owner, who we'll call Tubby, asked him to meet us at the store so he could check his inventory for anything else missing.

In his office was a heavy-duty commercial safe with a sign that read: *THIS SAFE IS NOT LOCKED. FOR FIRE PROTECTION ONLY. JUST OPEN THE DOOR.* Several merchants used their safes just for fire protection and didn't want burglars to beat, bang and ruin them trying to get them open.

We asked Tubby to open his safe and see if anything was missing. He said, "Naw, there's nothin' in there."

I'M PEDDLIN' AS FAST AS I CAN

"How about checking anyway, just to make sure," I said.

"It's okay," he said, causing me to wonder just what he did have in there he didn't want me to see. Finally, I opened the safe myself. Stacked on the top shelf was a sizable pile of cash. Later, when counted, it turned out to be $17,000.

"What's that?" I asked.

"What's, what?" Tubby answered.

"The money," I said.

"What money?" Tubby said.

Sometimes I'm a little slow but it finally came to me. "So any money in that safe's not yours. If there is cash in there, someone else put it there. Maybe the thieves, had a guilty conscience. Maybe the Safe Fairy. But it's definitely not yours?"

"Never seen it before," Tubby said. "Maybe it's yours," he said, hopefully. But I didn't go for that. Not that I couldn't have been bought but when a cop takes they own you. And it was gonna take a helluva lot more than 17K. (*I will admit it was tempting. At the time, I'd just bought a model home in Brookside for $10,999 and had two mortgages on it. That was a lotta money, then*)

So we sacked up the money, and put it in the evidence locker at the PD.

And why didn't Tubby own up to the cash being his? I remembered he'd recently been in trouble with the IRS for skimming off and not reporting profits. And, he was obviously doing it again.

A few months later the court allowed the City to convert the cash to its own use. Tubby never complained or mentioned it. . .ever. You could presume he saw the error in his ways and went straight.

But I doubt it.

RASCAL'S PLAN

Rascal was a big, handsome, youngun' out of Kentucky. I was interviewing him for a job with the Naples Police. Very likable, he'd made good guy points even before I found we might be related. We have common family ties: the Hatfield's of the *Hatfield and McCoy Feud* fame. During the interview I asked why he'd decided to move to Naples.

"Well," he said in his cornbread drawl, "I'm about marryin' age and when we were down here on vacation I noticed there were a lotta purty girls here."

No disagreement there.

"And, I also noticed there were a lotta rich folks here, too." Another affirmation from me. "That means there should be a lotta purty, rich girls here. So if you're lookin' for a wife and you want a purty one, you might as well get a purty, rich one while you're at it."

I laughed at his logic, figured he was yanking my chain, and later hired him.

Rascal was a good cop. Smart, dependable, fearless. And a better ladies man. In just a few months he told me he'd found his dream girl, was going to be married, and after that was going to retire from the police business. I couldn't believe it; Rascal worked faster than a *Fleet enema*. But he was true to his word and within a few weeks he was gone.

Rascal married the daughter of a big shot in one of the world's largest corporations. Wedding presents included a Porsche and a house three blocks from the beach. Plus, the best gift of all, his new wife who was not only beautiful but sweet and charming. We guessed Rascal would've married her if she was as poor as *Pitiful Pearl*. But, she wasn't.

We'd see Rascal around town now and then, but mostly lost contact. Then one day I received a call from him. "You remember when I retired from the NPD you said I was too young and would go back to work? Well, you were right. I did. I'm in the railroad business." He urged me to drop by his house and he'd explain. Who could resist?

His wife greeted me at the door, we exchanged pleasantries, and she, with a smile, pointed down the hallway to Rascal's office. I arrived at a large room that had been two bedrooms now remodeled into one. There Rascal was at work.

The entire space was filled with the largest HO scale model railroad layout I'd ever seen. A dozen trains chugged around the tracks, through villages, tunnels, and over bridges. Rascal sat in a cutout control space in the center, wearing an engineer's cap, bib overalls, and a red bandanna around his neck. *See*, he said, "I'm a railroad tycoon."

And so he was. We lost track of Rascal after that but I'm confident he's still working a plan somewhere. I suppose he's right, and that's the best way to go about this life.

But it's much more interesting doing it our way: just bumbling along and seeing what turns up next.

SPONTANEOUS ERUPTIONS

Some folks, when they're dealing with the cops, say some funny things. Part of the job's appeal, is waiting for them to happen.

We had a sweet old lady named Mary who was an Olympic level boozer. Sometimes she'd be sentenced to a few days and we'd have to lock her up. Our jail had two wings, with women and juveniles on one side and men on the other. There were seldom any women on their side. When there was, we'd make extra tours there to make sure they were okay, since they were probably alone. *(No video security cameras in those days)*

Mary, one day, asked why all the attention. "Just lookin' out for your well being, darlin'," the cop said.

"Well, that's sweet of you," the old dear said. "But if you find me dead, no fancy funeral, please. Just stick an old bone up my az, throw me out in the yard, and let the wild dogs carry me off."

Another winner was a lady who'd come to the station to report a rape. Turns out she was reporting it only because her husband had been told by neighbors that there was a husband-in-law who'd regularly been hammering his honey. The wife claimed it happened only once and it was a rape. The husband said if it was, she'd better damn sure come up with a police report.

"He forced himself on you?" the detective asked.

"Yassah, he do that, she said. Comes into my bedrooms, rips off my clothes, and jumps astraddle uv me."

"And this was all without your consent?"

"Show was. . .most of the time."

"Most of the time?"

"Yassah. I kept sayin' no, no, no, til he gots some of it in me then I say, Okay."

Then there was Wingding Whoops, who was known as Who Me? You could call to Wingding standing alone on the pitcher's mound in an empty Yankee Stadium and he'd look left, look right, point to his chest and say, *"Who Me?"*

One night we caught some thieves in the act of stealing materials from a construction site, a new hospital wing at NCH. We had two weasels in hand but the third had run into the multi-story addition. Since it was dark and the building's interior had been configured into over a hundred rooms, it would take hours and be very dangerous to search. We had a better tactic.

We called in a K-9 officer, Bob Melin. Bob decided to give the culprit a chance before he released his dog for a tasty treat. Turning on his car's PA System, Bob had his dog growl, bark, and snarl into the mike. The amplified sound was terrifying. Then Bob said, *"Come out now or I'm gonna turn the dog loose. You hear me?"*

From the bowels of the building came the horrified reply, *"Who Me?"*

After we stopped laughing, we sacked up Wingding when he bolted out the door, eyes as big as two fried eggs, sunny side up.

THE ADVENTURES OF FAST FREDDY-Part One

Our first hint that life with Fast Freddy was going to be different was his first night on duty. Fred, a former Chicago PD cop, came into the station toting a stuffed AWOL bag. When asked if that was his lunch, he opened it for display: his arsenal. Seeing our interest, Fred elaborated.

"This," he said, holding up a Colt Python with a telescopic sight "is for shooting snipers off roofs. And this," holding up a tiny semi-auto Beretta, "just fits right in a *crotch* holster." He then displayed his collection of throw-downs--cheap, untraceable, pistols used to cover your ass in shootings that weren't exactly righteous. Then the knives, from push-buttons to Bowies. Throw in some brass knuckles and blackjacks, and that was about it.

We laughed, thinking he was yanking our chain. He wasn't. "But, Fred," a bemused cop began, "we don't have a building over two stories in Collier County. Rooftop snipers ain't a big problem. And I don't even know what a crotch holster looks like, let alone how to put one on. . .if I wanted to."

Fred just laughed at our naivete, closed the bag, and went to work. And that was like nothing we'd seen either.

I got to know Fred very well. You couldn't help liking him, in fact, Sandy and I were married in his house. And who couldn't like Big'un, his singing dog. But he had a Chicago way of doing things that took some getting used to.

Once he dropped by my office and asked what was going on? I told him I was covered up trying to get statements on a rash of burglaries. The B&E's were in the Quarters and we had to get special statements there. You'd talk to a witness and they'd say: "*I didn't see nuffin'*." Then, come court time, they saw everything--that benefited the defendant. So we'd get what we called *I Didn't See Nuffin'* statements, making it hard for them to change their story in court. In this case there had been several potential witness.

"I can help," Fred said enthusiastically."Just give me a name."

Fred was a helper so I gave him a name, and told him I had no idea if the fella was involved, but I had to clear him.

"No problem," Fred said, and was gone.

About an hour later, I got a call over the desktop radio from Fred. There was a loud, unintelligible commotion in the background. Fred was breathless. "I got this guy here and I think he's clean, but I can work on him some more if you want." Then, I heard a terrified voice in the background, "*Please, Mistah Fred, don't hit me no mo'. I don't know nuffin.*"

When the shock wore off, I told Fred to let the poor guy go and 10-19 (return to station). He did and we had a long conversation about how they talked to suspects in Chicago and how they did it at the NPD.

I'M PEDDLIN' AS FAST AS I CAN

Fred was industrious. Besides being a cop, he had an auto body shop. His schedule was hectic. Five minutes til roll call, Fred would come barreling in, run to the sink and wash the shop dust and grease off him, then put on his uniform. No one did it like Fred. He had the thing in a kinda blanket roll, with his gun belt wrapped around it. He'd unroll it on the counter, start flapping it like he was dusting a rug, then put it on. He'd look wrinkled but the polyester was forgiving and, in an hour or two, he didn't look any worse than anyone who rolled their uniform up like a burrito.

And that was just the beginning.

THE ADVENTURES OF FAST FREDDY- Part Two

As mentioned before, Fast Freddy operated an auto body shop, along with his job on the NPD. He could be shrewd and industrious, and while the rest of us were living in modest Brookside Village, he lived in expensive Pine Ridge.

Fred's body shop skills were fantastic. He was particularly good at taking two or three wrecks and turning them into one beautiful car. I once helped him do this with a Corvette that had been crushed in a wreck. Fred bought two more wrecks and soon his wife was driving a cherry Vette.

I asked Fred where he'd learned how to do this work. He said, "Working in auto theft chop shops in Chicago, before I became a cop." Then he gave me a little Fred grin. I never knew if he was kidding me or not. And it was usually better not to dig too deeply.

Inquired once why he left the Chicago PD. He said he couldn't save up enough money to make Sergeant. Money? What? Yeah you had to pay the Lieutenant and it was just too expensive. I thought that was a joke until we hired another cop from there and he said the same thing. Rank was for sale. Who knows, but that's an odd coincidence, two guys, same story.

After a big storm once, Fred was elated. He'd found a Chris-Craft cabin cruiser that'd sunk at a private dock and he could buy it el cheapo. Fred had always longed for a Chris-Craft and he jumped on the deal like Porky on a double-cheese pizza.

I'M PEDDLIN' AS FAST AS I CAN

He spent hours water-pumping the vessel to float it and flushing the engine with kerosene to prevent the salt water from seizing it up. Finally, with it on the surface and Fred totally exhausted, he went home at about 3 AM. He returned the next morning to find the cruiser again on the bottom. He'd forgotten to put in the drain plugs.

Fast Freddy was a little too fast for our small berg and finally the NPD made him an offer he couldn't refuse; they'd quit paying him if he'd quit coming to work. He moved on to the Ft. Lauderdale PD. A buddy of mine, George Huffman, was concurrently on the FLPD with Fred. We heard that Fred was soon up to his old tricks and George confirmed it.

George said Fred moved the Chris-Craft to Lauderdale with him and stowed it on a side street, outside a shop he was renting. (*He was living there because he maintained his home in Pine Ridge, and drove back to Naples on his days off. He kept this schedule for many years*)

Soon Fred's living on the street-docked Chris-Craft was the source of complaints to the city, it being illegal and unsightly. When the cops came to check out the complaint, they found a clothes line strung the length of the vessel, from mast to rails, festooned with Ft. Lauderdale police uniforms. Seems it was wash day. Fred moved on to another agency shortly thereafter.

At least one other time he tried to launch the Chris-Craft in the briny deep. Again the boat sank. Fred had forgotten to put the drain plugs in again.

In part three we'll see where he ended up. You ain't gonna believe it.

THE ADVENTURES OF FAST FREDDY-Part Three

Fast Freddy moved to a small, new department near Ft Lauderdale in a city that had just incorporated. We didn't hear from him or about him for a while although he was still *living* in Naples on his days off.

Then came word that Fred had once again changed departments, this time to Dania. They must have liked him because shortly thereafter was news that Fred had been promoted to Sergeant. Soon after that came more astounding news.

I'M PEDDLIN' AS FAST AS I CAN

Shirley, my secretary, said I had a call from Chief of Police, Dania. He was on line one. She had a devilish little smile on her face. I picked up the line and was greeted with, "Hey, it's Freddie, what's happenin'?" Shirley started laughing and I almost tipped over in my chair.

Fred explained that he'd just been appointed Chief. But let him tell it. "They go through Chief's over here like they're rolls of toilet paper. Had like three in the last three or four months. Finally got down to me, being the Senior Sergeant." Senior Sergeant? Already? "Anyway I told them no thanks, I needed a steady job. But they told me if I didn't take it they'd fire me. So, what the hell?"

I could understand Fred's thinking about it not being steady work. Later, when I left the NPD, I was the first Chief to have left in good graces. All the others had been forced to retire or fired. A wise Sheriff Aubrey Rogers once told me he wouldn't have a Chief's job. "I only have to run for my job every four years. A chief has to every day."

A few weeks later I got another call from Fred. This time he wasn't so jubilant. "They're out to get me," he said.

"Fire you?" I asked.

"Maybe worse. I'm sleeping with a .45 under my pillow. Stepped up security in the office...maybe I'm just imagining, but..."

After talking to him a while, Fred changed his attitude and began joking about what he'd just been so worried about. I didn't know what to think, but was worried. By coincidence, we had a dick going to Lauderdale the next day to do some case work. I asked him to drop in on Fred and see what was going on. Two days later, I got the report.

"I think his ice cap's starting to melt, he's three cans short of a six-pack, know what I mean?" the dick said. "Had to go through seven locked doors to get to him. Seven. Had so many guns in there looked like a redneck barbecue. He's loosin' it."

Seems the job had claimed another good man. Fred was always unconventional. Wild. Erratic. But never paranoid. Yep, he had Chief's Disease. Thankfully, he didn't have to suffer long before they put him out of his misery.

I'M PEDDLIN' AS FAST AS I CAN

The last time I saw Fred he'd dropped in to see me at the CCSO. Emaciated and feeble, he was dealing with terrible physical problems. But, free of the Chief's job, he was a happy Fred once more. He died soon after.

Miss you, buddy. We won't see any like you again.

THE MYSTERIOUS GREEN BOX

There was a grand old gent, Harry Varner, who for many years ran the concession and bait shop at the Naples City Pier. He could be a curmudgeon but was easy to like and was a fixture on the pier.

I asked Harry one day what the contraption was that was mounted outside the shop wall, next to the railing. It was an olive drab metal box, securely locked, with a pipe extending down into the Gulf. It had a warning to not disturb, property of the US Government.

"Belongs to the Department of Agriculture, somebody like that," Harry said.

I raised my eyebrows, waiting.

"Don't know what it's for. They come by every so often and fiddle around over there with it. I never paid much attention. Countin' crabs or some such."

My interest aroused, I asked Harry to call me the next time the tenders showed up. In a couple of weeks they did. I hurried to the pier and found a man working with a crank that was in the opened box. Turning the crank raised a box out of the water and up the long pipe. The mysterious box was similar to a crab trap, but much more durably fabricated. After identifying myself I asked what he was doing.

"I'm taking the contaminate count," he said. "Trying to get a handle on how much DDT, fertilizer, mercury and other poisons have made in to the Gulf."

"How's that work?"

"We trap crustaceans in this box. Crabs, shrimp, lobsters, anything with a shell. Then we analyze them and see how many poisons are in their system. Crustaceans are one of the ocean's filters. Anything that goes into them, effectively, never comes out. Dies off in half-lives like radiation. By analyzing them, we can get an idea of how much poison is in the water."

"You mean shrimp and crabs are all full of. . ."

"Lobsters, too. Everything filthy in the ocean. And it stays in them."

"Should you eat them?" I asked.

"You do what you want. Me, if you notice, I have on rubber gloves. . .just to touch them."

I'm passing this on as a Public Service Announcement. Make up your own mind about munching on these critters. We do. Sandy and I celebrated our Wedding Anniversary last week by going to a favorite, The Red Lobster. She had lobster and shrimp.

Being the usual food wussy, I had a nice New York Strip.

LORD CALVERT'S BIG SCORE

The old City of Naples seal used to have palm trees, a pelican, and a boat on it. They left one off. The whiskey bottle. Booze barons were prominent citizens in Naples' history.

While working a burglary at the *Swamp Buggy Lounge*, near 4-Corners, I noticed a plaque on the wall that astounded me. It read, *Largest Retailer, Lord Calvert Whiskey*. I asked the owner Nick, *if this was a joke?*

"Hell, no," he answered, offended. "It's as legit as it gets."

Huh? In the 60's Naples wasn't exactly New York City. It wasn't even Ft. Myers. Sensing my disbelief, Nick explained.

"It's all those folks on Gordon Drive and in Port Royal. Lord Calvert is a good mixing whiskey and they do like their cocktail parties down there. Most homes are good for a few cases a year. It adds up. Adds up enough that, like the plaque says, for two years I've sold more than any outlet in the world."

Should've known. The area was a nesting ground for the Alcohol Elite. Just take a drive down Gordon Drive and and you'd find homes owned by the purveyors of *Busch, Miller, Pabst, Schlitz, Smirnoff, Falstaff,* plus family connections to

I'M PEDDLIN' AS FAST AS I CAN

Seagram, Canadian Club. Heublein, who owned Smirnoff, was one of the largest distributors in the world of alcoholic beverages.

Of these, our favorite was the Griesediecks, out of St. Louis, brewers of "Old Greasy Dick" beer. Answer a call at their residence on Gordon Drive and you'd better not try to get by with a *Grisydike,* or some other cop out that you could say without laughing. You'd be informed that the name was pronounced Greasydick, and they were proud of it. Good people, these.

And not just the rich folks contributed to record sales of liquid stupid. When raiding a homeless camp (bum's nest) off Airport Road where the poor unfortunates were spending more time breaking into nearby homes, than looking for work, we came upon a monument, of sorts. It was a pile of beer cans easily seven feet tall with a base circumference of about twelve feet. Had to be thousands. Had to've *cost* thousands.

We couldn't find a plaque.

SWEET HOME ALABAMA

Once, in the sixties, at a police seminar, I met two cops from Birmingham, Al and Bama, who were full of good humor and tall tales. A group of us were discussing how many cops rode in a police car in our particular cities. Cops, generally would prefer two, for safety and company. But most cities can't afford that so you go bare ass. The Birmingham boys were quick to point out that in their progressive city two per car was the norm. That's because they have to be able to read *and* write, Al explained.

They also passed on a war story. During this time of great racial unrest, Birmingham, a hub of hatred, was experiencing a particularly large, ugly, and dangerous demonstration. The cops were so overwhelmed by the mob that a class of recruits, from the academy, was drafted into service on the lines. They were young folks, mostly, with no police experience.

At one barricade the crowd became violent and a large, mean, protester began shoving a recruit. The recruit,

I'M PEDDLIN' AS FAST AS I CAN

frightened and confused, pulled his service revolver and shot said disgruntled citizen. The mob immediately dispersed in terror and the cops cordoned off the shooting scene, until supervisors could arrive. The first was a Sergeant.

"And what kind of weapon did this thug have?" he asked the dazed recruit. "Gun, knife, brick?"

"Uhhh, I didn't see anything," the recruit stammered.

"Come on now," the Sergeant urged, "*he must've had something.*"

"No...I..."

"*I said THINK now,*" the Sergeant said, up close in the recruit's face. Then, "You mull it over while I inspect the body."

The Sergeant moved to the face-down stiff, and half-rolled it over, probing underneath.

Then came the Lieutenant, same questions, same inspection. Then the Captain, the Major, the Colonel, more and more, questioning and inspecting until the recruit was so dazed he couldn't remember just what he had seen.

Finally the coroner arrived and flipped over the body to inspect for bullet wounds. Under the corpse he found, three revolvers, a switch-blade knife, straight razor, and an ice pick.

Al and Bama swore this story was the truth. But, Birmingham in the sixties? George Wallace's home state? They had to be kidding...right?

OPEN MOUTH, INSERT FOOT

Some fella said, *"You can keep quiet and some will suspect you're stupid. Or you can open your mouth and remove all doubt."* Words of wisdom verified here.

Det Mike Grimm and I'd been one step behind a slime ball. We wanted to jail him, but everywhere we looked he'd just left. Finally, we got a tip he was at a local boarding house. We beat it over there, met the landlady, and told her who we were looking for.

"He just ran in here, grabbed his belongings, and said he was going on a trip," the lady said.

I'M PEDDLIN' AS FAST AS I CAN

It was bitter-sweet news. Getting rid of him was about as good as putting him in jail. "Hope you got your rent money," I said. "We've been after him for a while and he's the sorriest, thieving, deadbeat scum we've ever seen. You're way better off without him."

The landlady looked at me in dismay. "*But, he's my son,*" she said.

Open mouth, insert foot.

Then there's the time my associate, Mr. Grimm, was working his part-time job as a barber. The shop banter was centered on sorry human beings. After the list of politicians had been savaged, Mike announced, "I have the world's champion sorry S.O.B. A drunken, lazy, piece of trash a dog wouldn't lift his leg on. Name's Piddlin' Paul Pooper the Plumber." Everyone laughed because Mike was right, Piddlin' Paul was renown for worthlessness. Everyone laughed except Mike's customer, who turned around in the chair and said, "*That's my Daddy.*"

Open mouth, insert foot.

Of course when you're flying on liquid stupid, the brain is disengaged. Two local boozers could tell you all about it. At the time they could've been called Stumblin and Dumb.

Both were at a dance at the *Cove Inn* when they spotted a Latin gent in formal wear, dancing with a beautiful woman. At the time, Latins weren't as common in Naples as now.

"Lookit that greaseball" Dumb said, "what the hell's he doin' in here?"

"And lookit those threads. What's he, the head waiter?" offered Stumblin. "Let's go kick his ass outta here."

Staggering over to the dancer, Dumb said, "We 'spect you better get where you belong, before we put you there."

The Latin's eyes flashed just a second before he said. "You men are obviously drunk. Why don't you go on, I don't want to take advantage of you."

"Take advantage of us?" Dumb said, "You Rocky Marciano or something?"

"No," his lovely dance partner said, "but he is Alexis Arguello, the World's Lightweight Boxing Champion."

I'M PEDDLIN' AS FAST AS I CAN

And so he was.

Open mouth, insert foot.

This wasn't their only really bad mistake. Another night, at the Cove, they perceived that a car had parked too close to them as they stumbled along, on and off the sidewalk. "Watch where you're going," Dumb yelled at the diminutive man that alighted from the diver's side, "or I'll come over there an kick your ass."

Immediately, the passenger's door opened and out stepped a large human being. "Why don't you pick on somebody your own size," he growled.

Since the two were pretty hefty themselves, this seemed like a real good idea. Later, in the hospital, Dumb said something like a cannon shot knocked him ten feet in the air. Stumblin said all he remembered was being crushed like the garbage in a waste management truck. It was a profitable lesson, however, both quit their drinking and became reputable citizens. . .and my good friends.

Oh yeah, the big guy. Dick Butkus, Chicago Bears.

Open mouth. . .need I say it?

A PRESIDENT'S VISIT TO NAPLES

In the early 60's we had a visit from the Secret Service. The President of the USA, John Fitzgerald Kennedy, was going to take an extended vacation in Naples. He was to stay on Gordon Drive, in a Gulfside mansion owned by a nationally known news correspondent. For now, the proposed stay was to be kept secret. At the NPD we were excited. Although Naples being a destination for celebrities was nothing new, we were talking about JFK, here in the Elephant's Graveyard. And whether you liked him or not--many cops didn't--it was still an honor to host the President.

This was going to take a lotta work. Most of it directed toward converting the property so that it afforded maximum protection for the President. We were amazed at what that required. One reason this particular home was selected was that the owner was a friend of the Kennedy family. But, more importantly, it had a huge iron gate, gate house, and an imposing wall across the front. The gate house was large enough to quarter several SS Agents. And the residence was stone, built like a fortress.

Communication and protective systems were other required additions. About thirty telephone lines were installed--this was to be a working vacation--plus a number of antennas, radios, and a state-of-the-art security and fire alarm system. The system included closed-circuit TV, seldom seen at the time.

Then the front gate, already massive, was reinforced. And the rear, Gulf side of the property, was fenced off. Emergency routes to the hospital and for evacuation were mapped out. The files were checked for known wackos in the area. A lotta work!

Over the years, when other Presidents or family visited, we learned that this dedication on the part of the Secret Service was a constant. After all, these are folks who have sworn to shield the President from harm with their own bodies. Stopping bullets and all.

Nothing is left to chance. When Mrs. Mamie Eisenhower visited each year, a special medical device was rented and placed in the NCH in the off chance she would need it for some rare malady she sometimes suffered. Later, a wealthy Naples patron learned of this and bought one for the hospital.

Anyway, finally the work was completed and we awaited the scheduled arrival of THE MAN himself, just a few days off. He never made it. I'm sure he would've were it not for a scheduled visit he had to make just beforehand.

A short stop over in Dallas, Texas, where all his future plans were abruptly canceled.

HAROLD YOUNG

When folks ask me who's the best investigator I ever knew, I always say his name was Young. That gets a laugh, then I explain. Harold Young. Since it's possible we're related, both coming from the same neck of the woods, we call each other Cuz.

Cuz worked for the CCSO, eventually heading Homicide. He once ran for Sheriff and did very well against the

I'M PEDDLIN' AS FAST AS I CAN

machine. His downfall was that he was too good a cop, too diligent.

Harold has fantastic intuitive skills. I remember one case in which a child had been abducted and its possible location was a large section of woods. While everyone meandered around, Cuz just walked in, went straight to the child and made the rescue. When asked how he did it, he shrugged, said, *Don't know, just knew where she was.*

He's so honest and personable that folks he has sent to prison consider him a friend. There would have been no limit to his accomplishments if it hadn't been for the Benson case.

This was Naples biggest case ever. Three major books were written about it. At one time a movie was in the works. It involved the tobacco rich Bensons and a greedy son who blew up his mother and nephew and disfigured his sister with two car bombs.

As an ironic aside, Steven Benson had researched the murders until he thought it was a perfect crime. Read books on bombs, concocted alibis, the works. His gigantic ego led him to believe no one would figure it out. I was working in the office that day, and asked a rookie who'd been at the scene what was going on. He said, "*Some A-Hole blew up his mother.*" One of our least experienced cops knew at first glance who was guilty. Perfect crime. Right.

Still, proving it was another matter. But Cuz worked tirelessly, found where Steven bought the bomb casing, discovered the motive, and had a good case. The State, however, was reluctant to prosecute. Since this was high profile, they wanted a slam dunk. Benson would have high-priced defense lawyers, there would be national exposure, a loss would be embarrassing. So, satisfied they didn't yet have enough evidence, they sat on it longer than Cuz could tolerate. A highly contentious pushing and shoving match ensued. When the smoke cleared, the State had successfully prosecuted the case, Benson was in prison--where we pray he's regularly bent over by the other inmates--and Cuz was out of work. It was one of those you don't mess with Mother Nature things. His totally unwarranted firing was a dramatic loss to local law enforcement that has never been filled.

I'M PEDDLIN' AS FAST AS I CAN

Harold's now a private investigator. Again, probably the best.

WHAT'D HE SAY?

When you get in the cop business one of the first things you have to master is how to talk on the radio. Then most agencies used the universal 10 Codes, later popular on the CB bands. The police version was longer and had some additions.

With the 10 Codes, there were the Signals. Basically, 10-Codes described actions: 10-4 (*OK, Will Do*). Signals described things. Signal-20 (*Mentally ill person*). The codes were used so often they were usually mastered in just a few days. But not always.

My favorite dispatcher, Sandy, one day received an alarming call from the Chief. *I'll be Signal-7 at the Pier*, he said. This meant literally that he would be a *dead person* at the pier. There was cause for alarm. The Chief was a retired Army officer who was in way over his head. He had dermatitis from stress, was buzzed from noon on, and acted irrationally most of the time. Was he sending some code that he'd been kidnapped? Was he going to kill himself? Or, after all these months did he still not know the codes. An officer sent by Sandy to check, found it was the latter.

And he never did learn them. Each evening, when he went home, he checked out with, *I'll be Signal 7 (dead)*. Not 10-7 (*out of service*). Then invariably, shortly thereafter would come a transmission from an anonymous patrol car, *Yeah, Signal 7 from the neck up.*

Another thing that rookies had to learn was how to read the master index cards. We were computer-less and personal records were kept on 3 by 5 index cards. When a cop on patrol called in a 10-28 or 10-29 asking for a verification of person's identity, the dispatcher searched the files, located the card, and read back the requested information.

This wasn't always easy. Much like the texting shorthand of today, there were contractions and codes used to save space on the cards. A very young Byron Tomlinson, who later became one of the NPD's and CCSO's best officers, got

I'M PEDDLIN' AS FAST AS I CAN

tripped up on these one night. When asked for a info on a Wilson, Byron replied "Ronly Oonly Wilson."

It took a minute for the requesting cop, and everyone else who was listening, to figure out what Byron had done. Then the laughter broke out. He didn't know that initials were indicated as initial, then (only). So, R(only) O(only) became Ronly Oonly. A name he had to live with for some time.

SLIPPERY SHENANIGANS, Part One

Big Earl was a reluctant Romeo. A devout family man. But being tall and handsome, with a magnetic personality he attracted women like teenyboppers chase a rock star. Or so it was rumored. Earl'd admit nothing and laughed off any allegations. And maybe he was telling the truth. But, the male of the species has a certain weakness. . .

Once a complaint against Earl was filed by a woman claiming to be a spurned paramour. This foolishness was absolutely none of our business but a Lieutenant decided to investigate and because of who the Lieutenant was, Earl could be in trouble. Said Lieutenant we'll call Ed Numnutz, was a nitpicker of the worst order. Too many of his cells had been spent building his imposing body, leaving his brains account bankrupt. He did have the good sense to be born with political connections, hence his rank and comfortable position.

My desk was right outside the Lt's then, and Earl walked by me on the way to his lynching. He gave me a shrug and a tight smile. Fifteen minutes later, he emerged from the office, gave me a thumbs up and a sly smile.

He was followed by Lt. Numnutz, who sat down at the chair beside my desk and shook his head, obviously distraught. "I feel like an A-Hole," he said. I fought an urge to tell him I could see how that could happen, kept quiet, and listened.

"I call poor ol' Earl in there and start gettin' on him about the woman chasing thing, and he breaks down, almost in tears, and tell's me it has to be a lie because he's not even capable of anything like that. His equipment was blown off by a hand grenade in the Korean War. I just feel so bad, embarrassing the poor damn guy."

I almost strangled, choking back laughter, excused myself and went into the restroom to let it out. Had it been anyone but Numnutz, they might have questioned a few inconsistencies. Aside from the fact that Earl was in the Navy, where they throw few hand grenades, his service was after Korea. Then there were his children, of which one son could've been Earl's younger twin. And you might wonder how in hell he passed the police physical with no landing gear?

When questioned later, Earl said, "He must've heard me wrong, I'd never claim that. Only a fool would believe it." Then that smile.

He had one more in him. Another high ranking officer, Woody Proboscis, suspected that Earl was a Cooter Cop. He called him in for a dressing down, or worse. This was ironic because Proboscis was a notorious midnight creeper, hammering a particular woman with great regularity. I overheard this conversation so can vouch for it.

"The word's out you spend a lotta duty time chasing women," Proboscis said.

"Who would say that?" Earl asked, seemingly devastated by the accusation.

"Well, rumor," Proboscis admitted.

"Rumor? Oh, hell, then I won't worry. You hear all kinds of rumors. Why I even hear a rumor the other day that the troops kept a log on you, where you spent your lunch hours, and late evenings. Some place down off Broad." (*Where Proboscis' sweetie lived*)

The color left Proboscis' face. Earl continued, "Course that's just a rumor, one I immediately discounted knowing it had to be BS. And I'm sure you've dismissed the one about me, too." Whereupon, Earl got up and left, leaving Proboscis looking like he'd just stepped barefoot into Sylvester's litter box.

Again, that choking sensation, causing me to retire to the restroom before the roaring laughter took over.

I'M PEDDLIN' AS FAST AS I CAN

SLIPPERY SHENANIGANS, Part Two

She was a young, pretty Dispatcher who we'll call Hope. Catch me, molest me, hope I trip. Hope was very popular because she was a sexual liberal. A serial slut. She didn't discriminate. She wasn't particular. Short, tall, fat, skinny, young, old, Hope was ready to bump uglies with 'em.

When word of her public service finally reached the higher ups--always the last to know--the Perverted Puritan himself, Woody Proboscis, leaped into action.--probably feeling slighted because he'd missed her while carousing, himself.

Woody, at first, tried grilling likely Lotharios, none of whom had ridden in on a melon truck. No luck. In desperation he went to Hope. A pitifully inept interrogator, he talked all around the subject but couldn't get right down to it and never would've had not Hope, herself, figured out what he was fishing for. "*Sexual relations? Sure. With who? Have to think on that, there've been several. What's the big deal, did it off duty, used birth control pills?*"

It took some coaxing and a promise that she wouldn't be fired, before Hope came up with a list of playmates; About twenty! And she'd only been employed by the NPD two months. When the glaze finally cleared from Woody's eyes, he realized he'd struck the mother lode. But what to do with it? He couldn't fire them all, he'd have to shut down the agency. However, if he caught one in the act and made an example of him the others would be so terrified they'd no longer stray from the righteous path. At least for a few days. So Woody told Hope to keep their conversation a secret and put his plan in action.

Of course, unlike the upper echelon, the lowliest cop knew everything that happened the instant it happened. And it didn't hurt that Hope told them everything she knew and that they should cool it for a while. This caused Woody many lonely evenings hidden in the bushes across from Hope's 10-42 (*house*) waiting to catch a copulating cop.

So there was a stalemate. Woody wasn't getting his example and the cops weren't getting any. Something had to give. Salvation came in the form of an officer who loved an

I'M PEDDLIN' AS FAST AS I CAN

outrageous practical joke nearly as much as he liked sex. We'll call him the Masked Man, since he was certainly that.

At the time, diminutive motorcycles were popular. An adult could ride one but it looked like a St. Bernard trying to mount an armadillo. This didn't deter the Masked Man. In fact, it enhanced the effect he was seeking. Picture Woody in the weeds, swatting mosquitoes. He hears what sounds like a lawnmower in heat screaming down the street. Then he rubs his eyes in disbelief. There's a large human being, in a gorilla mask and pork pie hat, riding a clown's motorcycle. The gorilla parks on Hope's front lawn, knocks on the door, and is welcomed inside.

From then on Woody's plan was doomed. Realizing the Masked Man obviously knew he was watching and had made a fool of him just took Woody's heart out of the work. And when he found the cops had long ago discovered his surveillance spot and were using Hope's rear door, which was in a blind spot, Woody shut down the operation.

The problem, if there was one, soon solved itself. Hope turned in her resignation stating it wasn't any fun now working for the NPD. She moved on to the Sheriff's Office known, at the time, for their liberal fun-and-games policies.

Photo on next page, NPD in 1971

Row 1, Hartmann, LaRochelle, Graham, Aldacosta, Horrom, Woodruff, Sprinkle, Sack, Dasher, Robinson, Barton.

Row 2, Young, Coopersmith, Atkinson, Burton, Tiffin, Trifiletti, Lester, Dampier

Row 3, Jessup, Nicholson, Tomlinson, Ferrell, Bartlett, Davidson, Parker, Muir, Spohn

Row 4, Harris, Kreider, Feltman, Burdette, Rittersdorf, Claveau

Row 5, Grimm, Baughman, Olson, Keene, Collins, Kee

4th PRECINCT

MY FAVORITE DISPATCHER

Dispatchers have a tough job. They have to learn how to speak in an arcane tongue. They must be able to deal with frenzied people on the phone, who are in life-threatening situations, and give them sound, protective advice. They coach anxious mothers with unexpected deliveries. And, they bear the wrath of A-holes who got a well-deserved ticket.

Another thing they sometimes deal with is boredom. This leads to pranks.

We had an crotchety, old dispatcher named Nick. Nick didn't like many folks, but he despised our new Chief, a retired Army colonel who was a pompous turd. And the feeling was mutual. We'd just had a new five-button phone system installed, providing four more lines. When a call came in for the Chief, the dispatcher would put the party on hold, call the Chief and tell him what line to pick up. *Call for you, Chief.* Simple enough, right? Not if Nick had your number.

Course, Nick would do it when there was no call, just a lit button on the line he'd punched. He'd listen for the Chief

I'M PEDDLIN' AS FAST AS I CAN

to pickup, then he'd begin tapping the buttons machine gun style. The Chief, trying to follow the lights, went insane. You could hear him bellowing down the hall. Finally, to cover himself, Nick would complain to the Chief that the new phone system sucked. Then, privately, have a good laugh.

But paybacks are hell and Nick had his own nemesis to deal with: another dispatcher, a fella named Bob Nicholson. Bob was even older than Nick but with the exact opposite temperament. While Nick was loud and volatile, Bob was calm as a clam. For some reason Nick disliked him almost as much as he did the Chief.

Our swivel chairs then, didn't have a simple lever to adjust the seat height. You had to get down on your knees and spin a wheel on a threaded post until it was the height you wanted. Bob made sure that the seat was lowered to the bottom just before Nick went on duty. This put Nick's chin at desktop height. Nick would be infuriated. Being old, and a little rotund, he couldn't bend over that easily.

We had a middle-age gal named Dorothy who was a smoking fiend. But, she only smoked at work. Never at home or anywhere else. When asked why she just didn't quit all together, since she didn't smoke most of the time, she'd say, "I don't need it at home."

And there was Betty Jo, a hard-worker who struggled for years making ends meet on a dispatcher's salary. Until she married a rich man.

And we had June Holzhausen, who anchored the station for years. She was a walking demographic directory of Naples.

Then, there is my favorite dispatcher. The first time I saw her, literally, I knew she was going to be the most important part of my life. She was a petite, lovely little woman and an excellent dispatcher. She could handle the most distraught callers and had an encyclopedic memory for names and people. Perfect for the job.

Course, in just a few months I had to fire her. They had this rule in the City, nepotism, that relatives couldn't have a worker/boss relationship. The rule also applied to wives and husband. *So when we were married...*

I'M PEDDLIN' AS FAST AS I CAN

That was many, many years ago and she's still my favorite. . .everything. Sandy. Her picture is at the top. See what I mean?

Sandy's Photo by Ray Barnett

THE SHORT REIGN OF THE PORNO PERUSER

Naples once hired a retired Army officer as Chief of Police. His military service record was brilliant. His list of commendations, illustrious. His bravery, unquestioned. He lasted six-months as the Chief. We'll call him the Colonel.

In a month, the stress of the job had given him such severe dermatitis that his hands looked like pink oven mitts. Then his cocktail lunches stretched to most of the afternoon. His love of *liquid stupid* finally led to his premature downfall. Loaded, while speaking at a local women's club, he salted his address with raunchy officer's club humor, using all the filthy language in his soldier's arsenal. Next day he was gone.

One of the things that drove him over the edge was that he couldn't separate political rhetoric from genuine vows of intent. When the movie *Deep Throat* was screened locally and all the Council members ranted about how deplorable that was, the Colonel thought they were serious. He immediately instituted a crusade against porno.

To advance this war he sent me to the *Book Nook*, on 5th Ave South, to buy a copy of every adult magazine in the place. The Book Nook wasn't a porno shop, but a complete magazine store with a huge inventory. It was a downtown landmark and meeting place. Speaker of the House Tipp O'Neill, during his frequent visits to Naples, hung out there. They did have girly magazines, but discreetly displayed in the rear of the store, in an Adults Only alcove.

When I came back with a stack two feet tall, the Colonel was elated. His suspicions had borne fruit. The filth was ubiquitous. Now he had to study these vile publications and determine if they met the standards of pornography. And study he did. Until the pages were as fluffed open from frequent turning as a Sears catalog in an outhouse. And there were always several open on his desk.

To make matters worse, he kept them stacked on the front of his desk, where anyone siting in the visitors chair had to look over them to see him. At the time, being Assistant Chief, I shared his office. It was great fun to see how long it took a visitor to notice that they had to peer over a copy of *Naked Nubile Nymphs* to talk to the Chief of Police. This went on until the City Manager happened by one day, took the chair, looked down, and erupted into a giant um pah storm.

The knockout blow for the porno war came when Judge Harold Smith reviewed the affidavits for a warrant to arrest the owner of the Gulf Gate Theater for showing Deep Throat. The Judge, a man of common sense and earthy wit said, "Where's the warrant for the other fella?"

The prosecutor was confused. "What other fella?"

"The one who held the gun on these people and forced them into the theater to watch this thing. Case dismissed." (It was rumored that the good Judge had personally evaluated this film. Several times)

We did learn from the Colonel. The porno law required that you use the community standard to determine what was acceptable in your town and what wasn't, Miami probably being different from Gobbler's Knob. Determining that demanded a lotta study. We would study the subject matter, particularly 8mm films, for hours trying to classify them. *It was grueling work but somebody had to do it.*

My favorite was the one with the dwarf and the fat lady. It was titled *Where There's A Woodie There's A Way.*

GRAVE ADMISSIONS

The Naples PD never scrimped on schools. I attended Homicide school at the Univ of Louisville, Polygraph school in New York City for six-weeks, and Investigators school at the Univ of Georgia for two weeks. This was an excellent school. We were taught by true experts in each field. Most classes were overseen by federal agents, but the actual techniques used were demonstrated by felons who had gone straight. Safe cracking was taught by a safe man. Residential burglary, by a burglar. Counterfeiting by a counterfeiter. And so on. The absolute best way to learn the business.

I'M PEDDLIN' AS FAST AS I CAN

We each had our own room on campus and the tuition was zero. The adult education building and classes were funded by Kellogg's, the cereal maker. The excellent meals were free. Really first class.

We had cops from around the country. In the evenings, it was common to gather for bull sessions. There was always lots of liquid stupid (booze) present. War stories proliferated. As an example, I told how we would catch a suspect, put them in the front seat of the cop car, wrap the mike cord around their arm and tell them they were hooked up the lie detector. Whenever they lied, the red light on the box would come on. This was really just the transmit indicator on the radio that came on when we surreptitiously keyed the mike.

"Did you break into that building?"

"No, Sir."

Key mike, light comes on. "You're lying to me."

"Well, uhhhhh. . ."

This, believe it or not, was very effective and not much of a departure from how the real polygraph is sometimes used by inept examiners.

Two detectives from New Orleans, however, took the *tall tales gold cup* one night. We were talking about how frustrating it was to know someone was dirty and not be able to make an arrest. Perhaps a burglar, who escaped your grasp for months, stealing thousands of dollars worth of property while you built a case.

One of the dicks from NOPD said they had the same problem, but, fortunately, they had the stupidest thieves on earth. They were often found, drowned in Lake Pontchartrain, after stealing more chain than they could swim with. A great quip. We all laughed.

I remembered this several years later when the FBI conducted a massive investigation of the New Orleans PD, charged with gross corruption. The list of crimes was endless. What caught my attention were several bodies of missing criminals that turned up in Lake Pontchartrain. Wrapped in more chain than they could possibly swim with.

It seems that once again, at the school, the real experts had spoken.

HARRY THE HANGER

Harry was a sho'nuff paper hanger but don't ask him to do your wall paper. Harry's was the kind of paper hanger that's cop's jargon for bum check artists. Worthless check utterer. Forger. And Harry was at the top of his class.

It was an easier and more attractive job in the sixties. Many of the banks were private or state banks, not national banks insured by the FDIC. Rinky-dink operations. Cashing a check was a casual affair. If you'd left your checkbook at home, most stores had counter checks you could use. Counter checks were in a check's regular format, but minus the name of any bank. You just filled in the name of your bank, the amount, and signed it.

A friend once argued that you didn't even need a counter check. You could write one out on a piece of paper. To prove it, we walked up to the Bank of Naples and he did just that. No problem.

So, in this grand world of slack security, Harry made his living. A charmer, with a gift of BS, he was perfect for the job. Seldom was he even asked for ID. And some folks he'd skinned refused to press charges. His problem was he was too honest, many times using his real name, leading to many stints in jail.

Although a born and bred Naples *Cracker,* we weren't the only ones who got to enjoy Harry. I received a call from a used car dealer in Texas. Wanted to know if I'd ever heard of Harry. "You didn't take one of his checks did you?" I asked.

He said. Harry'd left it for payment on a car he bought. "I don't usually do business like that, the dealer said, but he was so damn likable. Told me he was driving back to Naples to see his sick mother. Wanted to take her for a ride in a nice car before she died. When I found out the check was no good, I called you."

"What'd you sell him?" I asked.

"Can't miss it," the fella said, "Caddy limo, black, 'bout as long as the Orange Blossom Special."

I'M PEDDLIN' AS FAST AS I CAN

I had to laugh. I'd seen Harry driving it the day before. Gave me a big wave, tooted his horn.

Later Harry was on the road gang, working on Davis Boulevard, opposite the entrance to Brookside Village. There used to be a bar there called the Village Inn. The guard, who sat in a truck out of the sun, and half-watched the crew of all trustee convicts, noticed Harry's crew sitting down. He went to check. They were all drinking cold beers. "What the. . .?" he said.

"I bought it at the Village Inn," Harry volunteered. "Nothin' goes down like a cold beer when you're hot and sweaty."

"Right," the guard said, "just walked in there in your prison stripes and he gave it you, you not havin' no money an' all."

"Oh, no," Harry said, "I wrote him a check."

And damned if he hadn't. The bartender, when asked what possessed him to take a check from a convict said, "I don't know. He seemed like such a nice fellar."

HARRY THE HANGER Part Two

When you're a true legend you live in memories well after you're gone. My post on Harry has prompted reports from other cops who remember him.

Dave Dampier reminds me that when Harry went to court for he *Road Gang Beer Check Caper* he had a unique defense. He told the Honorable Richard Stanley that he'd plead *not guilty* because it was a post dated check. Post dated checks couldn't be prosecuted under the law. The rationale was that the writer, when warning not to cash the check until a date in the future, was admitting the check was no good at the time it was written. So the receiver should never have taken it.

The Judge asked Harry how it was post dated. Harry said to "Look in the little fish on top."

At the time, Bank of Naples checks had a fish logo. The judge looked and written in small letters in the fish was post

I'M PEDDLIN' AS FAST AS I CAN

dated. Everyone had a good laugh over that one. Except Harry, who went back to jail.

Then there was the time Ray Barnett used Harry as an undercover operative to make street drug buys in Immokalee. Ray had moved on from the NPD and was an investigator for the CCSO. He had a distinguished career there, ending up as a Chief.

Ray said Harry, with his winning ways, was making buys faster than *Slick Willie* could catch an intern. Trouble was, Ray found out, he was also writing bad checks all over Immokalee at the same time. But what were you to expect? That's what Harry did.

Harold Young reminded me of Harry's crowning glory. That was the time Harry went into a store in Immokalee and cashed an FPL electric bill. Yes, that's what I said, cashed an FPL electric bill. And this, again, was when he was on the road gang. *A working convict!* Prison clothes and all. Don't ask me how he did it. And we can't ask Harry. He's hanging paper on that big bank in the sky.

ANOTHER SILLY SALESMAN. AND CUSTOMER

We were besieged by yet another salesman. He was selling this new, powerful, defense spray.

"This product is guaranteed to knock your adversary to his knees," he was blowing, *"no matter if he's drunk, high on drugs, or crazy as a monkey on a motorcycle."*

"We got that stuff already," I said, "and even when it's new it doesn't work on most people. And when it gets some age on it, you might as well spray them with milk." It was true. This was just at the advent of defense sprays and they were concocted from tear gas. A good idea but a bad product.

Undeterred, the salesman plowed on. "But sir, this is made from capsicum, chili peppers. Not what you're speaking of."

"You mean like that pepper spray the mail carriers use on dogs? That's no good, either."

"Still not the same thing, this is--"

I was tired of listening to him and decided to embarrass him by showing just how puny his product was. "Okay, I said, let's give it a field test. We'll go out back and you can spray me with it."

The salesman was aghast. "Spray you? Oh, no, I wouldn't recommend that. No, I wouldn't do that."

Finally I badgered him enough that he gave in. The guy was genuinely trying to protect me but I couldn't see it. Chili peppers? Stuff you can eat? How bad could it be? We'll say it was one of those logical dysfunctions that *seem like a real good idea at the time.*

We went out back, I made ready about ten-feet in front of him and he let go. (I think he used as little more than necessary because I was such an A-hole.) And the next thing I knew I was on my knees, couldn't breath, and my face felt like it had been painted with acid. Some of the worst pain I've ever felt. But, in fifteen-minutes it was over and aside from feeling really dumb, I was fine.

You see, the new amazing product was *Cap Stun* and let me endorse its effectiveness. Works on most people except an occasional PCP maniac or psychopath. We bought several cases.

The troops, of course, were not satisfied until they'd done their own field tests. It was a bad time to bow up at a cop, all of whom had their finger on the button, looking for an excuse to hose someone down. And on the midnight shift, you couldn't find a possum or armadillo that didn't have their little fists balled up, rubbing their eyes.

THE WILD SWANS ROUNDUP

Down in Port Royal's Lantern Lake area we had a problem. Swans. It was nesting season and swans are particular about where they nest. Like to try out lots of places before they find the ideal one. Trying out involves ripping out and mashing down existing foliage to form the nest. Unfortunately, at Lantern Lake they were doing it in folk's manicured flower beds.

The calls to curtail this vandalism poured in. And, of course, since no one else wanted anything to do with it, they landed on my desk. Not exactly the exciting police work you see on TV but, truthfully, indicative of most of the crap cops have to handle.

I didn't want to involve the troops in this silliness, so I gathered up our animal control dude, one Mr. Clarence Sack, and headed out on our mission. First stop was *Jungle Larry's African Safari* (Caribbean Gardens). We wanted to know if he'd take them after Sack sacked them up. Larry said he'd be glad to, but was busy and couldn't pick them up for a day or two. I told him we were in a hurry and we'd just do it ourselves. Looking back, I'm sure he had a fleeting smile on his face.

We proceeded to Port Royal, located our quarry and Sack moved in. He went at it barehanded and soon found out you didn't just pick up a swan like a duck at the farmer's market. Swans are big. And strong. And they have beaks and stuff. Sack soon fled to his truck and locked himself in.

A crowd had started to form and was enjoying the show. This embarrassed me and I decided to tackle the problem myself. After all, Sack was an elderly, frail cat who could be butt-kicked by an aggressive egret. I was young, big, and strong. This was man's work.

Bad mistake. The swans put such an az-whuppin' on me I was soon scratching at the door of Sack's truck, begging him to unlock it and let me in. While the crowd roared, seeming to enjoy seeing the Chief of Police humiliated by two swans.

When I regained my courage, and the swans had gone back to cruising the pond, I asked one of the neighbors if I could use his phone and called Jungle Larry. I told him what had happened. He asked, innocently, "You mean you're not ready to make delivery?" Then he burst into laughter.

"Thanks a lot, pal. Why didn't you tell me how mean those suckers are?"

"Well," Larry said, gasping between laughing fits. "I figured you knew, being in such a hurry to pick 'em up and all."

"Obviously, I don't. What do I do to capture 'em? Shoot 'em with a dart? What?"

"Naw, just get behind them, reach down and grab their wings near the body and fold them back. It won't hurt 'em, or

I'M PEDDLIN' AS FAST AS I CAN

you. You get their wings like that and they lose all their strength."

Damn, if it wasn't true! We captured the birds, delivered them to Jungle Larry, and the rich folks in Port Royal's paradise were as happy as Jimmy Buffett with a cheeseburger. Jungle Larry let me name the two critters, Wayde and Lori, after my two little children at the time.

And it only took Sack and me a couple of weeks to heal up.

ELEMENTARY, WATSON

In Port Royal there were some normal size homes, some cottages really. They were located around Lantern Lake, off Galleon Drive. Half Moon Drive was there. Though the homes were small they weren't indicative of the size of the owner's wallet.

I was working a larceny there. The new owner, Mr Bell, had just moved his furniture into the cottage. When he tired of unpacking, and decided to make himself a drink, he noticed several bottles of scotch were missing.

I asked who moved him and he gave me the name of a nationwide mover. He was confident they were not responsible, because of their name. Said he'd been in the house several days before the movers arrived and the scotch had probably been missing beforehand and he hadn't noticed it. To the contrary, the movers were my first suspects.

Mr. Bell, didn't know that the highly skilled movers were picked up at the local labor shed when the driver got to his destination. In Naples these experts hung out under a shade tree near River Park Apartments. Anyone who wanted a day worker could go by there and pick one up.

I asked Mr. Bell if his milk was missing. He checked his refrigerator and came back with a confused look on his face. *Yes, it's gone. How'd you know that?*

"No problem," I said, "be back shortly."

Within an hour I had returned most of his scotch and had two moving experts in jail. Amazing detective work? I wish. Just knowing folk's habits.

I'M PEDDLIN' AS FAST AS I CAN

All the experts at the labor shed were black. Black folks like to drink scotch and, you guessed it, milk. I simply went to the labor shed, found out who'd gone with the mover that morning, found them--*drunk on liquid stupid*--and sacked p them up and the remainder of the scotch.

Mr. Bell thought I was Sherlock Holmes. I neglected to tell him what I've just told you. I did ask him, "All that Scotch was Bell's Scotch. And your name is Bell. You don't own it do you?"

Mr. Bell laughed. "Lord no, wish I did. I just own Bell Aircraft."

JACK BLISS DOES IT AGAIN

Before Jack Bliss was the NPD's first full-time detective, he pushed a cruiser, just like a lot of us. One early morning he fell in behind a Cadillac, driving fitfully toward the old Beach Club Hotel, near the Naples Pier. The vehicle would speed up, slow down, and ride on both sides of the road. Jack flipped on his siren and red light.

The driver paid no attention and continued to meander down the road. Finally, Jack pulled up beside the Caddy and shined his door-mounted spot light on the driver. The driver uttered some curses and pulled over.

Jack pulled in behind the drunk, and was alighting from his vehicle, when the Caddy took off again. This time Jack forced the car to the berm by wedging in front of it. He approached the car again.

The driver was a distinguished looking fifty-ish gent, in a dinner jack and wilted bow tie. He gave Jack a surly look. "Well," he slurred, "I guess you think you're the big frog in this small pond."

"Let me see your license," Jack said.

The drunk ignored him. "The big law and order man, arrest just about anyone you want?"

"Anyone that needs it, Let me see your license."

"But, I bet you lay off anyone important, has some horsepower, don't you?"

I'M PEDDLIN' AS FAST AS I CAN

"Oh, I wouldn't say that," Jack said. "I've arrested the mayor, a few city councilmen, a movie star once, a priest. . ."

"Yes," the driver smirked, "but I'll bet you never arrested one of these." Whereupon he fished a card from his wallet and handed it to Jack. The card identified him as a U.S. Senator from the mid-west.

"No sir," Jack said, opening the car door, fishing out his handcuffs, and grabbing the driver by the arm, "but it was right at the top of my *TO DO LIST."*

Jack always was an equal opportunity destroyer.

RACE ELATIONS

The sixties were a sad time, but humor could also be found. In sometimes unlikely places.

After MLK was killed we had a few disruptions in quiet ol' Collier County. Once Sheriff Doug Hendry deputized all the NPD cops and we went to Immokalee where the good citizens were trying to stir up a race riot. Back then, during picking season, Immokalee was mostly black, not Hispanic as it is today.

We didn't know who to trust. The blacks didn't want us there, and neither did the rednecks, thinking we were in some way helping the blacks. Go figure. And some *Deliverance* type threw a brick and another took a shot at me. Couldn't see who did either, but their aiming mechanism didn't work any better than their brain. (Later we were able to play a little catch-up so the evening wasn't a total loss)

Back in The Elephant's Graveyard, there was trouble at the *W.T. Grant* store, then in the Naples Shopping Center. A respectable size crowd of black folks had gathered and were beginning to chant and grumble about not being allowed to eat in the restaurant there. The manager, Jim McGrath, came out and asked, "Have any of you tried?" *Uh, nope.* "Well, where'd you get the idea you couldn't eat here? I'm in the business of doing business. You got a dime, I've got the coffee. Come on in."

Talk about somebody peeing on your campfire. Dropping your gooey marshmallow in the sand. So much for that

I'M PEDDLIN' AS FAST AS I CAN

demonstration. The stately Mr. McGrath was later a Naples City Councilman.

Then, the best of all. On the day MLK was whacked we were concerned there would be trouble in our ghetto, McDonald Quarters. We didn't want to show up in force and provoke an incident so we sent Det Ray Barnett over to have a look-see. A little later, one of the cops came and got me. "You gotta see this," he said, laughing.

We went to Miz Lillie's *Green Top Social Palace* where voices raised in song could be heard from within. A large crowd was singing an impassioned *We Shall Overcome*. Directing this impromptu choir was Det Ray Barnett. I gave Ray a questioning look.

Ray shrugged, said, "They didn't know the words."

And, overcome we did.

THE WRESTLER--NAPLES STYLE

A recent film, The Wrestler, brought to mind the Naples PD's experiences with pound and pretend. To help raise money for PAL, we used professional wrestling shows as one of many sources. The wrestling folks were great to work with. We would supply the place, security, sell tickets, and help put up and take down the ring. We kept the concession money and were guaranteed a certain amount even if the house was empty. They kept the ticket proceeds. Great deal.

Course we were soon insiders and our suspicions were confirmed; pro wrestling was a well staged show. We also found these showmen were tremendous athletes. For example, a 300 lb man on top of the corner post, back-flipping down on a supine associate, landing and not hurting either, required great athletic ability, strength and skill.

The wrestlers were all some of the nicest people you'd ever meet. As with many big folks, that don't have to prove a damn thing, they were, off-stage, invariably gentle giants. Yep, it was just a grand show. But some folks took it seriously.

Once, just before showtime, the manager of *The Samoans* gave me a desperate call. Their car was broken down just South of town and they needed help getting to the venue. No

I'M PEDDLIN' AS FAST AS I CAN

problem. I sent an off-duty cop and car out to pick them up. When knowledge of this became public, some people tried to put heat on me. Helping these criminals. Should have put them in jail when you had the chance. I tried to explain, without giving out the staged secret, that these guys were the main event and we needed them. No good. So, I just wrote the whiners off as what they were: Azzholes!

The Samoans, you see, were *heels,* wrestling talk for bad guys. Good guys were called baby faces. Heels were usually the most experienced and controlled the matches. Howsumever, *The Samoans* were so good at their act that people really hated them. That was common.

Once, before a match, one of the bad guy managers, *Sir Oliver Humperdink,* came to me several times to insure there would be a cop nearby when he performed all his dirty, ringside tricks. He was genuinely concerned. *Some of these rubes think this is for real. They try to HURT me.*

This truth was brought home shortly thereafter. In Ft. Myers, one of the heels, *Sonny Big Cat King* if memory serves, was leaving the ring when a fan stabbed him in the azz. The cops tried to arrest this fool and a riot ensued. Several people were severely injured and spent time in the hospital. This included a few cops.

Like the man said: *There's no business like show business!*

SEEMED LIKE A REAL GOOD IDEA AT THE TIME

Sometimes folks, without due consideration, do things that seem like a real good idea but lead to disastrous consequences. Former Chief Ben Caruthers reminded me of one such incident.

Naples had a hard-scrabble *Cracker* family that caused cops to assume a defensive posture anytime they saw one of them coming. The two sons, in particular, were notoriously combative hell raisers and were both unaccountable to any deity of common sense.

One night the eldest, who we'll call Luther, his puny cognitive resources further addled by a gallon or so of *liquid stupid,* decided that he would benefit from a circumcision. I doubt the possibility that a doctor and hospital should be involved ever crossed his mind. Luther's mind didn't work that way. He was impulsive, even when sober. Drunk, he was Pavlov's dog. So, he went to the beach, took out his Buck knife and began trimming away. This, of course, brought forth a gusher of blood and Luther barely made it to the hospital alive. He did live, of course, protected by the *Angel of the Drunk and Stupid.*

Later, if asked by hospital personnel what provoked him to engage in such insanity he would've said the magic words: *Don't know, seemed like a real good idea at the time.*

I know this will come as a terrible shock, but even cops make bad mistakes. Yes, it's rare but it do happen. Take the case of two from the CCSO who were chasing a speeder out the East Trail. The driver was the then Sheriff. (It was not Aubrey Rogers) He ordered the Deputy to fire on the escaping vehicle. Shoot it's tires out like he'd seen in the movies. This was a time when cops could shoot just about anybody or anything for any reason.

The Deputy rolled down the window, unholstered his revolver, leaned out and fired a round. Anyone who has ever fired a revolver at night knows there is a lotta smoke, fire, and sparks that come out the barrel and cylinder. When you shoot into a wind coming at you at 80 mph it blows back and burns the hell outta your hand. Causing you to want to let go of the thing quickly, which he did. The gun, crashed to the highway, destroying it.

Yes, yes, I know it never happens in the movies or on TV. And on TV little people regularly *Kung Fu* big bad people, guns have unlimited ammo, and all crimes are solved in an hour. Our Deputy, however, was in the real world and when he retrieved his revolver, the barrel now bent to the Southeast, he must've had one fleeting thought; *Seemed like a real good idea at the time.*

THE BUM PATROL

Once, in the mid-eighties, I was assigned a unique job: The Bum Patrol. I was to count all the "homeless" in the Naples area. The purpose was to evaluate the magnitude of the problem, which everyone knew was growing. It was an education.

First thing I found out was that many of these folks were not victims of the economy or misfortune. They were homeless because they chose to be. They were bums. There was a good infrastructure in place for legitimate homeless people, with the Salvation Army leading the list. Also, several church and privately sponsored programs. Many bums, however, wouldn't go near these help projects because they found something very unsavory about them: *they wanted you to work. To help yourself. To hell with that.*

And not all were bums, without means of support. A large number were dropouts, folks fed up with everything: family, job, the works. Among these we found two retired cops, on pensions, who lived in the woods because they were sick of society. Seen too much. Another guy was a former chef for the Ritz Carlton. Several had been business people. And many were construction workers who would come to Naples in the winter from frozen-out northern jobs. They lived in tents and travel trailers in the woods to save money. They would set up a respectable, though illegal, camp and never cause any problems.

Naples is a favorite spot for bums. We found several with travel guides they had been given in shelters in Washington, D.C. that told how to find Naples and what to do when they got here. Such as, go the St. Vincent De Paul and get free cookware and a chit for free breakfast at the White House Restaurant. St. Matthews House will give you free meals, no questions asked. You can camp in a wooded lot near there. You can go such and such and get free clothes. Go to the ER for free medical care. And they were provided directions to prime camping areas, such as near stores, beside a beautiful pond.

We found several large camps with fifty or more folks living there. Found out they had homemade warning devices to let them know when someone was coming. This was usually a dried palmetto frond, laying in the path. Stepping on it made a loud crunch. Some used beer cans strung on a fishing leader. Hit the lines, the cans would jangle.

I'M PEDDLIN' AS FAST AS I CAN

Many were enterprising. They'd steal enough construction materials to build lean-to's. One even had a four-poster bed, a sofa, and chairs. Many had lawn chairs stolen from folk's yards.

But, ah, for the romantic, vagabond life.

THE BUM PATROL--Part Two

There's one group of these romantic vagabonds we failed to mention; criminals, psychopaths, every deviate and disreputable on the dodge. Presenting a threat to the public, they could also be deadly to their fellow "campers." Preying on the weak, any loner who hadn't allied himself with another bum, could count on being robbed or beaten at will.

Ever wonder why these folks carry all their clothes around on them, worn in layers, and tote all their belongings in a purloined WalMart cart? Have to. Anything left back at their camp, is long gone.

The most common malady was alcoholism. Every camp we raided featured a huge mound of discarded beer cans. For most, all activity for the day centered around scrounging enough money to buy enough booze to set things right. Begging was popular. One bum, you had to admire, shunned the signs displayed by many: *Will Work For Food.* (They wouldn't) *Vet Needs A Hand. Hungry, Please Help.* He sported a sign that proclaimed: *Why Lie. I Need A Drink!* And he collected more coins than anyone else!

St. Matthew's House had to be the Four Seasons of Bumdom. Bums from all over the country could tell you about it and give you helpful hints. There's a field nearby where you can camp. Or just roost in one of the neighbor's hedges.

This generated a minor crime wave. Homeowners near the nests found anything left untethered was soon gone. No bicycle was safe. Mail boxes were raided. Cars B&E'd. And in nearby stores, shoplifting doubled.

Some were entrepreneurs. One character, Frank Allen, was from a reputable local family, but had gone astray in his teen years and gradually drifted from the jail to the woods. Frank set up a clandestine bicycle shop off Halderman Creek,

I'M PEDDLIN' AS FAST AS I CAN

where a bum could buy a stolen bike at a bargain price or have minor repairs made. He would also barter, trading his wares for stolen booze or whatever. He operated several years before he was discovered and added to the jail population.

That was over thirty-years ago. I counted about 1200 critters in the Naples area. Best I can tell, it hasn't changed a damn bit today.

YOUR TAX DOLLARS AT WORK

Aside from the Councilman's crackpot idea that we patrol on bicycles--for which this work, *I'm Peddlin' As Fast As I Can,* is named--there have been other gems from the *outer limits.*

In the late fifties it was decided that the NPD could save money by using Nash Ramblers as patrol vehicles. It would also shut up the local Rambler dealer who complained he didn't get a fair shake with mostly Chevrolets and Fords being used.

Ramblers were cheap, no frills, mid-size cars. They were so underpowered they couldn't out drag a codger in a wheelchair. And they weren't built to withstand rough use, let alone 24-hour-a day police duty. But there they were.

They did have two good features. They sipped gasoline and the front seats folded back into a comfortable bed. The bed was great for civilian use, but in a police car? There are two primary things a bed is used for, sleep and sex, both of which you're not supposed to be doing on duty. But we all know human nature.

The Ramblers began to fall apart before the new car smell was lost to the ambient cop car stench of drunk puke and urine. The folding front seat back had a bad habit of converting into a bed anytime you hit a bump. The thing just collapsed backwards. This could really pull your pucker string. And that of any backseat passenger, too. Talk about texting being a distraction.

The vehicles were so cheaply built that our huge cops, like Fred Scott, just crushed the seats until they were flatter than

I'M PEDDLIN' AS FAST AS I CAN

a cop's wallet. The next guy on duty had to stack up cushions, like a child's seat in a restaurant, to see over the dash.

Durable? A collision with a possum could require a tow truck.

Long-lasting? The poor, feeble engines were history after 40,000 miles.

Then there was the *Flash-O-Matic* automatic shifter. A push-button device built into the dash, it matched the reliability of the rest of the vehicle. Often, when the button was pushed, it would fall through, and disappear inside the dash. Real handy. . .unless you wanted to change gears again.

Finally, an always enterprising Det Jack Bliss, came up with the answer. By writing the specs for patrol car bids using a normal sedan's wheelbase, the stubby Rambler would not qualify. And so the cops were able to go back to just worrying about the bad guys trying to kill them. Not their own cars.

WHO WAS THAT IN THE BOAT?

One of the unique things Naples Cops experience is running into celebrities. Naples has always had it's share, either visitors or residents, and the interaction is inevitable. But usually not expected.

Riding with our boat man, Joe LaRochelle, one day I spotted a yacht, that looked to be a 100 footer, tied up off the Naples Yacht Club. It was a beautiful sleek vessel and I asked Joe if he knew who it belong to. He smiled, said he did, and headed that way. Pulling along side we were greeted by a lady I recognized from the movies and TV. She was a singer named Frances Langford. Was on the Bob Hope Show and others. She greeted Joe like he was an old friend and asked if he was ready for his *toddy*. Joe laughed like that was a grand joke--though I suspected it wasn't--and introduced me. Then a gentleman stepped to the rail, and after being introduced, I could see why the craft was so splendid. His name was Mr. Evinrude. Yep, the one who owned Evinrude outboard motors.

Another day I was working on a series of thefts in the old boat yard that was replaced by *Tin City*. I interviewed the

I'M PEDDLIN' AS FAST AS I CAN

honcho, then talked with folks in the yard, working on their boats. In one slip was a large and beautiful sailing yacht. On board was what looked like a scruffy deckhand, attending to the bright work. (To you land lubbers that's polishing the brass) I boarded the craft and, after asking my police questions, mentioned how attractive the boat was, and asked what brand it was. A Chris Craft, the deckhand said.

Surprised, I said, "I didn't know Chris Craft made anything but power boats, cabin cruisers, like that."

"Oh, no," the deckhand said, "if you're willing to pay, they'll make anything you want."

Finishing my work around the yard I walked back to the honcho. "Saw you talking to the deckhand over on the Chris Craft," he said.

"Yep," I answered, "didn't know they made sailing ships."

The boss laughed. "Well, if you own Chris Craft like that deckhand does, they'll make just about anything you want."

Another time we had two itinerant thieves steal a yacht out of Port Royal, sail it to New Orleans, and wreck it. When I was doing the initial report I asked for the name of the vessel.

"Easy to spot," said the owner. "On the transom there's a big Daisy flower painted with the letter "B" on each side. I though a second, then, Like Daisy BB guns?"

"Yes," he smiled, "*I own Daisy.*" And so he did.

THE GIRL BESIDE THE ROAD

Yesterday, I had the honor of participating in a ceremony to remember a fallen officer. His name was Louis Collins and I worked with him many years ago. The ceremony was at the Naples Police Department, my old home, where I had not been for many years. It brought back old memories.

This is the week when we honor our fallen brothers and sisters. And, it has to make you ponder why anyone would choose a profession such as ours. Many years ago, when I had just made Detective, I was asking myself the same question.

I'M PEDDLIN' AS FAST AS I CAN

Struggling to keep my family together, working two or three jobs to make ends meet, putting in 12-hour days with no overtime, was making me wonder if I'd taken the right path. That was on my mind, one night, on my way home to Brookside Village. My thoughts were interrupted by some movement in the weeds on the side of the road, just before the Royal Harbor entrance.

Pulling the car over, I could hear murmuring from a huddled form in the tall grass. It was a young woman who crossed her arms in front of her face and whimpered as I got close. I held out my badge so she could see it and said, "It's okay now, I'm a cop. I won't hurt you."

She studied me with terrified eyes for a moment then rushed to me and hugged me and began crying in earnest. Tears of relief. It turns out she had been raped and dumped beside the road like one might dispose of an empty beer can. Her assailant had done unspeakable things to her with a broken pine bough.

Standing there with her clinging to me, her horrors for the moment lessened because she knew there was a *cop* there, I knew I could never do anything else but this. No matter what it paid. No matter what the hours. No matter what the price.

All cops who stick on the job have this same, private, defining moment. There's a fancy word for it: *epiphany*. One day a special time will come that will cause you to look back and remember yours. Look forward to it.

"We're gonna get the bastard that did this to you," I said to the girl. "And when we do, he's gonna pay. He's gonna really pay."

And *we* did.

And *he* did.

THE MIDNIGHT STREAKER

Dollar Down was a Naples car salesman, long ago repossessed by the Man Upstairs. Or, most likely, the Man Downstairs. He loved beautiful, fast, sporty cars. And beautiful, fast, sporty, women. Especially if they were parked in someone else's garage, the danger making the adventure more exciting. Or so he said. One night, he got all the excitement he could handle.

The current object of his lechery was a pretty married woman we'll call Mustang Sally. She was a bad choice since she, too, had a more-the-merrier attitude and her Hubby kept close watch on her. At the time, Hubby suspected Sally was dallying and decided to set her up and see. Told her he had to go out-of-town on business. Wouldn't be back until late the next evening. He reasoned when the cat's away, the mice will get drunk and party naked.

That very evening, Hubby returned, unannounced, and caught Dollar in the front seat of his Mustang, engine revved and locked in high gear. Hubby ratcheted the shotgun he was carrying, and Sally and Dollar both instantly slammed it in Park. And before Dollar could say I've done stepped on my carrot he was outside in the bushes, trying to figure how he was going to make the two miles to his home with no money, clothes, and bare azz naked. You see Hubby had expelled him from his house as he had found him, keeping his wallet, car keys, and sporty car salesman clothes.

That night we received several calls from folks in the area who were sure they'd seen some naked prevert vault their rear fence. Or run from bush to bush across the neighbor's front lawn.

Later that night Hubby called us reporting he'd found clothing, a wallet, and keys outside their bedroom window. He suspected a *peeping Tom* who'd been frightened off. One of those real sickos who strip down naked while peeping. We took the clothing, found a car matching the keys parked nearby and showed up at Dollar's front door.

He'd just made it home and was a sorry sight. Bedraggled and barely coherent, he was trying to explain to his wife why he'd come home at 4 AM in a towel--he'd stolen off a clothes line--with scrapes and scratches from galloping through the woods, no money and no car. We got him aside and he confessed what had really happened. A later interview with Hubby confirmed his part. Mustang Sally had nothing to say.

Sometimes justice works itself out better than the courts can. Mustang Sally stayed with Hubby, changed her ways and became a happy homemaker. Or, at least she pretended she was. We couldn't find anything Hubby had done wrong. Matter of fact, we admired his MO. And Dollar Down had been punished enough during his midnight ramble and future hell-to-pay with his wife.

We know that because *The Midnight Streaker* was never seen again.

Fingerprint Classification School taught by the FBI in mid-60's.

Left to right, FBI instructor, Mike Gideon, Jim Scaggs, June Holzhasen, Mike Grimm, GD Young, Dottie Koester, Ed Downing, Bob Steele, Dave Dampier, Chief Ben Caruthers

Bob Steel later joined the Marines and became a hero, pulling passengers off a plane that caught fire on landing. He was killed in a rocket attack on the barracks in which he was staying in Viet Nam. The barracks were for those awaiting transit back home after serving their tour.

5th PRECINCT

FRED SCOTT

Fred Scott was a good 'ol boy from Helena, Georgia. What we call a *Wide Body*, he would've been an imposing presence on an NFL line on any Sunday. He worked for the NPD in the 50's and early 60's, until he was shot in the arm by a fellow police officer, who, mentally ill and violent, also wounded Chief Ben Caruthers.

Fred loved country music and asked Sam Bass, a master, to musician and fellow cop, to teach him how to play the fiddle. Sam, who was later elected to the *Florida Country Music Hall of Fame*, obliged and pretty soon Fred was sawing out a near-recognizable *Orange Blossom Special*. Problem was Fred's wife couldn't tolerate the squeaks and squalls that are attendant to novice fiddle playing. She banned Fred to the front porch. Until the neighbors enjoyed about as much of his music as they could stand. So Fred moved into his car.

I'M PEDDLIN' AS FAST AS I CAN

This could've been a good compromise today, but then, Fred's car was a VW--don't ask me how the giant even got into it--and it had no AC. But, you could see Fred in it, parked in front of his house, windows steamed and rolled up and the car bouncing up and down like a clogger at a hoedown.

The wounded arm troubled Fred the rest of his life, causing him to wake in the middle of the night with fearsome pains. It wasn't uncommon to run into him at one of the all-night burger joints, getting a little snack so he could go back to sleep. A snack for Fred was three hamburgers. For him, a burger was a two-bite *hors d'oeuvre*. Two bites. Washed it down with a couple large Cokes. And, of course, some fries on the side.

Like many giants, he was gentle, kind, and soft spoken. We still miss him.

RAID ON THE SNAKE FARM

Our narcotics unit had been working jointly on a case with the Feds and CCSO. A LSD lab had been located just north of Bonita Springs, in an abandoned serpentarium. The caretaker of the place was supposed to be a chemical genius. A test tube dude who was cooking enough LSD to have every head south of Atlanta seeing technicolor bunnies in their yogurt. One early morning we moved in.

The serpentarium, never anything but a third-rate sideshow, was just one house-size main building with a few trailers out back. We found the chemist, Karloff, busy at work in his makeshift lab. He was congenial enough but one of those "geniuses" who has all his furniture in one corner of the attic. At chemistry; a whiz. Remembering to eat, bathe, and sleep; dumb as dirt.

As an example, he told us he was being paid $125 a week. That for cranking out a hundred-thousand in dope every few days. But he was content, getting to live in one of the trailers free and, of course, there were all those snakes he could play with. And snakes there were.

I'M PEDDLIN' AS FAST AS I CAN

Like many snake nuts, he was not too good at keeping track of the critters. All of the cages in the building where open and Karloff was a little vague about how many had been occupied to begin with. They come and go. But out front was the kingdom of creepy crawlies. A pit, about thirty-feet across was full of rattlesnakes. Several hundred. They writhed and slithered and hissed in a giant ball that looked like squirming intestines. It took one of our cops, Ken Ferrell, several hours to shoot them all.

Karloff was mainly concerned that his friend, Clyde, would be well taken care of in his absence. And that we be careful when sniffing around the shed at the foot of a commercial radio tower on the back of the property. The owner of the snake farm still had some stuff stored there. We checked there first.

Opening the shed's door, we found it loaded with crates, oozing a substance like honey. It was old dynamite, disintegrating, with the nitroglycerin dripping out. Dynamite in its most unstable form. Fortunately, there were no blasting caps or the radio waves could've blown Bonita Springs off the map. We called the ATF folks, immediately.

Now to Clyde. We presumed he was a pal of Karloff's. We moved to the trailer where Karloff told us Clyde was asleep in the bedroom. Entering quietly, we eased open the bedroom door. We could see a huge lump under the covers, and peeling them back found a 250 pound python. He was asleep, having just had a tasty snack, a cow, something small like that. Maybe a Volkswagen.

We had a problem. What to do with Clyde. We tried to find a zoo or someone who'd take him but no luck. And Ferrell was eyeing his gun again. Howsumever, the expeditious federal legal system saved him. Karloff'd been taken to Miami, had a hearing, his bosses posted his bail and he was back at the farm while we were still snake wrangling, collecting evidence from the lab, and helping ATF guys tip-toe around the dynamite.

Karloff went straight to the bedroom, and hugged and cuddled Clyde. Clyde opened a sleepy eye and, I swear, seemed to smile at his kookie keeper. And I got all teary-eyed, being a sucker for happy reunions.

AN INCIDENT ON THE PIER

It was the seventies. The Naples PD was preparing to move to the new headquarters building on Goodlette Road. We were handling the records personally, to retain integrity for future court use. The old, old records were in our makeshift storeroom, one of the women's jail cells that was never used.

Sifting through the old stuff was as education. Most everything was written in the *Blotter*, a large bound book like those used in old-time hotels. The simplest of entries were used, complaint number, date, time, name, one-line description of the event, action taken. If further information was needed, you'd find an attached sheet of paper. This system was used until Chief Ben Caruthers upgraded to a modern records program, in the early 60's.

Reading one of these attached reports--probably from the thirties or forties--we were taken up short. It had been written by an officer whose name we did not recognize. It read, essentially, like this:

Received call that there was a nigger on the pier. Arrived and found subject. He was from a shrimp boat anchored nearby. Nigger was jumping off the boat, swimming to the pier, climbing up, then jumping off the pier and swimming back to the boat. Told nigger he couldn't do that, to stay off the pier. Went back to station. In a few minutes I received another call that the nigger was doing it again. Went back down there and found him on the pier. Shot same.

That was it. No addendum's. No further explanation. No nuttin'.

Of course, at the time, nothing further would have been necessary. It was another time in another world.

INCIDENT ON THE PIER--Part Two

Some explanation can be made as to how the shooting on the pier could've happened. At the time, there was a "no ass whoopin'" provision in the State Statutes. This meant that you could use any force, except deadly, to make a misdemeanor arrest. Wounding was okay. If a felony arrest,

I'M PEDDLIN' AS FAST AS I CAN

any force including deadly. Misdemeanors are petty crimes. Felonies are serious, like rape, robbery and murder.

So, because of the brevity of the report, we don't know if our cop was just arresting a violent subject or he killed him just to keep in practice. It wasn't that uncommon for some thug to get shot trying to whup a policeman.

To protect their health, officers would shoot a violent subject in the leg to take all the fun outta him. One of my best friends had to do this once. Confronting a large, mean, and violent street ape, who could've whupped half the NPD, my pal had to shoot the turd in the leg to make the arrest. Repercussions? None, it was the law. All that was required was a one-line addition to the arrest report: Had to shoot subject to effect arrest. As it turns out the shootee also was armed with a Beretta. I still have it. There were other wild and woolly times. This next incident I'll relate reluctantly since it was before my time and I didn't see it. But, I've talked to so many who did, I'm sure it happened.

A scumbag had killed a highway patrolman in Ft. Myers. The cops chased him and got him holed up in North Naples, mostly woods at the time. A Deputy went in after him, found him, and you could hear a muffled pistol shot. Then, *Police, halt, halt.* When the coroner came and inspected the body, a star-shaped blackened wound was noted on the murderer's temple. This is a sure sign of a contact wound. (*The gun placed on or very close to the point of entry*)

The Deputy said he'd spotted the perp running away, and commanded him to stop. The perp turned and the Deputy, thinking he was armed, shot him. Uh-huh. However, the coroner looked at the body, shook his head and said, *When are these A-Holes gonna learn you can't run from the police.*

I never had to kill anyone but, during this liberal shoot-em-up period, was involved in two incidents where I shot at fleeing felons. One was a drug dealer, the other wanted by the FBI for bank robbery in Ohio. Had to shoot at them because they were both outrunning me in a foot race. And we couldn't have that. Both put on the brakes when the lead whizzed by, deciding they'd rather rot in the jail than in the ground.

I'M PEDDLIN' AS FAST AS I CAN

Fact was they made bad choices. I was so winded and shaky from the run I couldn't have hit 'em with a cluster bomb.

POLYGRAPH SECRETS

When you run a lotta polygraph (lie detector) exams you hear way more secrets from folks than you want to. Mostly from the honest people. Criminals are intent on holding back everything to try and beat you. We call it "puking up your guts," telling any guilty secret you have so it won't influence the outcome of the test. Yep, after a while you start to feel like a priest.

Who they've been sleeping with on the side. What they'd shoplifted from the dime store when they were twelve. Stuff you don't want to know. Then there's the stuff that makes you think.

I was running a head waiter from an up-scale Naples restaurant. Although it had nothing to do with the crime we were investigating, he started relieving his conscience about things he'd done in the restaurant that he wasn't proud of. "When someone would whine about their food not being just like they wanted it, we'd take it back to the kitchen and spit on it. . .or worse."

"Okay," I said, trying to move on, "about the theft. . ."

"Course, it wasn't just me did it. Most of 'em did."

"Well, that must've been before you made it to the classy joints, when you were startin' out in the greasy spoons," I offered.

"Hell, no," he said, "the fancier the restaurant the worse they were. Chefs get the big head. Don't want anyone telling them how to cook the food and God help anyone who complains. I've seen 'em--"

I cut him off, not daring to hear anymore since I often ate in restaurants. Fortunately, I'd never sent anything back to the kitchen, having a garbage can gut, and feeling sorry for hardworking waiters who don't cook the stuff but still catch the heat from A-Hole customers.

I'M PEDDLIN' AS FAST AS I CAN

Always remembered what the fella said. And laugh to myself, in restaurants, when some pompous ass berates a poor waitress because his food doesn't match his delicate sensibilities. *Take it back!* Makes me hope the Chef gives it a good stir with his Johnson.

I know of one restaurant owner in the sixties--had a very popular place near 4-Corners--who'd start the day cooking a big pot of soup, and spit in it, muttering, "Damn slobs don't know what's good." Never ate there and was glad when he moved on to a much hotter kitchen.

Then there was the cook we had on a Marine base. About 300 lbs--we called him Buddha--cooked with his shirt off, over a grill, sweat dripping down on the food. If he caught you checking him out, he'd grab a ball of hamburger, put it under his greasy armpit, flatten it into a paddy, and toss it on the grill.

So remember, if that steak wasn't just the way you like it and you sent it back. . .*Bon appetit!*

JD AND THE MACON MOW DOWN

Interstate 75 South was built in segments over a number of years. For what seemed like forever, we had to drive to Tampa to get on it then get off at Macon, Georgia, where it ended. One summer JD Spohn took it on his way to a vacation in Kentucky. The evening after he left I received a call from him.

"Got in a little scrape," JD said, "some guys tried to rob me up here in Macon."

"Rob you?"

"Yeah, at gun point. Three of 'em. We got lost looking for 41 after I-75 ended and pulled off the road to look at the map. Next thing I know, here's these A-holes pointin' a gun at me."

Now, if I was gonna rob someone I'd pick maybe, Dirty Harry, the 5th Marines, somebody easy like that. Not JD Spohn. There was a joke around the PD that there was a standing reward for anyone who could catch JD unarmed. Once, I thought I had him. Driving by his house in Lake Park, I saw JD mowing his lawn. He was wearing typical JD attire: a 10 gallon hat, no shirt, Bermuda shorts, and cowboy boots. I pulled into his driveway and approached him. "Looks like I got ya, JD," I said.

"How's that?" he asked.

"Caught you without a gun."

"Don't count on it," JD said, producing a .38 from his boot and a Derringer from his back pocket. That was JD. And this is the same fella three fools in Macon, Georgia decided to rob. Another *Seemed like a real good idea at the time.*

"So what happened? You okay?"

"Oh yeah. I just reached down and got my .357 off the seat beside me and shot 'em. Here, the local cop wants to talk to you."

An officer, who identified himself as a Lt. from the Macon PD came on the line, confirmed JD's story and added, "We're gonna have to hold him here until we finish the investigation. Got three of 'em here with bullets in 'em. But, it shouldn't be too long. I'll call you back."

Then the phone went dead and I began to wait, fearing the worst. Georgia was the same state that locked up one of the CCSO Deputies in the same cell with the prisoner he was transporting until Sheriff Doug would wire them the $100 bogus traffic fine.

But, I didn't have to wait long. In less than two hours JD was on the phone again. "Everything's okay," he said. "Here's the LT."

I breathed a sigh of relief. "Looks like your man did the right thing. All checks out. But it makes ya wonder when these Nigrahs are gonna learn you can't rob white folks and not pay the price."

And with that the incident was over. JD went on his way and had a grand vacation. He wasn't the kind to worry about a few perforated bodies. He did ask me not to talk about the incident as he was afraid the City might not understand. I didn't, until now. JD is long gone and part of NPD history.

BE REAL CAREFUL WHAT YOU WISH FOR

I'M PEDDLIN' AS FAST AS I CAN

We once had a local merchant, Wilbur Whinesap, we just couldn't please. Although his business was on 5th Ave South, one of the most highly patrolled streets in the City, there were never enough patrols. Response time to his numerous, petty, complaints was never fast enough. He appeared at City Council budget hearings complaining the cops were overpaid and there were too many of them. In short, he was an Azwipe who needed an attitude adjustment.

One early April morning, about 2 AM, I was doing a plain-clothes bicycle patrol of 5th Ave So. We'd had some trouble with attempted break-ins to the rear doors of the businesses and wanted to put the turd responsible where he belonged; *Under the jail.*

Cruising silently down the alley behind *Ingram's Hardware* I noticed a rear door cracked open at a nearby business. A wedge of light was spilling out in the alley. I got off my bike, took out my revolver, and crept up to the door. I would've called in on my handheld radio for backup, but we didn't have such toys at the time.

There's an old adage; Be careful what you wish for 'cause you just might get it. The truth of this was about to be demonstrated.

Looking through the crack in the door, I could see a seated W/M hunched over a desk. He was diligently sorting through a stack of papers. And I recognized the man. Not a hoped for burglar, but maybe better. Wilbur Whinesap.

As it turns out Wilbur was working late to beat the deadline on filing his income tax. Engrossed in his labors, he had no idea I was there. So I crept up behind him, stuck my gun in his ear, and shouted "*Don't move or I'll blow your head off!*"

Mr. Whinesap complied, becoming rigid as a cadaver in a crypt. Nothing moved. Except his bowels, which after a great rumble filled his drawers. I said, "Oh, Mr. Whinesap, excuse me. Saw the door cracked open and thought it was one of those burglars you're always complaining about." Then, the stench in the room unbearable, I beat a hasty and happy retreat.

I'M PEDDLIN' AS FAST AS I CAN

Wilbur, on the other had, was evidently pleased that his wish for better police protection had come true. We never heard from him again.

AIR DOUG

You had to call Sheriff Doug Hendry a good pilot. Meaning his number of landings equalled his number of take-offs. No crashes. Yet, some of those who flew with him might take exception with that evaluation. And, in fairness, Doug was Evil Knievel in a cockpit.

I worked up the nerve to fly with Doug twice. No, that's not exactly true. Doug told me I was gonna fly with him twice. You didn't argue with E.A.

The first time we were trying to locate a Signal-10 (stolen car) that'd been dumped in the woods off Airport Road. The thief had described where it was, but we couldn't find it. Doug decided we'd locate it by air, and Chuck Whidden would take our directions and lead the ground search team. Doug put his big paw on my shoulder and said, "It's your car, let's go."

It was a city case, but the CCSO had caught the perp. We worked very closely together in those days. Strength in numbers. So, I couldn't very well refuse without sniveling and groveling and begging in plain sight, so, trapped, I climbed in the little Cessna and we were soon over the scene.

The car was easy to spot from the air and we tried to explain to Chuck how to get there. But the path was a bit convoluted and Doug finally announced over the radio, 'I'm gonna spiral down over where it is. Let me know soon as you can figure out where I'm pointing to."

That said, he dipped the nose of the plane, and began a corkscrew spiral over the area. We kept getting lower and lower. Nothing from Chuck. Still closer to the tree tops. I began searching for a parachute or some toilet paper. Still nothing. Finally, to keep from screaming in terror, I gasped, "Isn't there a limit as to how far you can dive down like this and still pull out of it?"

"Yup," Doug said.

"And how far is that?" I wheezed.

"Oh, hell, we got another 20, 25 feet left." Then he laughed and pulled the plane up, the engine shuddering nearly as bad as my body. Had I not asked, and allowed him to give his punch line, I'm convinced we would have made a much bigger impression on our target.

Another time, we were looking for an escaped prisoner in the Naples Manor area. Neither we, nor the ground search team were having any luck. Doug decided we needed to regroup. "I'm gonna take 'er down," he announced and I anticipated a turn toward the airport. Not so. He was gonna land it on the streets in Naples Manor.

Still silently cursing myself for being fool enough to go for a second ride with him, I asked, "What about those power lines down there?"

"No problem," Doug drawled, "you just fly over some and under the others."

And damned if he didn't.

AIR DOUG Two--FLYING CIRCUS

Sheriff E.A. "Doug" Hendry wasn't the only winged warrior who could make you want to keep your feet on the ground. Over the years there've been several.

One, we'll call Flip Flanagan, loved air searches. Flip liked to fly low so he could get a good view of the ground. Trouble was, one day he concentrated too much on the objects on the ground and not the tall things he was flying over. Like trees. He dipped his wing, to get a better look at something, caught the tip on a tall pecker-pole pine tree, and did a series of cartwheels with the Cessna. Had it been a gymnastic completion he'd probably earned 10's. But it wasn't. He ended up with a lengthy stay at NCH and the CCSO bought a new single-winger.

Flip had another plane crash on the runway. Who taught Flip how to fly? Good ol' E.A., himself.

One of my favorite pilots, Sonny Smirnoff, was probably the best I've ever flown with. A Vietnam vet, he could control a copter like no one else. I flew with him countless times, and was always comfortable that a talented master was in control. To my recollection he never had an accident.

I'M PEDDLIN' AS FAST AS I CAN

Not all were so thrilled with him. Sonny, you see, was a notorious boozer. And he liked to warm up his personal engine, pre-flight, with a tankful of his own high octane joy juice. Said he got the habit in the war zone where he not only had to worry about keeping his bird in the air, but dodging enemy rockets and bullets at the same time. Yep, that'd sure put me on a barstool.

About the time Sonny was doing his thing there was a scandalous story in the news about airline pilots. It seems that after their regular re-certification test, one airline had required their pilots to take a surprise breathalyzer test. An embarrassingly large number failed. They had, however, flown the prescribed test route perfectly.

Then, the airline had retested them, making sure they were sober. The same bunch now couldn't pass the test. They could do it drunk, but not sober.

So maybe Sonny knew what he was doing.

THE GREEN BAY PORKERS

In the early 70's the wives of PAL coaches or mothers of players held a football game against the Barnett Bank of Naples softball team. So it was a softball team, close enough. Ours, was no team at all, just a bunch of wives in PAL uniforms. The cheerleaders were the men, dressed in wigs and cheerleader dresses. What parts of them that would fit in. It turned out to be a vigorous and enjoyable contest.

Concurrently, the City had been on the cops and firemen to improve their physical condition. Most of our folks were strong as grizzlies, but some were a tad round. Inspiration hit. Why not have a football game between the NPD and the NFD. A great way to exercise and have fun at the same time. The game was on.

We were practicing at Cambier Park one evening when a group of thugs from East Naples approached us. How would the bad ass cops like to play some real men? *Bring 'em on* was the immediate response. We needed a tuneup game anyhow before we tackled the Firemen. The rules were to be regular flag football rules. No tackling. Blocking was fair. The play was dead as soon as the flag--a rag type thing--was stripped from the runner's belt.

We kicked off to East Naples, and a runner broke down the sideline. That is until Byron Tomlinson hit him with a vicious tackle. *Whoops,* this was flag football. But, we knew all these jerks from arresting them and didn't like any of them. And they weren't big fan's of ours. So the fight was on.

I noticed C.H.Dasher with a thug under each arm, banging their heads together. Barrie Kee, a giant, was sitting on two more, squashed under his bulk into the dirt. He was alternatively selecting body parts of the two and twisting until they screamed like sirens. Man-to-man scuffles prevailed all over the field. Finally everyone ran out of gas and the East Naples thugs limped home. So much for tuneups.

When time for the real game arrived the rules were the same as the practice game. Our team was named the Green Bay Porkers, with our lovely wives as cheerleaders. We also had a real pig named *Arnold* as a mascot. And after the kickoff the game proceeded pretty much as the rules defined. Our offense was built on a running back who'd played college football, Charles Barton. Charles was so fast we relied on two plays: Charles Left and Charles Right. No one could catch him.

Soon the blocks became a little more vigorous and flag was forgotten and tackles ensued. Although no fights occurred, it wasn't for sissies.

Some of casualties were our kick-off artist, Ken Claveau, who charged the ball, gave a mighty kick, and missed the ball. This hyper-extended his knee and he was on crutches for some time. Richard Aldacosta got his back knocked out of whack and walked for months with his chest seeming to be six-inches East of his rear end and legs. Byron Tomlinson busted his knee, requiring surgery to repair. There couldn't have been a contestant who wasn't hobbled for a few days.

When the bills for our game came in, the City lost interest in exercise programs. As I recall, they were over 60K, a lotta money for the time. That didn't count lost recuperation time and workers comp.

There was never a rematch.

COPTICAL ILLUSIONS

We were getting complaints that there weren't enough cops. Or they weren't patrolling like they should be. You never saw one. Must be asleep at the station house or dunking donuts at some fat factory. It wasn't true. We had, in fact, more uniformed officers than we really needed and they patrolled with regularity. But, when you live in a town with folks with lots of time on their hands, be prepared for nit-picky complaints. I wasn't quite sure how to correct the false perception.

Then, there was a story on the evening news about how the police in Japan were using marked cars with dummies in them, dressed as cops, to slow traffic. They were relying on what's called in the cop business the *halo effect*. The halo effect is what causes drivers to be on their best behavior for about 15 minutes after they see a police car. The Japanese figured out that the mere sight of the seemingly occupied car would slow traffic on speedways, and placed them, accordingly.

The concept is still in use. Many times the car you see parked in the median of a busy highway is empty or may have a dummy in it. There are those detractors who say that anytime you see a cop car there's a dummy in it. But they don't say it to our face.

Then there's the Sheriff's eye-in-the-sky thing you see parked sometimes in shopping center parking lots. The giant preying mantis-looking contraption may or may not be occupied, but what auto burglar or mugger is gonna risk finding out.

Howsumever, the Japanese thing got me thinking and I made one small change to the appearance of our marked cars. And, it wasn't a month until the accolades starting coming in about how much better our cops had been patrolling. You saw them everywhere.

How'd we do this? Our cars were marked with a silver badge insignia on each front door. It was about 16 inches tall and you couldn't read the lettering a few feet away. So, we

I'M PEDDLIN' AS FAST AS I CAN

added 10 inch letters down the side that read POLICE. Something you could see. And folks did, and the halo effect kicked in.

Just a few Coptical Illusions.

ALWAYS WANTED TO BE AN INGANEAR AND NOW I ARE ONE

We had a Councilman once who considered himself a traffic expert. And a law enforcement expert, once telling me that he had no *actual* experience but had watched every episode of *Dragnet* and *Kojak* on TV. *If I'm lyin', I'm dyin'.* Fact was, if you put his brain in a mosquito it'd fly upside down and backwards.

The Honorable Numnutz had come up with a new plan to control the raging traffic problem in sleepy Naples; Make every intersection a 4-way stop. It was his most imbecilic suggestion to date.

The City Manager sent it to me to review for the next council meeting. He told me, privately, "This is ridiculous, but it's gained favor with the council members. Sounds good and they don't want to explain why they didn't vote for it. But I'm not about to spend thousands of dollars erecting unneeded stop signs that people will want taken down in a week. See what you can come up with to dodge this absurdity."

I told him *thanks a lot* and broke out the safety manuals and state statutes, hoping to find salvation. And, I found it in the most unlikely place.

At the next council meeting, I gave my report. "According to traffic engineering manuals, the 4-way stop is a control option used only as a last resort. They are confusing--no one's sure who goes next--and slow traffic to a crawl. Infuriating to motorists."

Numnutz roared into action. "You read traffic engineering manuals? A cop?"

"Not just a cop," I said, "I'm also the City of Naples Traffic Engineer." There was a rumble in the chambers, before Numnutz retaliated. "Ridiculous! We have a City Engineer but no Traffic Engineer."

I'M PEDDLIN' AS FAST AS I CAN

"According to Florida Statutes you do," I said. "They read that if a city has no Traffic Engineer the Chief of Police shall inherit those additional duties." And it was true. So the proposal died on the strength of the *Engineer's* recommendation. Seems if someone gives you a title, you automatically become an expert. That, or own a brief case, suit, and are from another town.

I acted as Traffic Engineer until the city hired one. Made many rulings that were never questioned. And never got one damn cent for holding down two jobs.

GREAT WHITE HUNTERS--BAD BLACK CAT

Jungle Larry gave us an urgent call. One of his black leopards had escaped from his cage at the African Safari, now the Collier County Zoo. Some of the fences were only eight feet high, an easy leap for such a cat. Escape could have deadly consequences since the property was bordered by residential neighborhoods.

We gathered up every available officer, and after raiding the armory, headed to Jungle Larry's, loaded for leopard. Some CCSO Deputies joined us. Once there, Larry gave us a profile of what we were after. This caused some of our hunters, who were used to whacking out animals who couldn't fight back, to have second thoughts about our impromptu safari.

Black leopards, sometimes called Black Panthers, Larry warned, were incredibly dangerous. They liked to leap from trees on their next meal and once on you, owned you. They could run about 35 mph. They were very stealthy, when stalking, they were virtually silent. They could hide in the foliage within inches of their prey and you'd never know it. And if we didn't capture the critter before dark--it was late afternoon at the time--their black coat would make them invisible.

Larry showed us the leopard's cage, which had been baited with meat and other goodies to try to entice it back in. He again warned us to be very careful. And thus, scared to death, we broke up in three man teams and began a search of the preserve.

I'M PEDDLIN' AS FAST AS I CAN

Jungle Larry's had been *Caribbean Gardens*, a botanical show place. A virtual jungle, there were acres of green stuff where the leopard could hide. We headed out on the defined paths, keeping our eyes open and our pucker strings tight. But after a few hours of plodding along, with great trepidation, the cop's perverse sense of humor took over. One of the group would grab a vine hanging from a tree and give it tug, causing the leaves to rustle, terrifying his partners. Another would throw a rock in the underbrush, sending cold chills up backs. Or a joker would make low, growling noises.

One Deputy took a break and, unknowingly leaned up against a lion's cage. The lion roared in protest and the Deputy had extra laundry that week.

It was getting close to dawn and, with no luck, we regrouped near the leopard's cage to decide what to do next. Standing there talking, someone yelled, *Watch out Ken!* Ken Ferrell spun around and faced the snarling black beast charging out of the bushes. Ken leveled his riot gun, and blasted off a round, knocking the leopard butt over bucket. But the cat regained its footing, and streaked for its cage, where Jungle Larry quickly slammed the door.

Ferrell's double oo buck load had, thank God, stopped the cat in mid-leap. Yet, the cat had run away. You just don't run away from a direct hit from a shotgun loaded with double oo buck. On close inspection, Larry found two pink skin marks on the leopard's head where pellets had bounced off him. Otherwise he wasn't even scratched. The leopard remained at the zoo for many years and bore the two white skid marks on his beautiful black hide until his death.

We took the shotgun shells to the range and found that at a distance of about 10', Ferrell's range to the cat, there was a hole in the shot pattern. A hole just right for a PO'd black leopard to slip through.

We changed brands of ammo real quick.

JOE HUNTER

Florida once had the Constable/Justice of the Peace system of law enforcement, especially in rural areas. Collier

I'M PEDDLIN' AS FAST AS I CAN

County was divided into three JP Districts, each with a Constable and Justice: Naples, Immokalee, and Everglades. This was a fee system, in that what pay the Constable and JP made was predicated on fines, and fees collected for serving process. The obvious fault was if you were arrested by a Constable you were damn sure gonna be found guilty by his JP or neither got paid. The shameful system had pretty much died out by the late 70's in Florida along with municipal courts and jails. It was used longer elsewhere.

Collier County wasn't as crooked as most, with stop signs behind bushes or traffic lights hidden in trees. And unlike Georgia, a Yankee license plate didn't guarantee a traffic citation.

One of our last Constables was a colorful gent named Joe Hunter. Joe's law enforcement career included stints as a wildlife officer, Constable, CCSO Deputy, and Detective with the Ft. Myers PD. The character actor, Warren Oates, always reminded me of Joe. Both had a Depression era look about them. Tough, shrewd, enduring.

Joe was a teller of wild tales, usually about himself and always true. He once, while a wildlife officer in Everglades, was forced to transfer to Monroe County in order to escape the Seminole Indians. It seems Joe had become amorous with an Indian maiden, making him very unpopular on the reservation. Joe told me they were gonna capture him and take him to the *Green Corn Dance,* a powwow where important matters were settled. Among them justice for offenders. "Hell," Joe said, "I was afraid they were gonna stick-roast me like a possum, something like that." So he lit a shuck and beat it to another county until the war drums quit beating.

Most of my dealing with Joe happened when he was a detective with the FMPD and I with the NPD. All were entertaining and unique.

As an example, I was working on a B&E and had a suspect in Fort Myers. Calling Joe, he erupted, "I know that bunghole and he's probably good for it."

I cautioned that he was one of several suspects, but Joe advised me to scurry up to Ft. Myers and we'd talk to the

I'M PEDDLIN' AS FAST AS I CAN

rascal. There, Joe walked up to the front door, kicked it off its hinges (first time I'd ever seen that done) and strode inside. He grabbed a terrified man up from in front of the TV, talked to him until the suspect collapsed, then began a search. His search technique involved turning every thing in the house upside down. Everything!

Finally, panting from the exertion, he turned to me, said, "He don't know nuthin' or he'd have coughed it up by now," and he started out the door. I looked around in disbelief at the tornado-like destruction and the lumped up suspect. "Don't worry," Joe said, "he ain't sayin' a thing or he knows I'll come back. Would you want me to come back?"

I had to admit he had a point.

WILD BILL ON THE TRAIL TO MIAMI

Before there was an Alligator Alley most traffic from the Southeast Florida used US 41, the Tamiami Trail. And sometimes folks, for any number of reasons, used it to try to outrun us. Go barreling down 41 with us in hot pursuit seeing who either blew an engine, ran out of gas, or wrecked first.

It wasn't unknown for a NPD or a CCSO cruiser to chase a culprit all the way to Krome Avenue (Highway 29) in Miami where they were greeted by an FHP roadblock. That's if they could get by the most formidable obstacle in their path: Dep. O.B. "Bill" McCrea, stationed at Everglades City. Bill owned the South Trail. And if he was on duty, no one got by him.

One evening, after midnight, I was on the east Trail, just beyond Boat Haven. I heard a rumbling engine sound coming up beside me. It was a new Mach I Mustang being piloted by a young rascal in a Marine uniform. He looked over at me, smiled, and insolently flipped his cigarette at my open driver's window. Then he burned rubber and took off like Uncle Dudd when he got caught in the Widder's bedroom. Bap, zoom, gone.

Well, I couldn't have that so I showered down on the Dodge 440. The car wasn't sickly by any means. A local FHP Trooper, Ed Crawford, had souped his up until it ran over 140 mph. But in mine it was boys versus men racing the

I'M PEDDLIN' AS FAST AS I CAN

Mustang, which was soon a diminishing dot on the highway ahead. Time to call for reinforcements. Radioed Dispatch to call the CCSO and see if Bill was on duty.

Soon he was on our channel with his distinctive voice, flat, deep, and loud. Had to be. Bill drove at horrendous speeds with one hand on the wheel and the windows rolled down. He had to talk loud to overcome the wind rushing by in the background.

I explained the situation to Bill. He said, "I'll be waitin'."

About twenty minutes later Bill radioed a short message, "He's here when you want him."

I hurried on down to the Everglades substation in the old Courthouse. I passed the Mach I parked beside 41, steam wisping from under the hood.

The Marine was handcuffed to an oak chair, shivering like a dog passing walnut shells. "*Heeeeee shot at me,*" he whimpered, "*shot my new car.*"

"My car was parked aside the road," Bill drawled, in plain view with the lights flashin'. "You didn't slow down so I had to get your attention." And that's what Bill had done. Stood out in the middle of US 41, cranked a round into his Winchester Model 94, put one right into the radiator of the speeding Mach I.

Remembering, at the time we didn't even think that was such an unusual thing to do.

WHO CHECKED THIS CHECK?

Ray Barnett reminded me of one of our favorite cops whose son, at an early age, made his mark on the other side of the law. The teenager, who we'll call Smoothie, like all good con artists was likable to a fault. And, very convincing for a high school age youngster. Had good taste in automobiles, too. Liked the sporty models.

Smoothie was also enterprising. Being a cop's son, with meager financial resources didn't pose a problem. Not when he found out about checks. To Smoothie checks were money you printed yourself. So, one day he walked into a local car

I'M PEDDLIN' AS FAST AS I CAN

dealer, selected a new sports cars, paid for it with a check, and drove off.

That worked so well, he went in the next day and bought a brand new truck. With another bogus check. He didn't get to put many miles on either vehicle before the local constabulary put him back on his bicycle.

My wife Sandy, who worked in local banks for years, called to mind a fantastic dude called *Mr. Ouse*. This slippery gent, in one day, passed over twenty bogus checks on 5th Ave South. Dapper, in a golfer-outrageous sport coat and slacks, with a brilliant smile and slight Irish accent, he could bilk a leprechaun out of his pot o' gold.

We became aware of Mr. Ouse only after he had passed a dozen or so worthless checks. This was after one of the victim merchants actually looked at one of the things. Detectives prowled 5th Avenue looking for a man in golfing togs, which was like identifying one particular petunia in a patch. Back at the station, clerks were on the phone, alerting merchants to the scoundrel.

Had not a teller, at Naples Federal, finally looked at what she was asked to cash, he could have done his work and left town. Which, being an itinerate thief, was his plan. The teller looked at the check, said *You've got to be kidding,* and called the cops. We were nearby and arrested Mr. Ouse before he could scamper away.

And how had our check artist signed these checks that'd been so widely accepted? *Mickey M.Ouse.* The NPD detectives and alias Mickey Mouse had a good laugh over the caper down at the station house. Just before we locked him away.

BUGGED BY PALMETTOS

If you look up "ubiquitous" in a dictionary you should find a picture of a Palmetto bug--the Asian Water bug. The cockroach on steroids. That is, if it's a Florida dictionary. They're ubiquitous! And, sometimes found in the strangest places.

A State Fish and Game officer, Snook Bucktail, could tell you all about it. We had the Hoppe's and patches out one morning, cleaning our guns, when he dropped by the NPD. "Mine might could use that," he said, pulling his S&W from the holster. If he had re-floated the Titanic, there couldn't have been a rustier piece of metal.

In fairness, Snook worked on salt water quite often and it will rust a blue gun fast. Stainless weapons weren't in production at the time, so we all had to be vigilant against rust. But damn. His looked like the anchor on the Ancient Mariner's ride.

Then, when he tried to open the cylinder, it was rusted shut. He had to beat it on the corner of the desk to release it. And, when it finally creaked open, out strutted a Palmetto bug from an empty chamber in the cylinder. Seemingly perturbed that he'd been evicted from his home, the bug ran up Snook's arm and crawled in his shirt pocket. Seemed to know the territory real well.

Another time, Snook stopped by wanting to bum some fresh ammo. "Sarge told me to change mine out. Said it had more moss and mold on it than granny's Cooter. Guess it is a little raunchy. But, I'm a little short on cash this week. Wonder if. . .?"

We said *sure* and got some out of the ammo closet. When he opened the leather ammo pouch on his gun belt, out walked a Palmetto bug. He looked at it, then at us, and stuttered, "Now that ain't the same one. . ."

But you couldn't have found a cop that would've bet on it. One said, "You keep bringing your pal around least you could do is introduce us, tell us his name. We'll get him some coffee and a donut."

Note: (Why did Snook's revolver have an empty chamber?) At the time, some cops still had old revolvers that didn't have a hammer block built in. The block prevents a dropped gun from firing. One of our officers, Lou Collins was killed in just such an accident. So, as a safety measure, they would just load five bullets and leave the chamber under the hammer empty. (This is still practiced by some with Colt .45 revolvers and black powder guns. Same reason)

And, a COOTER is a genus of pond turtle, especially in Florida. Granny was an animal lover.

What did you think it was?

ED CRAWFORD, FHP

Ed Crawford was a Trooper with the Florida Highway Patrol when I got in the police business in 1963. Then, they shared a desk at the NPD. The desk was also used by the wildlife officers and the FBI when needed. These were all agencies that didn't have local offices.

Ed was the personification of the FHP Trooper. He was stern, had little to say, and was the scourge of bad drivers. The FHP had a system in place to insure their Troopers didn't turn into slackers. They were assigned a monthly quota of tickets they had to meet or they got transferred to Florida's equivalent of Lower Slobovia. They didn't need the quota with Ed. He was the first cop I ever heard use a famous cop wisecrack. Ed'd stopped a mouthy speeder who disparaged him with, "Well, I guess you got your quota for the day."

To which Ed replied. "Nope, we don't have a quota any longer. Now I can write all the tickets I want."

Ed was a strong fella, too. Once an enraged motorist bowed up at him at the NPD, and said, "I'm gonna kick your ass."

Ed grabbed him by the neck, with one hand, lifted him in the air arm's length and said, "Well, come on down here and do it."

He was also innovative. He modified his radio car, a Dodge 440, so it would exceed the 120 mph top end. That model had a speedometer that had a horizontal, sliding bar to indicate the speed, instead of the round, regular model. Ed took the stop peg off his so the indicator could continue past 120. Then he wrote on the glass over the meter, 130, 140 and 150. And the meter would get there.

I understand he has a son in law enforcement. Hope so. If he's anything like his Dad we can sure use him.

PENNY ANTE JUSTICE

I'M PEDDLIN' AS FAST AS I CAN

Judge Richard Stanley had his own way of doing things. He'd dole out special conditions to his levied periods of incarceration. *Thirty days on a diet of Gerber's baby food.* Or, *Corporal punishment consisting of so many licks with a belt, administered in the courtroom.* Or, *Keep the cell in total darkness.* Yep, Richard, or *Wretched* as he loved to be called, was an original.

Once a game violation case came before him that evoked his special conditions. Dorkwood Dickhead was a local game warden. Being a game warden requires special sensibilities because of the vagueness of the laws and sometimes unique circumstances. And a little common sense comes in handy. Dorkwood, without exception, possessed none of these traits. He was nit picky and picayune, and was popularly referred to as a *Prick with ears.* It was an appropriate epithet.

In the case in question, Dorkwood had a man for possession of three cottontail rabbits. The man had no valid hunting license so Dorkwood charged him and took the rabbits as evidence. The poor defendant stood before the bar, a downtrodden soul, who obviously had intended the bunnies for his supper. He readily pled *Guilty* to the charge. Whereupon, Dorkwood related the man's dastardly deeds to the Judge.

Judge Stanley, looked at the defendant for several long seconds then adjudicated the case: *On your plea the court finds you guilty, and fines you two cents for each rabbit. Pay the clerk six cents.*

Then he turned to Dorkwood and gave him that look that you never wanted aimed at you. A look that would wither an oak tree. Then, with the brutal sarcasm that only *Wretched* was capable, he said. "And for you, Mr Dickhead, bring me some more of these cases."

Dorkwood Dickhead beat a hasty retreat from the courtroom, amid rumbles of muffled laughter.

And he didn't present any more bunny cases.

JUDGE HUGH HAYES

Officer Gerald Rittersdorf came into my office at the Naples Police Department and dropped a bomb. "Just gave that new Judge a traffic ticket," he said. The new judge was a young Hugh Hayes. Although giving a judge a traffic citation was perfectly legal, it was considered bad form, at least. This was a person we were going to have to work with and, considering the egos of some judges, crapping in their flat-hat could have disastrous consequences.

But Rittersdorf was famous for arresting those who usually received special consideration. He'd arrested a local priest for DWI. Twice. And, although only giving him a warning ticket, had lectured our boss, the City Manger, at a traffic stop. "You think you being the City Manager impresses me, think again."

"I thought, after I'd given the Judge the ticket, maybe I should tell you about it," Rittersdorf said. *Yep, so I could get a head start on looking for a new job.*

Just about then, my secretary Shirley, came in and said, "Judge Hayes is out here and wants to see you."

"Well," I told Rittersdorf, "I guess we're gonna find out real quick what kinda man we have for the new Judge." I told Rittersdorf to go back to his duties and I'd take care of it. Reluctantly.

Judge Hayes came into my office. I'd met him before, but we weren't friends or close associates. He came right to the point. "One of your officers just gave me a traffic ticket and I want to know where I pay it."

"Well, uhhhhh. . ." I muttered, trying to read his attitude.

"No, I was speeding," he said, "and I deserved a ticket. Your officer did exactly the right thing. I'm going to be presiding over a court that will hear cases just like like this. And if I can't be fair in my own case, how could I be expected to be fair in anyone else's." And pay up he did.

That day I formed an opinion of Judge Hugh Hayes. This time they got it right. A good, decent, intelligent, and equitable man. Just what a judgeship requires.

We found out later he could sure come in handy in other situations. Once, while presiding over a case with a rowdy defendant, the defendant went nuts and attacked the bailiff. The defendant was strong and mean and violent and the bailiff was having a time with him. Thankfully, help was on

I'M PEDDLIN' AS FAST AS I CAN

the way. The bailiff was dumbfounded to see his assistant was the *Honorable Judge himself*, piling on the rowdy and helping to subdue him.

Yep, I found out about Judge Hugh Hayes years ago and have never had reason to change my opinion of him. The perfect man for the job.

THE GREAT DUDA RAID--Part 1

At one time, my wife Sandy was a payroll clerk for A Duda and Sons, then the world's largest farming operation, having properties all over the world. They were good employers and offered their employees excellent benefits, especially insurance. They could do this because they had a controlling interest in Hartford Insurance. Their operation in Naples was several miles out on the East Trail. I got to know several of the folks there, especially their farm boss, Lamar.

At the time Hubert Humphrey, running for president, had a traveling circus going around where he was exposing the terrible conditions migrant farm workers endured. Although being a migrant worker wasn't a cushy job, being a construction worker, and many other occupations weren't any fun, either. And the migrant's irresponsible lifestyle appealed to many. Especially wetbacks who didn't like to stay in one place too long.

Hubert's circus did uncover some sad cases but mostly the idea was to gain publicity for Hubert. And, he didn't want too much lemon in his hot toddy. Tom Morgan, a local reporter for the Miami Herald, accompanying Hubert on a tour of a destitute woman's home in Immokalee, opened up her refrigerator to take a picture of how bare it was. He was astounded to see that it was packed full of groceries. And the heifer weighed about 300 lbs. No starvation going on here. He pointed it out to Hubert, who quickly slammed the door shut and moved on to another building.

Closer to home, at Duda's all of the pickers made more money than Sandy. All. They also enjoyed free health care at the County's expense, and got food stamps.

At the start of one picking season Lamar showed me the family housing units the pickers could use. Looked like a motel. They were all freshly painted, had good appliances--some new--and were as nice as many low-cost motel rooms. He said we'd look at them again in just one month.

In that short time the buildings had been destroyed. And anything that would hold a clothes hanger was festooned with new clothes. Never seen so many. They'd even pried the doors off the refrigerators and used them for a clothes closet. Lamar just shook his head and said, *This is how you get the slum housing Hubert's crying about.*

THE GREAT DUDA RAID--Part 2

Seeing property trashed the way the migrant's had done at Duda's wasn't anything new. While attending polygraph school in NYC, a Lt showed me some of my tax dollars at work. It was a multi-story apartment building that had been renovated under HUD for low cost housing.

When we went inside the stench was unbearable. He showed me why. There was an air shaft in the center of the building that each apartment on that floor had windows on. The garbage was stacked up over the third floor windows, where tenants had just thrown it out into the air shaft.

As for the apartments themselves, anything that could be removed had been. Copper plumbing, dry wall, appliances, sinks, toilets, even the tiles on the floor and carpet had been stolen. When the tenants took everything out they could sell, they moved.

This project was paid for with tax dollars. Most of the tenants had been illegal aliens. The renovation had happened less than six-months before.

Sandy told me that most of the workers at Duda's had to be illegal aliens since they all had phony Social Security numbers. I used to tease Lamar about this, and he would deny it--with a wink. I told him, as a joke, that he'd better quit lying to me or I'd get revenge.

One day I had one of those *The Devil Made Me Do It* moments. I was on the East Trail and Duda's was coming up. Sandy and I were having trouble making ends meet. With four kids and several doctor's bills a cop's and her salary didn't go far. And what hurt was that we were also paying the doctor bills for these illegal aliens.

So I flipped on the blue lights, turned on the screaming siren and raced into Duda's parking lot, skidding to a stop. In the fields I could see migrants running in panic in every direction. It looked like when you pick up a board and the ants have built a nest under it. Or, maybe like a soccer game. Anyway, I guess they figured it was an Immigration raid to sack them up.

Probably was a silly thing to do. But it sure felt good. Lamar told me it took a week to gather 'em all up from the woods and get 'em back to work. But they did come back. And we're still paying for them.

SNAKE MOBILES

Most folks with good sense stay as far away from snakes as possible. And others carry them around in their cars.

JD Spohn once ran over a rattler, and was so impressed with its size he threw it in the back of his station wagon to show to his family. JD lived in Pine Ridge by then and in rainy season the rattlers would migrate from the marsh lands--where Pelican Bay is now--to the high ground in Pine Ridge. It was common to run over these brutes, some as thick as a coal miner's arm. And when you ran over one it was like running over a tree limb. JD had one of these. Spying one of his neighbors he pulled in the driveway and yelled, "Look what I got in back." The neighbor came over, looked in the back and said, "What? An empty K-Mart sack?"

"No, the snake! The rattler." JD said.

"*Snake!*" the neighbor said, taking a quick step back. "No snake back here."

The neighbor later said he'd never seen JD move so fast. Out of the car, pulling his .45, pointing it in every direction, realizing the rattler he thought was dead had only been stunned.

Finally, JD gingerly opened all the doors, stood back and waited until the rattler came slithering out. Whereupon he made sure it came to an untimely demise.

I'M PEDDLIN' AS FAST AS I CAN

Another time, a man was taken to the station on suspicion of larceny and was being interviewed while his truck was being searched. "Tell who ever's searchin' that truck not to open that box in the back. There's a rattlesnake in it." *Huh? "A rattlesnake."*

When cops went to confirm, sure enough, in a chest-high wooden box, was a rattlesnake. Never found out why he was carrying it around. A pet, a close friend, a relative, who knows. But there it was.

Then there's the cop that stopped a fella on the East Trail for a speeding violation. Writing the ticket, he could hear movement behind the driver in the back seat. Looking inside, he saw a large burlap bag with something squirming inside it. *What's that?* he asked the driver.

"Oh, it's about twenty, twenty-five moccasins I picked up this evening out in the Glades."

"Moccasins? You mean Cottonmouths? Snakes?"

"Yep. I gather 'em up and sell to Ross Allen at the Serpentarium. He milks 'em or something to make antivenom."

"You ever get bit?"

"Ever once in a while, but the pay's real good."

Not good enough for this old hoss.

JOHN HENRY'S BOX OF ROCKS

John Henry lived in the Naples ghetto and worked for McCormick excavators for years. He was a huge man with a bear-like physique and prodigious strength. Which he used to great advantage. And he was a pretty good thinker when it came to not letting his job interfere with his precious off time.

Ernest McCormick would tell two stories on John Henry that illustrated the latter. A dump truck was down with a cracked engine block. The new block had been delivered and was waiting to be moved onto the workbench. Ernest collared John Henry late in the day. "John," he said, "gather up two or three of your partners and put that engine block up

I'M PEDDLIN' AS FAST AS I CAN

on the bench. Then, you can go home." John grumbled an okay and went to the shop.

About five minutes later, when Ernest was locking up the office, he saw John walk by. "Goin' to get some help?" he asked.

"No, suh," John said, "I be goin' home."

"What about the block?"

"It's up there."

Astounded, since John was the only other person there, Ernest raced back to the shop where he found the block sitting on the bench. "What the. . .?" he said.

"Just be one engine," John said. "I do it myself."

Another time Ernest told John Henry to go get a dump truck full of rocks. It was early on a Saturday, and Ernest said John could go home when he picked up a truck full. At the time the fields around SR 951 were scattered with coral rocks, free for the taking. John left on his task. In less than two hours he returned. Ernest couldn't believe it. Loading a truck full of the melon-size rocks should take hours. Suspicious, he looked in the truck.

What he saw made him laugh. The truck was full, alright, with about ten huge boulders. "Didn't say how many," John Henry said. "Just you wanted a load."

John Henry was a lucky man, too. One Saturday night, in McDonald's Quarters, an angered drunk pointed a sawed-off shotgun at John's belly and pulled both triggers. Nothing happened.

When we arrived, John had the assailant in one hand and the shotgun in the other. We relieved him of both, checking the gun to make sure it was unloaded. There were two 12 gauge double OO buck shells loaded and each had a dented primer where the firing pins had hit them. The detective checking the gun figured the clown had tried to shoot John Henry with two empty shells. But, he ejected them and found they had never been fired. He replaced them, cocked both hammers, aimed the shotgun at the ground, and pulled the triggers. It fired instantly.

Go figure. We never could.

KEN CLAVEAU

After watching carefully choreographed demonstrations of five-year old girls slinging grown men across the gym, and confronting Karate "experts" in real life, you have to come to several conclusions. Great way to get in shape? *You bet.* Teaches admirable principles that aren't usually followed? *Yep.* A good way to get your butt kicked if you try it on someone who really knows how to fight. *Oh, yeah!*

That is unless you are a real Karate master like Ken Claveau was.

Ken came to the NPD from Chicago. He was a fit-looking guy but his appearance was no clue as to what a bad dude he could be. Ken was a devoted student of Karate. And a master. He could do things that you only saw Bruce Lee do in the movies.

Stand flat-footed, jump up and kick the ceiling? *No problem.* Break bricks with his hands? *Sure.* Deliver a knockout punch with such speed it couldn't even be seen? *Yep.* Several saw him do just that one night while arresting a combative turd at the Anchor. Or, to be factual, several *didn't* see him do that. They were looking right at him, but they didn't see a thing. One second the fool had bowed up at Claveau, the next he was in sleepy land at Ken's feet.

When the City decided to reconfigure and replace the old parking meters of 5th Ave South, Ken got permission to help on the project. The meters were clamped onto 3" steel pipes. His removal technique was to kick them off. That's what I said, kick them off. Said it was faster than using wrenches and all those other tools.

One night, while off duty, Claveau and his pal, Karate student, and fellow Naples PD cop, Ken Ferrell got into a altercation at the Rainbow Restaurant and Bar. When one of their antagonizers decided to beat a hasty retreat to his car, they went to work on said refuge. Although, the car later looked like it had been pounded with sledge hammers, only their feet and hands were used. Looking at the car, you were chilled to realize that a human body could do that to metal.

I'M PEDDLIN' AS FAST AS I CAN

Ken worked for us a few years, then went on to another agency. He died from a heart attack before he reached middle age.

So, the moral of this story is be nice, stay outta fights, and if you get trapped into one, hope it's with one of those little girls in the Karate contests on TV. And not with a Ken Claveau.

CLOSE CALLS

In the cop business you run across things that can strengthen your resolve that somebody up there may be watching out for you. Here's a couple that convinced me.

One of our cops, Mr Lucky, was in the River Park Apartment complex answering a complaint about some Saturday night rowdy. It was a common occurrence. He was told this particular turd had threatened several folks with a machete. They pointed to the direction the culprit went so Lucky went thataway, too. As he was going around the corner of a building, he stumbled on the gravel and dropped his flashlight. Bending over to retrieve it, he heard something whoosh over his head, then a loud clink, and sparks. Jumping back he saw the assailant had ambushed him. Had he not bent over, to get his flashlight, the machete would have decapitated him.

The machete had been swung with such force that it was embedded in the mortar joint between the blocks. Lucky, grabbed his attempted murderer, and put him under arrest. Unfortunately the assailant stumbled several times on the way to the patrol car, sustained injuries about the head and shoulders, and had to be patched up at the ER.

All cops will tell you that most of us die in ways the public would never guess. Shot by John Dillinger? Waylaid by a Machine Gun Kelly? Nah. Number one is in cars crashes. Number two, is answering domestic violence complaints. One of my first ones taught me that lesson.

I was answering a complaint in River Park Apartments (same place) concerning a man beating his live-in. When I arrived they had taken it out to the street and the man was sitting on the woman's belly. He had her by the ears and was

I'M PEDDLIN' AS FAST AS I CAN

smashing her head on the asphalt like he was trying to crack a coconut. And, it was working. You could hear a wet, mushy sound with each blow.

I piled on him and pulled him off. He was drunk, and big, and mean and I wished I'd jacked him with my slapper first. He was truly an all-day-sucker and I was beginning to think my coconut would be the next one cracked. Then, I heard a wonderful sound. An approaching siren. Concurrently, I felt something hit me on the back and heard the woman scream, "*He killin' my man. He be killin' my man.*" Then the cavalry arrived and order was restored.

When I caught my breath and sorted out the madness I was astounded. What I felt hit my back was a butcher knife the woman I had saved had tried to stab me with. What saved me was the fact that it was one of those old ones with two rivets holding on the wood handle. The wood had rotted away and when she tried to stab me the handle gave way, the blade hit me at a glancing blow and swung back on her, cutting her severely. I mean really cut her, which was some small consolation.

I looked at her and at the knife, a big *what the* in my eyes. "*You was hurtin' my man,*" she jabbered.

First off I wondered what fight she'd been watching, then, why she didn't try to stab this asshole, that was trying to bash her brains out, instead of the guy that saved her.

Sgt. Robert Dennis told me why. "Domestic violence complaint. They'll turn on ya every time. Just like breakin' up a street fight. Pretty soon both of 'em are on ya." Always remembered that. And I'm still here.

FLATT AND SCRUGGS

Lester Flatt and Earl Scruggs were a big deal after The Beverly Hillbillies hit TV. Their tune, *The Ballad of Jed Clampett,* was the show's theme song. And their *Foggy Mountain Breakdown,* then atop the record charts, was featured in the film Bonnie and Clyde. Everyone knew it, except folks in Naples, as we found out the hard way.

Always on the prowl for a quick buck to fund PAL kids football, Sam Bass, then the NPD Chief, said he'd heard Flatt

I'M PEDDLIN' AS FAST AS I CAN

and Scruggs were gonna play Ft Myers soon and had an open date after. He said we could book them cheap.

Sam knew this because he was a long-time country music musician himself. He was in the loop. Sam made the phone calls to Lester's wife, who was their agent, we made arrangements to use the Naples High School football field for the concert, and the deal was set.

The night of the concert things started out awful and ended up worse. Flatt and Scruggs were late. Had there been a crowd they might have become unruly, but there wasn't one. Maybe 100 people showed. It was a financial disaster before the show even started. Our only hope was the concession stand.

The band finally arrived, Lester and Earl in the back seat of the Caddy. They were in bad shape, looking like two wilted lilies on a week old grave. Turns out, they'd gone out fishing in Ft Myers that day, had too much booze in the treacherous sun, and were very sick puppies. They were, however, troopers and climbed to the stage and began their show.

The show was bluegrass perfection, Lester picking the guitar and singing, and Earl untouchable on the banjo. They took turns, however, waltzing off to the wings to puke up their guts. Lester alternated his trips barfing or taking long pulls from a fifth of liquid stupid. The audience never caught on and loved the show. We did, too.

Afterwards, Sam, after counting up the proceeds, found we were about $50 short of the agreed fee. Always resourceful, he wrote them a personal check with instructions not to cash it until he covered it the next day. They agreed, and accepted the post dated check which was worthless. But good ol' Sam made it good.

Flatt and Scruggs went on to the Country Music Hall of Fame, Sam Bass to the Florida Country Music Hall of fame, and the rest of us found better ways to raise money for PAL.

POLICE ACADEMY ON A BUDGET

In 1963 Chief Ben Caruthers sent Dave Dampier and me to the Broward County Police Academy in Ft Lauderdale. At the time getting to go to a police academy was a novelty. The

I'M PEDDLIN' AS FAST AS I CAN

state didn't require it and most sheriffs and chiefs were *agin'* it. Losing an officer for several weeks just so he can learn his job? Waste of time!

Our salary at the time was about $281 a month. That was for as many hours a day that it took in the six-day week. It cost me $100 a week to leave electronics for the police business. But I never regretted it.

The City gave us a per diem budget of $15 a week. We'd get up early Monday morning and drive to Lauderdale, via US 41 and SR 27, in Dave's old Dodge sedan. Wasn't any Alligator Alley. We'd come home on Friday afternoon.

Stretching the $15 was a trick. We rented a cheap room within walking distance of the FLPD. But you have to eat, too. Thank God Dave was a hunter and had a full freezer. I don't know where he got all that deer meat--and I didn't ask--but it kept us alive. And Dave, having grown up in hard times, knew a million ways to vary the menu. We had venison burgers, steaks, stew, soup, you name it. Breakfast, lunch, and dinner. If we'd had a freeze he'd have made ice cream out of the stuff.

And damned if it wasn't good. But, one night a week we splurged and went to the Burger King for a Whopper and the works. Man does not live by deer meat alone. But he could.

The academy was populated by cops from departments all over South Florida. Many were transplants from big northern cities. One, from New York City, quit in a rage when he found out there wasn't any "under the counter money for cops down here". "How the hell they expect me to live on this salary?" he bellowed.

And I remember the day the academy's Director, Lt Bob Smith, later the Ft Lauderdale Chief, interrupted the class with sad news. "President Kennedy's been shot," he said, his voice halting, tears in his eyes, "and it doesn't look like he's going to make it." We were stunned. No matter what your politics an attack on the President is an attack on our country. There was silence in the classroom until some dope from Plantation asked, "Do that mean we get to go home early?"

I'M PEDDLIN' AS FAST AS I CAN
MICK AND THE SPEEDOLESS KRAUTS

In the sixties the Germans began invading Naples. Started with day bus tours from Miami. They'd park at the end of 5th Ave South and go to the beach. Nice people. No problem, except for one small thing. They would change into their swim suits right out in the open. Shuck off their lederhosen and suit-up.

Until that time I was certain there was nothing uglier on earth than a fat, hairy, Frog in a Speedo, or whatever that banana hammock is the French wear. I was wrong. There's nothing worse looking than any fat, hairy, man *without* a Speedo. So when the calls came pouring in that the moon was rising over the beach, we knew it was a true emergency and beat it down there to deal with it. It took some time, and many trips, but we finally cured them of indecent exposure.

How'd they comply? With a beach towel. They'd wrap the beach towel around them and somehow squirm about, shedding clothes and adding clothes as they went. Then the towel would drop, and they were in swimming garb. Or, after the swim, back in street clothes. And you never saw a thing.

After that, Naples was secure from these *vile scenes* until folks found Party Beach, an island tip close to Marco. Something about the area, the sun, or too much liquid stupid, would cause revelers to shuck their laundry. Get sand in their Schlitz.

The CCSO would sorta overlook the indiscretions on the remote island. Especially, if it was a topless, pretty girl. After all, they were only partially breaking the law, still having half a bikini on.

One day CCSO Marine Patrol Deputy Bobby K spotted a group of five or six men strolling down Party Beach, sans drawers. He edged up close to the beach, and got the groups attention. He noticed that one, an extremely skinny and unusual looking dude, was trying to hide behind the others. Then he figured out why. It was Mick Jagger. And the Rolling Stones. Seems they were staying at the Ritz Carlton and playing a concert in Tampa the next day.

Bobby told them before he could *get any Satisfaction* they were gonna have to put their togs on and they complied,

I'M PEDDLIN' AS FAST AS I CAN

without complaint. Mick was very apologetic and agreeable. That wasn't a surprise. The Stones stayed at the Ritz often--some finally buying homes on Sanabel--and were known as primo guests. They would rent an entire floor and caused no one any trouble or made any goofy demands. They also liked to hang at Harold's Place, a small bar still on US 41, never causing a problem.

Some lesser rock stars could *rush* to take notice. Especially on New Year's Eve.

HOMEMADE KUNG FU

Cops, as a survival mechanism, develop their own self defense moves. CH Dasher, who could destroy any aggressor with his fists, had a little trick for his light work. He'd put a 38 cartridge between the victim's index and middle fingers and squeeze them like a nutcracker. He owned you then but if you were good he'd only squeeze until you whimpered like that Senator that got caught playing footsie in the restroom.

One cop, who we'll call RD, was a fan of professional wrestling. From TV he'd picked up the sleeper hold. This is now called a Figure 4 Neck Lock. Applied correctly, the carotid arteries are compressed and no blood goes to the brain. Soon sleepy time ensues. RD could knockout a thug faster than Hulk Hogan. The hold has since been banned because, in certain ethnic groups, the carotid is not too elastic. You clamp it shut and it doesn't flex back open when released. Then you've got a dead rowdy on your hands and lots of paperwork.

Perhaps, as some unjust Karma, RD was victim to a certain street Kung Fu move: the kick to the gonads. Another nutcracker, so to speak. Never saw a man get kicked in the sperm bank more often. And anyone who's had this happen to them knows it's just terrible. Again, unlike in the movies, it can have dire consequences. Last time I remember it happening to RD he had an extended stay in the hospital.

Course, some dudes are just so huge they don't need homemade Kung Fu. Take 6'4" 250 lbs Ed Jones. Ed arrested a coward one night who'd taken Karate lessons and was an expert at mule-kicking unsuspecting drunks in a bar. He'd

I'M PEDDLIN' AS FAST AS I CAN

done just that at *The Port Hole* and Ed had brought him to the station. There, Grasshopper decided he wasn't going into the cell. He struck a combative pose, gave a screech like when Granny sat on the toilet after Grandpa forgot to put the seat down, and yelled *Karate!* Ed looked at him, laughed, picked him up over his head and threw him like a dart into the slammer. His head hit the back wall and we weren't sure he'd ever get to be a Barroom Bruce Lee again.

So kids, this stuff can lead to early retirement. Don't try it at home. Unless you know someone who really needs a good whuppin'.

MAYHEM-WHAT REALLY WORKS

Watching a Kung Fu movie recently caused me to recall the training in self defense we received in the Broward County Police Academy in Fort Lauderdale. Back when the text was carved on stone tablets. It was a combination of mixed martial arts, and come-along holds popular at the time. I Remember Dave Dampier and I throwing each other around. And I particularly remember the last day of class.

"First rule," our coach, Payne N Misery, said, "is don't try any of this stuff unless you practice it diligently. My advice, unless you seriously want to study martial arts, is to pick up one or two favorite moves and practice them. For example kicking some puke's knee backwards, or dislocating his shoulder using a bar hammerlock."

"This ain't the movies," he continued, "and you ain't Bruce Lee."

How right he was. In the movies the Kung Fu'ers kick and punch the hell outta each other and come right back for more. In real life, land a good ol' country boy sucker punch and the show's over.

And if this stuff is so great, why don't the dudes in the UFC mixed martial arts battles do any of these movie gyrations. Cause they'll get your butt broken unless you use them against someone who doesn't know how to fight.

Howsumever, after Payne had made his cautionary statement, he picked two recruits to try to get one man out of a car. The driver, a Ft Lauderdale cop, just offered resistance, no offensive moves. He held the wheel with both hands and the two recruits couldn't move him.

The instructor laughed and said, "Now, after all these weeks of text book self-defense training, I'm gonna show you what really works."

He moved to the car. "See the mustache on the driver, get a good hold on it and pull. He'll follow right behind it. And, a quick finger to the eye will get those hands loose from the steering wheel. And an ear is a perfect handle. So's a finger in the mouth, like a fish hook pulling it sideways. These things work. But forget where you heard it."

These moves, and a few others, kept most of us out of the hospital. There were other cops who didn't need them.

TOM T AND HOW IT'S NOT DONE

Once, when Tom T. Hall was surfing the crest of his fame he played a show in Naples. It must've made him seasick. He wobbled and bobbled, slurred his words, couldn't focus his eyes, and needed assistance walking. Some suspected he might've pigged out on too much liquid stupid. But he could've been just sick and tired.

He was in good enough shape to spot a Deputy's wife and ask her if she'd like to come in and look at the trailer he was waiting in. She quickly consented and studied the place for near an hour.

When they finally emerged from the trailer, it was time for Tom T to perform. He had to be walked to the stage by two Deputies like a drunk being escorted out of a barroom. Then he was lifted onto the stage. There, he staggered to the center, mumbled some greetings and went into his first song. Sadly, he couldn't remember the words. Nor those to the second, or third songs. By then, the crowd had had enough and booed him off the stage.

I guess the high-point of Tom T's act was before he even got on stage. That being all the Deputies waiting for the Deputy, whose wife was in the trailer, to bust down the door and open up a can of Whoop Ass. Never happened. Another Deputy explained why later. "I know his wife. He was probably glad to get rid of her sorry ass for an hour or so."

I'M PEDDLIN' AS FAST AS I CAN

Also, knowing the woman, it sounded reasonable to me.

PS-I saw Tom T later, in Tennessee. He was doing a free charity concert for our Sheriff's Department there. Country music stars regularly do that up in Tennessee. The same day we had Tom T we had George Jones, Jerry Lee Lewis, and David Allen Coe who all performed free. And Tom T, that day, was in much better shape. His act was first class.

JD SPOHN AND MMMMMMEL TILLIS

JD Spohn was an inveterate RV'er. And he had a Fiat with a rattan flat roof that he towed behind his motor home. Never seen another like it. Camping in Pahokee, he was stopped waiting for a light to change. The driver of a pickup truck stopped beside him yelled over that he admired the little Fiat and his boss would love to see it too. JD told the driver where he was camping and asked who the driver's boss was. Mel Tillis, he was told. JD said "bring him on by and we'll have a toddy or two."

Sure enough that evening up pulls Mel, with his driver. As expected he loved the little Fiat and offered JD good money for it but JD loved the little car too much to part with it. Later Mel broke out his guitar and began singing around the campfire. All the delighted nearby campers were treated to a free concert. Two elderly ladies, walking back from the rest rooms, could hear Mel singing, too.

One said to the other, "Listen to that fella sing. He sounds just like Mel Tillis."

"Nope," corrected the other, "I've heard Mel sing a dozen times. That fella's no where near as good as he is."

Mel and the campfire group could hear this and all had a good laugh.

Another time Mel and Tom T. Hall appeared at the old Swamp Buggy Track. It was some charity event and both the CCSO and NPD volunteered security for the concert. Unfortunately, Mel was suffering from the flu. His assistant told us, "Don't worry, he'll do the show. Mel's a tough old bird."

When time came, he got out of his bus, supported by two men, and weaved to the back stage steps. There, the men

I'M PEDDLIN' AS FAST AS I CAN

boosted him up on stage, he straightened up, and walked to the mike. He said, "I hope you folks will excuse me tonight if I don't hit some of the high notes. I have a little cold." That said, he did his hour, with all the perfection one expects of a master. I doubt any member in the audience could tell how he was suffering.

His show over, he walked to the wings and collapsed. His assistants hurried him to the bus. One of the cops enquired, "Guess you're going to get him home to Pahokee for some bed rest."

"I wish," the assistant said. "He's playing Detroit day after tomorrow and we're on the road from here."

Always admired ol' Mel all the more after that.

THE CIA INVADES PORT ROYAL

Naples old-timers may remember that at the end of Gordon Drive there was once a trailer park. One of my friends grew up there. And, along the water, across from Keeywadin Island, there was a collection of boat sheds, tin buildings, and other unsightly shacks that today, the mere sight of would cause the elegant Port Royal residents terminal apoplexy. Right after Fidel came to power, these abandoned buildings were commandeered by the CIA. Or some federal spook agency we could never identify.

It started with a Fed visiting Chief Sam Bass with some odd demands. In the future, there would be large van trucks proceeding down Gordon Drive late at night. They would be driven by Cubans. The police should not stop them, follow them, or hinder their progress in any fashion. If one was stopped the driver would present a card on which was written Chief Sam Bass. That would serve as code that the driver was legit and part of government sanctioned operation. Huh? But after doing some checking Sam told us it was way over our heads and just to turn our backs.

One early morning, however, one of the trucks broke down on 5th Ave So and 3rd Street. In the process of helping to get the truck started one of our nosey cops--God love him--was astounded to discover that the truck was loaded with cases of

I'M PEDDLIN' AS FAST AS I CAN

ammo, clearly stamped US Air Force. Later we figured out where all this ammo was going.

The old shacks along the water soon sprouted signs proclaiming they were the home of Delta Enterprises, Trans-World Imports, and other exotic--and ridiculous CIA type names. Tied off in front of two of the building were thirty-foot power boats, with obvious cannons pointing to the rear. The cannons were covered with a form-fitting tarp mark Radar. *Right!*

Then the raids started. The boats would proceed out, head to Cuba, sit off-shore and blow hell out of Fidel's fiefdom, then return to Port Royal. Though they weren't advertised, it didn't take much to reconcile news reports with the disappearance of the boats for several hours.

And they kept up, which didn't surprise use. It was a well known secret that the government was training Cuban insurgents in the Everglades. Why should the midnight runs be a surprise?

The runs continued until the Bay of Pigs fiasco. Then, the boats and bogus businesses disappeared. Later we read that the Cuban general who had been training the troops in the Everglades had been put in prison.

Always caused us to wonder--and hope--the CIA was usually a little more covert than what they demonstrated in the Port Royal operation.

I'M PEDDLIN' AS FAST AS I CAN

BACK ROW: JUNE HOLZHAUSEN, MARVIN MAYO, GD YOUNG, CHESTER KEENE, BUD WOOD, BARRIE KEE, ED JONES
CENTER ROW: MIKE GRIMM, RICHARD DAVIDSON, WALTER OLSON, NICK TRIFILETTI, RAY BARNETT, JERRY WEINBRENNER
FIRST ROW: EVE TIFFEN, DOTTIE KOESTER, DAVE DAMPIER, J.D. SPOHN, BYRON TOMLINSON, C.H. DASHER, JACK BLISS

NAPLES POLICE DEPARTMENT

I'M PEDDLIN' AS FAST AS I CAN

Naples Police Department in the later 60's. Sam Bass was Chief at the time. Many of the officers mentioned in this book are in this photo.
Photo taken on the steps of the old City Council chambers, which also served as the Municipal Court.

Ed Jones, the son of long-time Chief Cale Jones

6th PRECINCT

HOMEBREW BURGLAR ALARM

In the sixties we didn't have all the electronic goodies we now enjoy. Having no handheld radios was particularly dangerous and inconvenient but we didn't know any better. When electronic assistance was needed you had to use the *Necessity Is the Mother Rule*. Ingenuity.

Sometimes you'd have a burglar who had a good thing going and didn't want to give it up. This was often true of dopers who, to satisfy their habit, would break into the same place, time after time. And they liked drug stores because that's where the mother lode for hop heads was.

We had one who liked the Rexall at 5th Ave So and 8th Street. Hit it every couple of weeks. We weren't equipped to run long surveillances and the little portable burglar alarms they have now hadn't been invented. So we became young Tom Edisons.

The telephones, back then, were all big, heavy, black rotary dial things. We decided to use one of its unique characteristics to make a burglar alarm. If you dialed all the numbers to the desired contact but didn't let the last number dialed return back to to zero point, the call wouldn't go through. As an example, dial 774-443 then dial the last 4 but don't let it rotate back, the line would stay poised to make the call, but wouldn't do it until you took out your finger and

I'M PEDDLIN' AS FAST AS I CAN

let the dial process finish. Folks used this trick all the time calling radio stations to win money. The next caller will win $25. People would wait around with all the numbers dialed, but their finger holding the last number back. When the announcer gave the word to call, they'd let go and the call instantly went through.

So we went to the Rexall one evening, selected a phone near a pathway in the store that had to be traversed, dialed all but the last number to the PD, tied a string in the finger hole, tied the string across the pathway, then went home.

The idea was that when the burglar broke in, in the dark, and went down the pathway, he'd pull the string loose from where we had it loosely affixed, the dial would rotate home, and a call would be made to the PD. Dispatch was instructed that if they received a call with no one on the line, send a car to the Rexall *post haste*.

Mickey Mouse rig, right? Rube Goldberg at his best. Redneck engineering. That ain't what the burglar thought when we caught him in the act. And we caught another, the same way, at the Moorings Pro Shop.

Next we invented the wheel.

FUTURE COP TRAINING

What kind of little boys and girls grow up to be cops? All kinds. I always liked to hire the ones who'd lived in the real world, knew how things worked, and were familiar with the system. Street wise. No one was gonna pee down their back and tell them it was raining.

One of my favorite cops, Byron Tomlinson, made money in high school by injecting oranges with Vodka and selling them to other students. Is there not some element of genius here?

Had a few others who were *Crackers*. To keep the old belly full in their youth, they'd skinned a few gators, sold a few hides, and taken several deer out of season. And fishing limits? Forget it.

Long as we're fessin' up, I have to make a few myself. Growing up post depression in Charleston, WVa, you forgot about trying to make a buck. A few pennies would do. To accomplish that, I used to go all over downtown stuffing toilet paper up in the coin return slots of pay phones. When the change and returned coins dropped, they remained up there atop the plugged slot. End of the day, I'd go by, remove the toilet paper, and collect my bounty. Which could be very good for a ten year old. Later, the phone company got wise and installed that rocker device in the coin slot to prevent stuffing it.

Then there was the bottle return thing. You got two cents for soft drink bottles and five cents for a Canada Dry ginger ale bottle. *Five cents!* Why you could by a candy bar, or an RC for five cents. Five more and you could add on a Moon Pie.

So I'd look for stores that stored their collection of returned bottles behind the building. It was usually fenced in but that was no problem for a kid. The process was simple. Climb the fence, liberate a few bottles, then, later, sell them back to the same store. Course, we spent the ill-gotten gains in that store so the owner didn't get hurt too badly.

Then there was the old Coke machine trick. Remember the old machines that looked like chest freezers. Had the drinks in there hanging on sliding rails. You slid the drink to the end of the row, put in a nickel, and pulled it up through a lock thing.

All that work wasn't necessary. Look for a place where the machine was out of sight--usually a service station--pop the cap on one of the Cokes with a bottle opener, insert a straw, and empty the bottle. *Ah, the pause that refreshes.*

Then for my favorite. Michael Jackson did not invent the moonwalk. Young folks like myself did. At movie theaters they usually had two sets of doors; one set for folks to enter the movie, another for those exiting. We'd wait by the exit door until the movie ended and the crowd was flowing out the doors. Then, we'd step into the crowd, and moonwalk backwards into the theater. Never failed!

Hope the statute of limitations has run out.

NAPLES' INVISIBLE STREET

I'M PEDDLIN' AS FAST AS I CAN

I Noticed recently that Collier County folks are still fighting about personal property vs public beach property. This particular fight was at the Ritz Carlton, but the battles and questions have persisted since before our family moved here in 1956.

Most of the disputes in the City were caused by realtors who told prospective beach front property owners that their lot ran from the street, Gulf Shore Boulevard or Gordon Drive, to the Gulf. This, of course, was a lie and led to calls to the PD with whines about people walking on their beach.

There's that *mean high tide* thing that's considered the true dividing line. But, witness the battle at the Ritz, calculating that takes an engineer or a Swami and a lotta time.

Quite by accident, we found out the founding father's foresight had made the problem non-existent. An old-time Naples resident called the PD one day and said he'd been reading about the disputes in the *Collier County News* and wondered if folks didn't realize that the beach was actually a platted street in the City of Naples. We went over and dug through the plats and durned if the fella wasn't right. It was also spelled out in the City Ordinances. Obviously, the founding fathers wanted to retain the Beach's use for everyone, not just a privileged few.

Its name was Gulf Street. All the Avenues in the City terminated at Gulf Street. The plat map clearly defined Gulf Street's right-of-way so conclusively that we kept a copy of it at the PD to show blubbering beach property owners just where their property boundaries really were. And they sure weren't out as far as the invented *mean high tide line*.

Once a NPD cop wrote a motorcycle rider a ticket for speeding on Gulf Street. And it held up in Municipal Court.

I've wondered over the years if the plat still exists, as platted or if some misguided or politically pressured weasels did away with it.

BOARD STIFF

Getting used to working a cop's varied 24-7, 365 days a year schedule is tough on some. Particularly, young folks

I'M PEDDLIN' AS FAST AS I CAN

having lived a normal life where the major holidays were always just that, and only vampires worked after the sun went down. We tried to make the adjustment as painless as possible at the NPD.

On Christmas and Thanksgiving we'd arrange the schedule so cops would double up on calls to allow the other half of the shift to spend a few hours at home. And, to those trapped in the office--dispatchers, jailers, and clerks--we sometimes provided a little liquid stupid to sweeten the lonely hours. Great discretion was used--*usually.*

The NPD jail didn't hold many real bad guys. Most were folks who drank too much, or were minor non-violent offenders who'd made dumb mistakes. Most of the time Andy Griffith would've been comfortable there. It was traditional that on Christmas we'd give the prisoners a snort or three of booze. The hooch was always plentiful, cases of the stuff being left off by local bars as Christmas presents.

Once one of the dispatchers had too much of the Christmas spirit and got all the inmates stoned. And just when the stiff-neck chief we called *the Colonel*--among other things--happened to drop by. One of the inmates was sitting with the dispatcher and upon seeing the Chief, jumped to his feet, grabbed the Chief and hugged him, exclaiming, "You're a great guy to take care of us on Christmas."

Old Leather Britches was astounded, dragged the inmate back to his cell, and returned mumbling, "If I didn't know better, I'd think that inmate was plastered."

Later that night, when the town went to sleep, cops came in and decided to help our young dispatcher, Bucky, celebrate. Bucky wasn't an accomplished drinker. The cops were. Soon one noticed that Bucky was petrified, staring into space. Concerned they may have killed him, he was taken home. It was said that Bucky was as straight and stiff as a 2 x 4 and when he kept rolling out of the bed, they just leaned him up in the corner and returned to the station.

Bucky survived and recently retired from the ranks of local law enforcement after a long and productive career.

PANTS ON THE GROUND:BARE FACTS

I'M PEDDLIN' AS FAST AS I CAN

It's nice to find out that suspicions you have that some folks are idiots have been confirmed. Such is the case with those who wear goofy clothing. Young folks have always worn fashions that adults disdained. Comes with the rebellion of growing up. But the clothing today is in the *Alice In Wonderland* realm. Makes you wonder if youngsters know the history of these fashions.

Let's take the baggy tops and bottoms. This hip-hop disaster came from street gangs. The ridiculous baggy drawers and loose tops serve well to hide weapons. And, they're really handy when you go on a shoplifting spree, to hide your purloined goods. So, if that's the image you're trying to project, *a lowlife piece of gang filth,* hang in there Numbnutz. You're gettin' it done.

Then there's the incredible *pants-half-down-shorts-and-ass-showing* look. Besides being the silliest style ever witnessed, it has to be the most aggravating to wear. Constantly hoisting your drawers so you don't trip on them has to be a pain in the azz. Literally.

Now comes the sweet part, where this style began. Years ago, before jail inmate's prison attire became the jumpsuit, prisoner's wore regular shirts and trouser's. They were worn without a belt, that having been taken away to prevent suicides. Hence, prisoner's usually had droopy drawers. But, some prisoner's dropped theirs much lower for another reason. It was a signal to other inmates that they were sissy boys looking for a "husband" or mate. Advertising.

Is that what the young folks of today are doing? Advertising to be a rump ranger's squeeze?

Let's hope they're just ignorant of history and don't realize where the style came from. However, to me, anyone who walks around showing their skivvy drawers is already halfway up Humpback Mountain.

KIM BOKAMPER

Mentioned before that we were always looking for ways to make money for our youth program, PAL. *The Naples Daily News* helped us with this one, a charity basketball game between the local sports scribes and broadcasters and the

I'M PEDDLIN' AS FAST AS I CAN

Miami Dolphins--off-season football team. I was appointed referee. This wasn't a problem as it was much like a Harlem Globetrotter's game, mostly fun and not much attention paid to the rules.

The game went well and the crowd was having a grand time. The Dolphin's players--about a dozen showed up--put on a great show, particularly since they were playing for nothing. And, being prime athletes, it was not surprising their basketball skills were superior. I was to find out, first hand, just how superior.

Just before the second half started, Kim Bokamper came up to me with a plan. Kim, is of course, the legendary Dolphin linebacker, who was part of their deadly Killer B's defense. He was a Pro Bowler, and at 6'6" and a muscled 250 you could see why. In the late 70's and early 80's he was at the top of his game.

He said, "Next time you see me bringing the ball down the court, run to the center jump circle, hunch over, and brace your hands on your thighs, with your back to me."

I looked at him with some trepidation.

"Don't worry", he said, "I'm just gonna jump and vault, over your head."

This was little comfort. I could just imagine him plowing over me like he did running backs. But, for the sake of charity, I didn't argue. And soon he had the ball, was charging down the court, and I assumed the position.

Gritting my teeth, I could hear the thundering of what sounded like a tornado behind me. Then, I felt one hand on my shoulder, saw his huge body pass over my body, and watched, dumbfounded, as Mr. Bokamper, raced to the basket and slam-dunked the ball.

Slam-dunked it! Not many *basketball players* could do it at the time.

Standing there looking stupid, one of the Dolphin's running backs joined me. "Kinda terrifying, ain't it?" he said. "Quick as a tiger, strong as a bull, and in a scrimmage, you look over there and see him and pray you don't get the ball. Cause you know he can outrun you, too. Yep, kinda scary."

Yep, it was.

I'M PEDDLIN' AS FAST AS I CAN

Kim Bokamper later retired and is now a restaurant owner and broadcaster for the Miami Dolphins. And, a first class citizen.

THE OTHER GREAT CANOE RACE

Over the years, *Naples Great Dock Canoe Race* has become a major event. On occasion, reminiscent of Key West's gaudy and raunchy events. This year was the 33rd Anniversary, the first held in 1977. Another *Great Canoe Race*, maybe best forgotten, happened about the same time.

Merchants were promoting a "Day" at the Central Mall, then located on the Northeast corner of Goodlette Road and US 41. The site now is home for a beautiful condo complex. As an added bizarre attraction, they asked Sheriff Rogers and I to compete in a canoe race. We were to cruise across Gordon River from behind the old *Pancake House* to the Central Mall landing.

I don't know how Aubrey felt, but I would've rather bedded a porcupine. When I saw the actual canoe, my apprehension increased. First off, I'm of the Richard Pryor school of seamanship. One of his friends once tried to coax him out on his boat. "Boats sink." Pryor said.

"I'm not talking about a rowboat here," the friend said. "My boat's a yacht, big enough to sail around the world. It won't sink."

"Is is bigger than the Titanic?" Pryor said. The canoe looked to me like a piece of watermelon rind fixin' to flip over and get me wet. And, propulsion for this craft was a paddle, resembling a badminton racket.

We were allowed to have one crew member and I knew mine was going to have to be a paddlin' machine. "Get Dan Crisp," one of the cops suggested. "Dan can paddle a canoe like Hiawatha."

It was a good suggestion. Dan was a big, raw boned athletic cop, who had mastered most sports. I asked him and he, with enthusiasm, agreed.

Race day, I asked Dan what our strategy was to be. "I'd rather do all the paddlin'," he said. "You'd probably just slow

I'M PEDDLIN' AS FAST AS I CAN

me down. So just pretend to paddle, and don't actually put the oar in the water."

When the gun sounded and we were off, Dan churned like a duck on Amphetamines and I pantomimed paddling. About halfway across the river we were 100 yards ahead of Aubrey. I showed Dan and he cooled it so we didn't embarrass the Sheriff. *Too much.*

At the landing, people were amazed at my athletic prowess. Of course, I had to admit what really happened. And I did admit it. *Just now, for the first time.*

NPD'S FIRST COMPUTER

We decided we were going to determine what violations were really causing traffic accidents, then direct our citations to those violations. This would require studying several year's worth of accident reports. Had the information been in a computer, it would've been easy work. But we didn't have computers back then.

Actually, we had one Radio Shack Color Computer. Might even have had a Commodore 64. And, recognizing computers would be important tools in the future, we had an officer assigned the ancillary duty of becoming conversant with the beasts. His name was Gary Phillips, and he enjoyed the work. But the task at hand was no match for our "toys." So we found another way to sort and collate the information. Our volunteers!

They could obtain the information manually, and since we had so many willing workers, it wouldn't be a burden on them. Like the Chinese proverb, *Many hands make light work,* thing.

Our new computer in hand we decided what info we needed from the reports. This was decided to be, primarily, time, date, location, and cause of accident. And the work began.

Soon the data was collected and we developed a way to deliver it to the cops. It went like this. When an officer came to work for the day he was given a sheet with various violations, times of day and locations. His mandate was, if he wasn't busy with other duties, to proceed to one of the

I'M PEDDLIN' AS FAST AS I CAN

locations in his district and look for the violations on the list. They didn't have to give the violator a ticket, but they did require at least a written warning.

What were the leading causes of accidents? Probably just what they are today. Illegal lane changes, following too closely, aggressive driving. 'Course today we have the worst hazard, cell phones.

The results? After one year, we were one of the few cities in Florida to reduce the accident rate. Reduced it. Unheard of for a growing city like Naples.

Maybe some folks should try it again. Should be easy with real computers.

THE KAW-LIGA KAPER

When Hank Williams wrote about the troubles of poor ol' *Kaw-liga*, he overlooked one. So we'll make the record complete.

Our Kaw-liga was a life-size wooden Indian that stood outside a tobacco shop on Park Street. Each morning the shop's owner would take the wooden warrior out of his shed, attached to the outside of the shop, and wheel him around to the front of the store. On closing, it was back in the shed. He led a pretty uneventful life until he ran into Gunzan Rozes, a rookie NPD cop.

Gunzan, assigned to the midnight watch, was struggling through his initiation onto the force. All rookies were teased and aggravated and some took it better than others. When the veterans found out Gunzan was "goosey" his initiation took a whole new turn.

One early AM. when the town was locked down and cops were struggling to keep awake, Gunzan became the focus of fun and games.Working downtown, he was on foot, "rattling doors." This is cop jargon for checking the back doors of businesses to insure they are locked. As he crept down a darkened alley, one covert cop threw an empty garbage can behind him, the crash and roll evoking in Gunzan pure terror and gastric distress. When he finally was able to catch his breath, he was amped up, his hand on his revolver. He

I'M PEDDLIN' AS FAST AS I CAN

squinted and roved the alley with his flashlight beam, trying to penetrate the spooky nooks and crannies.

When he got near Park Street, another cop kicked the shed door of the tobacco shop, then jumped out of site. Gunzan crept up to the door and, gun drawn, yanked it open. There he faced poor 'ol Kaw-liga standing in the darkness, arm up, tomahawk in hand. Gunzan fired one shot into Kaw-liga's belly before he realized he was killing a statue. He quickly shut the door and beat it out of the area. All the prankster cops did, too.

There was no report of the incident and none was asked for by Gunzan's superiors. The story became a legend, circulating around the PD for years. But no one would ever own up to being the garbage can slinger/door kicker or Gunzan Rozes. And I'm damn sure not gonna break the tradition now.

VOLUNTEERS

Bob DeVille, long-time manager of the Naples Shopping Center's Publix, loved to tell this story. He had a bag boy working for him that was such a joy to encounter that people were constantly trying to give him tips. The bagger, in his seventies, would decline, saying he was well compensated and it was store policy for employees not to except tips. That was mostly true. But not in this man's case.

He'd come to Bob and volunteered to sack groceries or do any other menial job that was open. Said he was retired, a widower, and needed to get out of the house. Didn't want to do anything complicated, just something to keep him busy. Bob, impressed with his sincerity, took him on and never regretted it. The volunteer had a genuine warmth and rapport with folks that soon made him an old friend to all who shopped there.

Bob said he could understand how the man had become a self-made millionaire. Yep, he could've owned the Publix. And he didn't need the tips.

We, at the NPD, were blessed with a number of volunteers, also. I was looking over the list one day when one name jumped out at me. *Quinn Tamm.* I found Dave Dampier and showed him the name. Dave smiled and said it was who I though it was.

Quinn Tamm had been the Assistant Director of the FBI under J. Edgar Hoover. After retiring, he became Director of the International Association of Chiefs of Police. In law enforcement circles, he was legendary. I told Dave I wanted to talk with Mr Tamm the next time he reported for duty. I envisioned a source of wisdom and expertise we could use. Wasn't to be so.

Mr Tamm only wanted something to do, not another career--or anything like it. Make busy work. He finally went to work on our huge card index file that listed, on 4 x 5 cards, every name and event we'd ever dealt with. There were thousands and they were invariably misfiled. And, he worked at it, happily, as his volunteer task.

Next, we'll relate how we found a way to put these volunteers to best use.

VOLUNTEERS Part 2

We received continual complaints about "speeders", particularly on Crayton Road in the City. It wasn't a genuine problem. The speed limit was 30 mph and few exceeded it. But the folks that lived along that street, with not much to do and a whole lotta time to do it in, invented a problem. As folks, with no real problems, are apt to do. So speeders became an issue.

The real problem was regular citizens can't estimate speed worth a flip. It takes cops a while to learn how. A bored citizen, lounging on their front porch, would perceive any vehicle traveling over granny speed to be *burning up the road*. Then they called in. And we would respond, and waste time trying to catch nonexistent culprits. Something needed to be done.

We came up with an idea to put our many volunteers to good use. We taught a handful how to use the radar speed reading device. Then, we'd put several of them, who lived in the Crayton Road area, out as a team to do traffic studies. They would record the speed of every passing car for a day. This was handled in shifts, so several had an opportunity to

I'M PEDDLIN' AS FAST AS I CAN

participate. It didn't take them long to realize that 30 mph on a residential street was a lot faster than they'd imagined.

Word got around their community, and our calls dropped almost to zero. After all, their own neighbors who'd recorded the speeds with a radar gun themselves had told them that speeding wasn't a problem.

That problem solved, the focus shifted. There was the belief that even though the drivers weren't speeding, they were causing too many accidents on Crayton Road.

Time to shift gears. We assembled another team of volunteers to go over the accident reports for the previous year and record all those that happened on Crayton Road or contiguous streets. Didn't take them long to figure out their accident rate was almost zero. And so another *serious* traffic problem was solved.

THE RAIFORD ROAD SHOW

The Florida State Prison at Raiford once had a program aimed at teenagers. It functioned by having real criminals tell them how crime had ruined their lives. Sort of a *Scared Straight* thing in more generic terms. It was a compelling effort and, I think, impacted some young folks.

This particular time the show was in Naples and was scheduled for Naples High School. There were six convicts, as I recall, who were serving time for an array of crimes; murder, rape, robbery, burglary, you name it. All, of course, had demonstrated they were trustworthy, and presented little or no threat or they wouldn't be out there. But, convicts are wily and you can't always tell what their real motives are.

They were, of course, accompanied by guards and traveled in a secure prison bus. When they arrived in the city they were working that day, each was handed off to a local cop, who was responsible for getting them to the venue and back. I drew a man who had murdered three people. He was a lifer with no chance of parole.

Sounds like a dangerous dude, right? Not always. Most of the time a murderer will never do it again. Their crime was one of passion. Something had snapped. Many times the victim had worked real hard, over time, to get themselves murdered. There are those that believe that anyone is capable of murder--under the right circumstances. I'm such a believer.

We're not talking about "hit" men here. Or mob or gang killers. Just the regular Joe who has stepped over the edge. Or was shoved over. Anyway, mine, as best I could tell, was in the former category.

Cars were short that day and I grabbed an unmarked unit that was not my own. I put the "speaker" in the front seat with me and we headed out for the High School. Everything went smooth until we hit 22nd Ave North. There, the City had dug up the street and it was poorly marked. I was almost on it before I saw the cavity and slammed on the brakes. When I did, the glove compartment door popped open. And laying in the glove compartment, within an arms length of the murderer, was a .38 S&W revolver.

We both looked at the gun, then at each other. Then my prisoner leaned back in the seat and raised his hands in a *I give up* position. I reached over and took the gun.

He broke the tension by looking at me, smiling, and saying, "Guess you're glad I'm reformed."

"Bubba, you can say that again," I replied. With complete candor.

WHY I WEAR A HAT

A few years ago, during my annual physical, my doctor said it would be a good idea for me to start exercising. Always a proponent of Mark Twain's advice, *Whenever I get the urge to exercise I lie down until it goes away*, I declined. But, under relentless pressure, I finally acquiesced to his request. That evening I went to our local gym and began some light weightlifting. Within a week I had a torn rotator cuff.

In about three months, when I'd recuperated from the repairs, the doctor suggested I take up walking instead. He is strictly against running--one reason he's my doctor--but said walking was a good compromise. In three months I was

I'M PEDDLIN' AS FAST AS I CAN

walking two miles each night. In four months I was having my knee carved on for a torn meniscus.

When I was ambulatory again, the good doctor said maybe I should switch to bike riding. I reminded him that I had been doing much better when I was a couch potato. He persevered, claiming the benefits to my heart would, in the end, allow me to rot in a nursing home long after my slovenly contemporaries where resting comfortably in their graves.

I rode the thing until I started getting prostate problems. The urologist said bike riding was the worst thing I could do. Look at that Armstrong fella, guy that won the Tour de Frog bike thing so many times. Prostate cancer caused by the bike seat. Try swimming instead.

So I'm floating here in the pool, no swimming, no kicking lest I rupture something else, trying to get to the point of this thing. Which is, while I was riding the bike I always wore a hat. A helmet. Here's why. The first vehicular death I ever worked was in Port Royal. An elderly lady was riding her bike, at a low speed, and ran into the curb while crossing the street. Couldn't have been going five miles an hour. Howsumever, over the handle bars she goes, hits on her noggin which cracks like a pistachio. This caused a subdural hematoma in her cranium. She went into a coma and died a few days later.

So, considering my record with exercise, a hat was compulsory. Should be for you, too.

GONE LIKE THE WIND

Once the Naples PD decided to enhance their First Aid capabilities. After getting each officer certified in CPR--advanced training and rare for the era--they installed extra equipment in each patrol car: a portable oxygen cylinder and mask and a blanket. The oxygen for those with emergency breathing problems and the blanket to warm victims subject to shock. Great idea. Except. . .

Each time a cop reached for the oxygen the bottle was empty. And you could never find a blanket. An investigation ensued.

I'M PEDDLIN' AS FAST AS I CAN

The oxygen bottles were checked for leaks. Negative. Maybe the heat in the trunk was too intense somehow killing the stuff. Nope. The refill cycle time was shortened. No help. What was going on? Finally one of the cops came clean.

Nothing smells worse than a rotting dead body and our sub-tropic heat steps up the putrefaction stench until it is unbearable. Unless you happen to have a handy oxygen bottle and mask in your trunk. On reflection by supervisors, it made sense and was probably a legitimate use. The second, and most prevalent use, was harder to justify.

The cops, always on the leading edge of shady technology, found out that a few whiffs from the bottle after a long night, or day, of boozing would help deaden the most dreadful hangover. Some argued this was a more essential need than masking rotten body stench. Hangovers happened way more often.

Then the blanket problem, where were they going? Never was resolved although some said many migrated to the trunks of the cop's private vehicles. Or their beds at home. Or were left in the bushes after a quick roll with a willing cop groupie. And it was said one officer's dog snuggled each evening on not one, but two of the purloined comforters.

Oh, well, the First Aid equipment seemed like a good idea at the time.

BACK ASSWARDS

Sometimes the protective devices we work so hard to put in place turn on us. Such is the case with the *Ten Codes and Signals* used by cops. Now the standard of the good buddies on the CB--10-4--they originated for law enforcement use. There was a code for most activities or occurrences. Easy to understand, foolproof. Almost.

Once got one a Signal 41, at the time Armed Robbery. It had just occurred at a local gas station. There was a good description of the vehicle, with a New York plate, and, as luck would have it, it was two cars in front of me. I pulled the car over, drew my gun and ordered the two male passengers to get out, hands up. They complied and I put them spread eagle, belly down on the highway. It was Summer and the

I'M PEDDLIN' AS FAST AS I CAN

asphalt was blistering hot. Or so they claimed as they squirmed around like worms on a griddle while I stood over them, gun cocked, ready to blow their felonious asses away at the slightest mis-step.

One of our cars pulled in for backup, and gave me a quizzical look. "You're a hard man, G.D." he said.

"Don't mess with armed robbers," I said.

"Armed robbers? Hell, they ain't armed robbers. Got in an argument with the station attendant, and knocked over the oil can pyramid display on the way out. Vandalism, at the most. I took the call."

Then I knew what had happened. Vandalism was Signal 40, Armed robbery Signal 41. The dispatcher had mis-read the signal list. It happened.

I got the two miscreants up, dusted them off, and arrested them for Vandalism, a very minor misdemeanor, about 100 miles away from Armed Robbery. They were two jerks anyway, but I would've have pulled my gun on them and put them on the griddle if I'd know it was a piddly offense.

But there's a bright side to most things if you dig for it. *No harm done*, my partner said in a low voice. "And you can bet your bippie this is two Yankees ain't never gonna visit Naples again."

EMBARRASSING MOMENTS

In the sixties, police cars were equipped with a electro-mechanical siren. A big, heavy thing, mounted under the hood, it spun a turbine-looking device that created a fearsome howl. It was just a giant version of the ones kids put on bikes that rubbed on the tire.

Starting at a low growl, it gradually built up to an ear-splitting scream and, when cut off, took forever to slow down and shut up. Now sirens are electronic, controlled from a panel inside the car, and feature a number of sounds. They are electronically amplified through a speaker and when activated start and stop instantly.

The old models were controlled by a foot-button on the floorboard, near the dimmer button. (Remember them?) Too

I'M PEDDLIN' AS FAST AS I CAN

close, you had to be particular that you stepped on the right one. And, of course, some times you hit the wrong one. Invariably, this would happen when you were in traffic with a built-in audience of folks keeping an eye on the cop car. Thinking you were dimming the lights, you'd stomped on the button and the siren took off. And wouldn't shut up.

So what's to do? I always pretended I'd just gotten a hot call, stomped the siren up to full speed, and beat it on down the road 'til I was out of sight and hearing range.

MOPERY WITH INTENT TO GROPE

Ray Barnett reminded me that cops in Florida, before 1972, didn't need to use the mythical charges of Vitamin Deficiency and Mopery when they wanted to slap someone in the slammer. There was always the Vagrancy law.

This is how it read: *Rogues and vagabonds, idle or dissolute persons who go about begging, common gamblers, persons who use juggling or unlawful games or plays, common pipers or fiddlers, common drunkards, and night walkers. Thieves, pilferers, traders in stolen property, lewd, wanton and lascivious persons, keepers of gambling places, common railers and brawlers, persons who neglect their calling or employment, or are without reasonable continuous employment. Persons who misspend what they earn. Persons wandering or strolling around from place to place without any lawful purpose or object. Habitual loafers, idle and disorderly persons neglecting all lawful business and habitually spending their time by frequenting houses of ill fame, gaming houses or tippling houses shall be guilty of vagrancy and subject to the penalty provided.*

Don't know about you, but I'm good for about ten of those things any day of the week. Especially the *habitual loafers* part. And in the days before our corrupt politicians had turned many Americans into legitimate homeless folks, there were the homeless that were really bums. Tramps. Well, vagrants. Except in Florida. Weren't allowed. We had a law against it. Don't know where they were, but they weren't tolerated in F L A..

I'M PEDDLIN' AS FAST AS I CAN

Vagrancy was a Florida Statute until the Supreme Court deemed it unconstitutional in February of 1972.

All good cops know that a liberal amount of discretion must be melded with common sense in applying the written law. They know that if they used *the letter of the law* no one could drive a mile or walk ten feet without being arrested for some violation.

We must have laws. But, *Damn!* How many do you really need to keep the lid on the garbage can?

IT'S THE LAW?

One day, while house cleaning, Dave Dampier and I came upon an old ordinance book for the City of Naples. Some of the laws were so incredible you had to wonder why they were ever written. Laws are usually drafted to regulate some public ill or danger. When reading these old timers, some, then still on the books, you had to wonder.

Here's an example, paraphrased: *No one shall drive a motor vehicle upon the streets of the City of Naples unless preceded, at a distance of no less than 50 feet, by a person carrying a lantern and announcing "Stand clear, motor vehicle."*

This would probably have been good advice when I was learning to drive, but I believe that was the exception. Someone suggested that early auto's frightened horses and humans, and the warning was necessary. Dave and I couldn't figure out why Naples would have such a law. Naples wasn't around in the early day's of those contraptions.

Another ordinance, that still befuddles me, read: *No one shall walk a lion in the City of Naples unless the animal is on a proper leash.*

Kinda makes you wonder what type of leash could control a lion. And who the hell had one they paraded down 5th Avenue South. When I lived in Hollywood, California, there was a dude that walked one down Santa Monica Boulevard, but that was Hollywood. You could see anything there.

We brought these arcane ordinances to the attention of the City Attorney, and they were removed.

I'M PEDDLIN' AS FAST AS I CAN

Naples lion? Could it have been an ancestor of Jungle Larry? Nahhhh.

LADIES PISTOL TEAM

Before the semi-auto Glock revolutionized police handgun use, you couldn't find many officers carrying anything but revolvers. Most departments banned the semi's use. The most common reason was that most cops qualified for handguns on the FBI's PPC course. This was a fifty-round exercise, requiring the officer to fire from different positions and distances from the target.

The favorite semi at the time was the Colt 1911 .45 caliber. The thinking was a .45 had so much kick a cop couldn't control it accurately for 60 rounds of firing. So, .38 and .357 were used almost exclusively.

Some always suspected that the real reason was that semi's were so unreliable. Their record of jamming and misfiring--due to user error--was horrendous. And, a .45 slug was a formidable load, big as a taxi cab. Remember, back then, the underpowered .38 was endorsed because it was safer if it got loose in public.

Anyway, during the midst of this Lowell Raines, a former FHP officer and then county maintenance supervisor, started a women's pistol team. His Deputy wife, Carol, was a deadly shot who went on the win the National Police Olympics. My wife, Sandy was a member, and I helped coach.

Most of the members became remarkable shooters. Sandy can still outgun me--and about anyone else. Aside from their practice schedule, they manufactured all their own practice ammo on Lowell's reloading equipment. Melted the lead, formed the bullets and seated them.

They competed in police matches across the state, even the NRA Nationals in Tampa. The string of fire was three of 90 rounds each with small, medium, and large caliber guns: usually .22, .38 and .45. Many only had two weapons so they fired the .22 and used the .45 for the medium and large bore strings.

So here we have women--Sandy is just over five-feet tall and weighs 100 pounds after a trip to Red Lobster--shooting

180 rounds from a .45. And mammoth cops, supposedly, couldn't shoot 50 accurately.

Sometimes we think up the dumbest excuses to get out of doing something we don't want to do.

THE PUSSY CAT BALL

The Naples Police Chief with the shortest reign lasted about six months. He was a retired army Colonel who both the City and he thought had the perfect background for the job. Wrong! Soldiers are stuck with who commands them. They can be put in the brig if they don't follow orders. Cops don't. To soldiers a Colonel is a person with formidable powers. The lowliest cop has more power than a Colonel. To cops a retired military officer is someone who used to have power. I worked for one retired Marine colonel who knew what he was doing. This one did not. And he lasted six months.

He did nearly everything wrong. On the one occasion he tried to do something right, it was a disaster.

To win over the cops who generally despised him, the Colonel decided he was going to have a party. Dave Dampier and I counseled him not to do it, that cops could get wild and woolly. He laughed off our advice. He'd been dealing with the "troops" all his adult life.

He didn't realize that the cops hated him because he'd been made Chief without ever being a cop--the ultimate insult to the rank and file.

Trapped into attending, Sandy and I arrived late and left early. On arriving, we found the Colonel's wife visibly shaken. A nice lady, who deserved better, she'd already become a victim of the rowdies.

Several drunken cops were on the their knees, on the kitchen floor, shooting craps. When a five was thrown, you could hear, *Fever in the cathouse, go ho, go.* One or two had puked on the carpet. Others staggered around like zombies, looking for more booze. Rude humor, in loud voices, ricocheted off the walls. It was obvious that the guests were being extra obnoxious on purpose.

I'M PEDDLIN' AS FAST AS I CAN

I gathered up Sandy and we ran for the hills. On Monday morning I expected to find an enraged Chief, taking notes on how he would extract his revenge. Quite the contrary. Sitting behind his desk, staring blankly at nothing, he mumbled "my *Pussy Cat* glasses." Confused, I went to find Dave.

"He had a set of Pussy Cat glasses--some piss-willy drink made with Early Times. The guys stole them all. Emptied his liquor cabinet, too. Don't know about you, but I'm gonna find something to do out of the office today. Maybe all week."

"Need a driver?" I said.

DUTCH TREAT

Police agencies exchanging officers, to broaden their horizons, is nothing new. In the sixties the London, England, PD (Scotland Yard) and New York PD swapped a few cops for a limited time. Trouble was the London cops, who didn't even have to carry guns in merry ol' England, soon jumped in the East river and swam East, terrified and trying to get out of NYC with their lives in tact. While the NYC cops, enjoying the vacation, were filing for extensions of duty.

The CCSO once did an exchange with the Netherlands. We received one male cop and a lady, who I'll call Gretchen Gootentah. Gretchen was a 6-foot-two blond beauty who spoke seven languages, had a Master's degree, and was a martial arts expert--as several CCSO kung-fuers who practiced with her could attest to.

Asked Gretchen one day how the Netherlands got away with legalizing marijuana and prostitution, two crimes that sap our police resources. She said they weren't legal, just overlooked. In the Netherlands if a crime wasn't really causing any problem they officially overlooked it.

As an example, you could have small amounts of marijuana with no problem. Even buy and smoke it in some restaurants. Police were not allowed to search persons for these minor amounts. But, you weren't allowed to deal marijuana or any hard drug unless you wanted to face severe penalties.

I'M PEDDLIN' AS FAST AS I CAN

Prostitution was the same way. Prostitutes openly advertised in display windows on the streets or solicited in public. No problem. Everyone realized that prostitution would never be stopped.

When asked what she thought of our methods, she said it seemed a huge waste of resources.

She might be on to something.

HENRY'S "BOG"

At a time when Henry Kissinger was damn near as famous as Donald Duck, he made a visit to Naples. Henry, former Secretary of State, Nobel Prize Winner, and purported horny old man, dropped down at the Naples Airport to grace some well-heeled locals with his words of wisdom, and collect a handsome honorarium. God knows who would be a party to such absurdity but, that's Naples.

Henry, well padded and impeccable in a tailored suit, alighted from the aircraft where a team of CCSO SWAT Deputies awaited. They were to protect him in case there might be a Cracker or two who would like to thump his pompous, annoying azz. Aground, he pointed to a leather valise, and nodding to a SWAT officer, grunted in his heavy Teutonic accent, *"Boy, my bog."*

Without missing a beat, the Deputy gave Henry a withering stare and replied., *"First off, I'm not your boy. Second, I don't do bogs."*

You couldn't say Henry wasn't a quick study. After first getting a look on his face like someone had squatted in his strudel, he recovered quickly, recognized his faux pas, grabbed his bag, and waddled on toward the terminal, surrounded by his protectors. One couldn't hear what he was mumbling under his breath but you can bet he wouldn't be contributing to the Sheriff's re-election campaign.

After several minutes of laughing when the SWAT guys told me of the incident, I found Captain Wayne Graham, then Commander of the team. *Tell me, it's true, Wayne*, I said. *Tell me it's true.*

Wayne just smiled. Which, was all I needed.

I'M PEDDLIN' AS FAST AS I CAN

I have no doubts, anyway. One of the first weapons a cop collects is a sharp barb for deflating those who have self-inflated themselves to obnoxious proportions.

I can just hear the air hissing out now. Sounds like the Hindenburg when it got pricked.

Dave Johnson had a version of the Henry story, too. He said he and Larry Hargrove once picked up Henry and took him to a Marco hotel. Henry tried to make a bellboy out of Hargrove, then turned on the TV and spent the evening offering rebuttal to the speech that was on; then President Jimmy Carter.

I'm glad he's not as popular as D Duck any longer.

THRIFTY (NUTTY) IDEAS

Government, constant bastion against frivolous spending of the tax payers dollars, sometimes is a little too thrifty.

There was a time when the CCSO would only use Firestone tires. Great tires, cheap price. The City would only use Goodyear. Cost a little more but lasted much longer. A friendly contention raged over who was right.

The argument was settled one evening when both NPD and CCSO cops chased a wild man in a Dodge Challenger up to Bonita Springs. Before the chase was over, the tires blew on all three CCSO cars in the chase and remained inflated on the Goodyears. By the end of the next week all Sheriff's cars were wearing Goodyears.

That's not to say the City was always wise in their spending. When the new PD was built on Goodlette Road our--the Police Department's--specs called for shades over the front windows. If not shaded, a clear view of the lobby and the Comm Center, with dispatchers, was available at night to anyone driving by or taking a gander from the adjoining neighborhoods. Across Goodlette was Naples' ghetto, McDonald's Quarters, not always the NPD's fan base. The City said blinds cost too much so we asked for dark solar film. The cost for this was minimal but some Council folks argued it was excessive. And they won.

During the first week we occupied the building, a rifle shot came zinging through the Comm Center one evening.

I'M PEDDLIN' AS FAST AS I CAN

Fortunately, no one was hit, but several did have to change their laundry. And, suddenly, the film was no longer too expensive. It went up the next day, right after the glass with the bullet hole in it was changed.

MORE THRIFTY (NUTTY) IDEAS

The City of Naples loved the new 1957 Chevy Impalas so much they bought three of them for the Police Department. And paid for them twice. It happened like this.

At the time new car dealerships were scarce in Naples so getting the Chevrolets was a trick. But a used car dealer, who we'll call Slippery Simpson, convinced the City he could get them a good deal on new Chevies. He'd once sold new cars elsewhere, he claimed, and had the inside track on obtaining all the new ones the City wanted. They bought his story, gave him three old police cars as trade-ins, and paid for the merchandise. Slippery told the City they'd have to pick up the cars in Lakeland, where he'd bought them, and made all the arrangements.

When the car picker-uppers arrived there, however, they where met with quizzical looks. No one, it seems had purchased three new Chevies for the City of Naples. Must be some mistake. So the City took delivery of three new ones anyway, and told the dealer there they'd forward payment.

Arriving back in Naples, a search for Ol' Slippery found he'd left town. Driving the then Chief Cale Jones' car he'd taken on trade. The car dealer in Lakeland finally filed a civil action against the City when they never received any money from Slippery or the City and the City had to pay up. Again.

Slippery was later caught out of state, but the money was long gone.

JACK, HARVEY AND THE O'DAY TWINS

Jack Bliss was the Detective who taught me to be a Detective. A big, rowdy, former Paratrooper, he had his own way of doing things. And a grand, dark sense of humor.

Harvey St Jean was the premier South Florida criminal lawyer. The subject of Calvin Trillin's *Harvey St Jean, He*

I'M PEDDLIN' AS FAST AS I CAN

Had It Made, he was at the top of the defense garbage heap in Miami. He was preferred by the criminal cartels. Until, in 1974, when someone shot him to death in his fancy car. The suspect was a Cuban cocaine dealer who claimed Harvey had stolen some of his money. Harvey? A lawyer? Why would he think that.

Harvey may have come close to his just deserts earlier, when he met Jack Bliss. Harvey defended two burglars who we'll call the O'Day twins. The O'Days had a neat little operation going. One would commit a burglary, while the other established an iron clad alibi. If caught, the one with the alibi would go to court. Who knew? They were identical. After he was identified, Harvey, their lawyer, would prove it couldn't have been him using the alibi. Worked great. Until they did it in Naples.

After stealing from a Naples hotel and getting caught, Harvey had gotten them off using the same trick. The O'Days walked. Not Guilty.

The gloating trio were on their way back to Miami when Jack pulled them over, miles down US 41, deep into the desolate swamp. Then Jack had a conversation with them that got their attention.

Jack was vague about what he'd told them, but when he loomed over you, and spoke in that flat, menacing, voice, accompanied by a wry smile, it amounted to one of those offers *you couldn't refuse.*

Like, Your visa to Collier County has just been revoked. And, *Do you know how many folks have disappeared in these swamps? Never a trace found after the gators ate their bodies. And, If you don't think I'm serious, just bring your az back over here and see.*

Harvey and the O'Day brothers never returned to Collier County. Knowing Jack, I wouldn't have either.

I'M PEDDLIN' AS FAST AS I CAN

I'M PEDDLIN' AS FAST AS I CAN

PHOTO--PREVIOUS PAGE--NPD ABOUT 1957
From left, *Ben Caruthers, Sammy McCaa, Ed Hellenek, Col Dirgin, Fred Scott, Chief Cale Jones, Ed Jones, Sam Bass, George McCrea, Robert Dennis, Oren Coates, Unknown lady, Ralph Cox*
Photograph taken in front of the old PD at 8th and 8th South. Building in now used by Fire Department. In the background the old water tower is visible, sitting on the site of the present Government Building.
Most of the officers are wearing cross-draw holsters, popular at the time, and their badge is on the right breast.

Jerry Weinbrenner instructing a Riot Control class in 1965.
From left, *Jerry Weinbrenner, Sam Bass, Dave Dampier, Chester Keene, Dottie Koester, JD Spohn, George McCrea, Nick Triffiletti, Barrie Kee, CH Dasher, Ken Mulling, Richard Davidson*

7th PRECINCT

PRINCE AND THE PUGNACIOUS PUKES

For years a fella named Ralph Cox ran a private security patrol in Port Royal. Ralph was an ex-Naples cop and was diligent in his work, coming out every evening and patrolling all night in a little Morris Minor. His partner was a huge German Shepherd named Prince. (*Ralph's son has been an NPD cop for years*)

After Naples slipped into a comatose state at about 3 AM, Ralph, and the cops on the night shift, would gather at 4 Corners, or the old Royal Castle for coffee, and for those truly adventurous souls, *a hamburger and a bowl of grease* (chili).

Prince was always good for a laugh. Ralph would position him so he could see his own reflection in a storefront window and tell Prince to attack. The dogs would go nuts, snarling, barking, slamming into the window with his huge paws and body until Ralph told him to stop. He was also fearless, one night attacking a 6' gator that was trying to cross 5th Ave So. In short order, the gator demonstrated how he could use his tail like a *Louisville Slugger* and knocked Prince into center field.

I always loved ol' Prince, especially after he saved my arse. Jack Bliss and I answered a call that there was a riot starting at the Royal Castle. When we arrived we found a group of whites and blacks making ugly faces at each other, just on

I'M PEDDLIN' AS FAST AS I CAN

the verge of exploding into a rumble. The cause was racial stupidity.

Back then, the Royal Castle had a back window that blacks used to place their orders. They didn't go inside, although they had every right to under the law. But rather than start trouble, they used the back window. To some drunken rednecks, that night, that wasn't far enough away. They wanted them off the property. The blacks declined. One redneck said he'd get his gun. One black said that was okay, he had a "shooter" in his car, too. That's about when Jack and I arrived.

Anyone with a lick of sense knows not to break up a fight. Most times, they'll both turn on you. But when you're paid to stop them. . ..

Jack and I were immediately surrounded by the nasty bunch. Jack said, "Get back to back and keep your gun handy. I'm not takin' any ass whoopin' for this money." I did as he said and was getting ready to start singin' *Please Send My Saddle Home* when I beheld a wonderful sight. Ralph hurrying into the parking lot, being pulled by a raging Prince. Seems they were stopping by for a snack and saw what was happening.

There are two things that will get an A-hole's attention: The racking of a shotgun, and the snarling of a police dog. One bark from Prince and the crowd evaporated. Vamoosed! *GONE*!

After that, I used to carry dog biscuits in my car in case I happened to run into my hero. I'd buy Ralph a hamburger every once in a while, too.

PAYBACKS ARE A BITCH

If Ed had been a wrestler, he'd have been labeled *Haystack* or *Man Mountain* or, at least, *Big Ed*. Because that he was. About 300 pounds with a neck like a keg of nails and fingers like smoked sausages. Mostly muscle, too, from his years of pulling the nets in his trade as a fisherman.

Big Ed was a mean 'un, with a disposition like a gorilla with hemorrhoids. Not someone to trifle with. He was a

I'M PEDDLIN' AS FAST AS I CAN

regular customer of the NPD or Sheriff's Office, usually producing a legendary encounter.

Once Ed had possession of a skiff thats ownership was in dispute. The boat was in the water near Boat Haven. Cops were trying to figure how to get the boat started, so they could drive it to the ramp and up on their trailer, when Big Ed arrived. He said he didn't have the keys with him, but that was no problem. And it wasn't. He just leaned over the seawall and lifted the boat, motor and all, up to dry ground.

Another time, we had a warrant to serve on him. It required him to go to jail and bond out. One of our biggest officers, Jack Bliss, went out to do the dirty work. Ed's tiny wife, Sweet Pea, greeted Jack at the door and warned him that Ed was asleep and didn't take kindly to being awakened. Jack told her he was just gonna have to be ticked off cause *this* wouldn't wait.

In the bedroom, he called Big Ed's name, eliciting no response. So, he put his hand on Ed's arm and shook him. Bad move. Ed spun around, clamped Jack's arm like a vice and said, "Don't mess with me when I'm sleepin'." Jack, in agony, replied, "No problem, Mr. Ed. I have a warrant for your arrest. When you get up, drop by the station and we'll process it." And that's how it worked.

Knowing all these tales, Dave Johnson, couldn't believe the message that was broadcast over his police radio. *Big Ed said he needs help, Sweet Pea was beating on him.* Sweet Pea? At about 110 pounds. Dave eagerly took the call. This was something he had to see.

He could hear Ed howling when he arrived on the scene. Going inside, he found Ed on the floor, his leg in a cast. Seems he'd broken it fishing. Standing over him was Sweet Pea, with an aluminum baseball bat, taking measured, hefty swings at the cast. She'd already busted it open and was now getting to Ed's beefy leg. He howled like a werewolf with each blow.

Dave, enjoying the sight, watched her deliver a little more agony, then stopped her. It seems Sweet Pea was playing catch-up for years of putting up with the brute. There's a lesson to be learned here.

That's the way it works with little women. Folks used to ask me who I was afraid of. "Sandy", I'd say. They'd laugh, Sandy, my wife, at just over 5 feet tall and 100 pounds, and me six feet and over 200. "It's true," I'd say. "Ever since she found out I have to sleep sometime, I've lived in fear."

A good thing to keep in mind.

WORST CASE OF WHAT?

After you spend a lifetime in the cop business surprises are few. They do come, though. Here're two that rattled my cage. You may find them hard to believe. Had I not read the actual court papers, I wouldn't have believed them, either.

The first happened over by Lake Okeechobee. I'd gone there to pick up a prisoner and got to telling war stories with one of the Deputies. He topped my best one all to hell with this.

A black man had been out on the town one evening and had consumed too much liquid stupid. Too drunk to make his way home, he hailed a taxi and rode it to his downtrodden project rental room. Arriving, he found he was short of money and decided to run for it and not pay. He didn't get far before the taxi driver pulled his trusty hog-leg and blew up his insolvent fare. Stone dead. The cops, of course, charged the taxi driver with Second Degree Murder.

A grand jury was convened to decide the matter. The actual decision read like this. No true bill. (No charges) *A negro shouldn't take a taxi ride he can't pay for.*

The second happened in Eastern Tennessee, near Etowah, where I worked a short time. I guess every law enforcement agency in the area had a copy of the coroner's verdict in this particular case, and every new cop got to read it. To sort of show them the lay of the land, I guess.

It seems a car with three black tourists ventured into a mountain village where blacks were not allowed. And yes, that was still possible in Tennessee in the 1960's. They entered the little town but never came out. Their Cadillac,

I'M PEDDLIN' AS FAST AS I CAN

with New York plates, was found abandoned. Now, driving a Caddy with New York plates would put you in disfavor in many places in the South, but one occupied by blacks was tantamount to loading up with vials of nitro-glycerin and doing a bungee jump.

The three missing folks were found hanging by their necks in a tree. This was the actual coroner's verdict: *Worst case of mass suicide I've ever seen.*

THE AMAZING PURPLE STUFF

When Jack Bliss taught me to be a detective, one of the grand things he showed me was what he called purple stuff. Like gentian violet, the granular treatment for fungal infections, it had a persistent stain and, when diluted, a little bit went a long way.

We'd use it to catch sneak thieves, pilferers, and such. Rub on a little of the powder, and just wait for normal sweat or any moisture to do its work. Pretty soon everything was purple and it wouldn't come off. I loved the stuff. Not everyone did.

Chester Keene remembers the irate mother whose toddler had gotten too close to a newspaper rack's coin box we'd doctored. Some jerk had been stealing the money from the ones on the street so we'd doctored a few. Poor little Junior had turned into a Purple Paper Eater.

Long after Jack had left, I was still using the amazing purple stuff, once to catch a desk officer who was stripping turned in "lost and found" wallets of the cash. I doctored some of the money in one with purple stuff dust, and when the dispatcher turned up at the end of his shift with violet hands, he also left our employ.

Later on we came up with state of the art purple stuff. We were trying to find out who was stealing gas from the pump both the NPD and the Fire Department used. It was located behind the old station and we filled police and fire vehicles using the honor system. Pump 'er full and write on a clipboard log how many gallons, vehicle number, and initials.

I'M PEDDLIN' AS FAST AS I CAN

Trouble was, the honor system only works if you're honorable and some cops or smoke breathers weren't.

If surveillance video cameras had been in use at the time, we could've sure used them. But they weren't. Black lights, however, that were really purple, were in limited use after the cops found out they would fluoresce (glow) on body fluids. We stole the idea from Hippies who used them to make Grateful Dead posters look really groovy. But what we needed now was a powder that would glow when diluted in gasoline.

Jack first suggested we save our urine and pour it in. Didn't work, too diluted in the hundreds of gallons tank. Neither of us were willing to donate blood or other bodily fluids--although the thought did cross our minds. I was kinda glad it didn't. Would've been hard to explain in court, pouring pee in a storage tank. Finally we found the new purple stuff, and a teaspoon full made a 1000 gallons of gas glow like a lightenin' bug in a coal miner's shorts. Dave Dampier remembers the name of the chemical I'd long forgotten. *Anthracene.* We poured it in and waited.

The next night we made a round of the parking lot with a portable black light. Two cars glowed around the gas cap. One car belonged to a fireman, the other to one of our civilian employees. Both fessed up to the thefts and the shortages stopped.

Mike Grimm remembers using it on a baited purse we put in the nurse's locker room at the hospital. One of the nurses had sticky fingers. Probably the one that emptied bedpans. Anyway, when Mike checked with the black light, the whole bathroom was glowing and so was she.

Great stuff, that purple.

CALE JONES
Cale Howard Jones was the first Naples Police Chief. He served for 31 years until his retirement in 1958. Before being appointed Chief, he was the Town Marshall. (Tom Weeks the *first* Town Marshall.) He still has the record for being the Chief with the most service in that position. And that's not easy to do!

I'M PEDDLIN' AS FAST AS I CAN

Cale and his family moved down from Jasper, Georgia in about 1922. He and his father and brothers worked on constructing the Tamiami Trail. Cale was known as a formidable "law and order" man who did what was necessary to make Naples a safe and peaceful community.

His son, Ed was on the NPD for a number of years and his nephew, Jimmy Jones, was on the Naples Fire Department and later was Chief of the North Naples Fire Department.

HEAVY'S FERTILE FEET

Cops get to see folks at their best and worst. And some characters that just make you scratch your melon and wonder under which category of *human being* they should be listed.

There was such a dude who was called Heavy, because of his size I imagine. He was just reasonably tall, but thick, his wrists and ankles like 4x4's. He was also a drunkard and brawler and thief, earning him frequent vacations in our jail.

For his health's sake, it was probably a good thing as he was filthy beyond belief, the stench intolerable. When he came to the hoosegow, we'd hose him down and clean him up as best we could so the other inmates wouldn't gag and heave up their weenies and beans.

Once, during this process, he removed his rotten work boon-dockers, and the sickening stink caused strong men to stagger and fall back. When told to remove his socks, he tugged at them but the foot part remained in place. On closer inspection we found he'd worn the socks so long, without removing them, they'd *grown to his feet*. Yep, grown to his feet. We had to take him to the hospital to have them removed. (*The doctor soaked them and scraped them off a little at a time.*)

Another time, during booking, he was removing the contents of his crusty wallet, and among the cards was a huge Palmetto bug. He gently took it out and put it on the

I'M PEDDLIN' AS FAST AS I CAN

counter as though it was a pet. Noting our stares he said, "What? I lives with 'em."

Thereby removing all doubt that what we suspected was certainly true.

NPD'S PRISON RELEASE PROGRAM

At the old Naples Police Building, at 8th and 8th South, the parking lot was in the rear, by the gas pumps. There was no rear door from the PD to the lot, requiring you to exit the front and hoof around the building. Inconvenient, and cops don't like that. So it was decided a door needed to be cut in the back wall, next to the parking lot.

As always, there was no money for the project. But, there was free labor available from the inmates. More specifically, the trustees, who could be let out of their cell with a reasonable expectation they wouldn't catch the next Bloodhound Bus to Slick City.

At the time we had only one who met the criteria. Hershel Hump, we'll call him, was a good ol' boy who was a victim of love. The love of booze, hooch, *liquid stupid*. He wasn't a pure dunce, but he wasn't going to be designing any rockets either. When he got a full gut of the *Anchor Lounge's* finest swill, he'd do anything. His last misadventure was DUI. He'd left the *Anchor* and made it four blocks to Four Corners, where he dutifully stopped for a red light. And waited. And passed out behind the wheel, earning him three months in the *Bastille*, of which he had 6 weeks remaining.

Chief Ben Caruthers told Hershel that if he'd cut a doorway thru the back wall, he could go home as soon as he was finished. Hershel jumped at the proposition and, with a two-pound hammer and concrete chisel, commenced with vigor.

Trouble was, the City Jail had been built to Federal Prison standards. The exterior walls were one-foot thick crammed full of reinforcing bars. At the end of the first day he'd excavated a hole about as big as a hamster's nest.

Hershel could've made a better deal if he'd waited a few years until the Sheriff's new jail was constructed. Some of the laborers on that project, figuring one day they'd probably be residents, mixed the mortar about ninety-percent sand and ten-percent cement. And they hid hacksaw blades in the

I'M PEDDLIN' AS FAST AS I CAN

mortar joints. The first night the jail was open, several convicts scraped out the mortar joints with spoons and escaped.

Not so the Naples Jail whose walls were *poured concrete*. So hard that Hershel was still pecking well into his fifth-week. And he'd only chipped out a hole big enough to allow the passage of a fat dog. With the prospects of him having to make *life* before the project was completed, some industrial saws were rented. And some welding torches to cut the steel.

And Hershel finally made it back to the *Anchor*. As irony would have it, when the new back door was completed, Hershel was one of the first customers to pass thru it. On his way back to jail.

HOLLYWOOD HOODWINKS

The movie people were in town again and we met their arrival with mixed emotions. Watching movie production was fun, but you had to watch it with one eye. And keep the other on the participants. They were notorious flakes. In the past they'd borrowed police uniforms from us, then tried to steal them. Once a swamp buggy they'd borrowed for some epic had disappeared. One group even stole a PAL football uniform. So, when Otto Preminger's people contacted us to work security for them, we were wary.

Otto was a big deal at the time, and his movie *Tell Me You Love Me, Junie Moon* was touted to be Oscar material. It starred Liza Minnelli, Ken Howard, and former pro football player, and later action star Fred "The Hammer" Williamson was a featured actor.

It was to be a standard deal, off-duty cops and the bill to be paid at the end of the job. (Now this service must be paid for in advance) The cops got to eat and drink the same thing the crew did. We agreed.

Things didn't start out well. One late evening I received a call urging me to go to the Anchor Bar and Lounge. Major faux pas. Arriving, I was greeted by the owner, Bill F, who was so distraught he could only mumble, "I don't even sell peanuts." An officer on the scene made things clearer.

Preminger, Minnelli, Howard, and Williamson had been drinking and dancing. Suddenly, Bill came up to them and said they would have to leave. When asked why, he said "Because of him," pointing to Williamson, who was black. This caused an um-pah storm, with Preminger yelling at Bill he'd never heard of such crap and Bill yelling for them to get out. By the time I arrived, they had left.

I talked to Bill who was still mumbling about not even selling peanuts. Finally, he calmed enough to tell me: "I can't allow niggers in here. You know the crowd here, I'd lose them all. And you let in one coon, pretty soon the place is full of them. That's why I don't sell food. Don't even sell peanuts. If you don't sell food, the Feds can't make you let them in."

Don't know if the "peanuts" thing was true but, at the time, having blacks and whites mingle in The Anchor, where liquid stupid flowed like tropical rain, could be a bad idea. The irony was, Williamson was a nice guy, educated--someone said he had a degree in architecture--and the Anchor crowd was delighted to have him and his celebrity among them.

The incident, blew over, and Williamson said *no hard feelings*. Had it been me, I'd have been real pissed off! Howsumever, Preminger was reticent on the issue, taking his revenge on Naples later.

HOLLLYWOOD HOODWINKS-Part 2

It seems Otto had chosen Naples for "the most beautiful skies in the world." And because it was far enough away from Miami that he could dodge the union, who he was in a bitter dispute with. Something about using scabs, non-certified movie makers in this most unionized of businesses. Or so we were told. Otto was saving money by using scabs. We found out later, he knew several other economies.

Well, the movie ticked on, with several scenes shot on the beach south of the pier, and at the Edgewater Beach Hotel, where cast and crew were staying. They were nice enough folks, except the self-important Preminger, and everything seemed to be sailing on like a fat duck on a smooth pond. Then one night, about two in the AM, I received a call from the desk man at the Edgewater. I'd talked to him previously and, not trusting movie people, asked him to call me if anything unusual went on.

"Otto and the whole crew have packed and are loading up. Most are gone already," he said. "Moved out like Oral Roberts' tent show when folks heard he'd healed that geezer in the wheelchair about 300 times."

"Be right down," I told him. I hurried but was too late. Located the desk man. "He pay his bill?" I asked.

"Nope, but his accountant left me his card with his office address on it, said to mail it there." I wrote down the name and address and phone number in New York City.

We, and everyone else, are still waiting to be paid. The firm, address, and phone number were bogus. The cards had been printed in advance so this scam was a premeditated act. We never caught up with Otto, but were glad to be rid of him.

After production, Lisa Minnelli, was quoted as saying she'd never work with the "tyrannical" director again. And the movie didn't do well at the box office. Most critics thought it was not Otto's best work. He had few good ones afterwards. I saw the movie and though the actors did an excellent job, the thing was so slow in many parts it'd put a junkie riding out a horse load of crystal meth to sleep.

HOLLYWOOD HOODWINKS Part 3

It was 1977 and they were filming a low-budget biggie called *Thunder and Lightening* in Naples. It starred David Carradine and Kate Jackson. And the director wanted to blow up a Cadillac on the end of Gordon Drive. Gordon Drive, an area so rich and uptight even the gentle Gulf Breeze squeaks like rusty hinges on a coffin.

"You wanna what?" I asked him.

"Blow up, burn a Caddy. Right in the middle of the street," he reiterated.

"Don't think so," I said. "First, there's the danger, then the damage to the street, then the explosion noise, then the lynching party that will form shortly thereafter. The director laughed. "No danger," he said, "very little noise, no damage

I'M PEDDLIN' AS FAST AS I CAN

to anything but the Caddy. Let me show you how we do it." And he did.

Charley Sanders, a Deputy with the CCSO, was rigging the car for the explosion. Charley had experience in such matters, having been a stunt driver, Nascar racer, and mechanical genius. He was also doing the stunt driving for the film.

Charley had disabled the hinges and placed hydraulic rams on the doors, hood, trunk, and bigger ones on the frame, shooting straight into the ground.

He also put a thing he called a cooker in between the front and rear seat, a round cylinder a little larger than a propane tank. Inside the open top's tray he put some sawdust and poured in a pint of gasoline. It would be fired electrically. I took Charley's word that most neighbors wouldn't even know the stunt had happened.

The Caddy was moved into position, the cameras rolled, and Charley threw a switch. The hydraulic rams shot into the doors, hood and trunk and they flew off the car. Simultaneously, the gas exploded inside the car sending a raging wall of fire out the holes where the doors had been. Then the two rams on the bottom of the car hit the road and the car jumped into the air. And there was no sound--it was added later--or damage, except to the car. I later saw the scene in the movie and was amazed at the seeming destruction, knowing how they'd done it.

So, a few days later, when the director wanted permission to machine gun all the front windows out of a house they'd rented on Gordon Drive, and assured me no actual bullets would be fired, I said "Work out, Bubba. No problem."

GUN CONTROL: A NO-BRAINER

Several years ago the Illinois town of Morton Grove was in the news for a new ordinance their City Council passed. No guns in Morton Grove. None! A little later, in 1982, Kennesaw, Ga passed a gun law, too. Theirs read, if you live in this town you'll damn sure own a gun and know how to use it. This dichotomy of thinking intrigued me and I began

I'M PEDDLIN' AS FAST AS I CAN

to track the outcome. Over the years, I've kept it up, the last check yesterday.

Morton Grove's robbery rate tripled in a short time. Their crime rate increased. Police officials there told me they were going to have to hire more officers.

Over the years several other cities in Illinois thought, for some reason, their crime rate wasn't high enough so they passed similar laws. As of yesterday, all have been rescinded. Except Morton Grove, who, evidently, can't recognize a stupid idea when they puke one up.

Kennesaw, on the other hand, had crime reduced so much cops there told me they was worried there might be lay-offs. This shouldn't be surprising. If you were a criminal would you rather burgle a house that you knew was free of guns or one that you knew had at least one gun and someone who knew how to use it? Duh! Criminals are cowards. They'd rather rob an 80 year-old woman than a 60 year-old man. Unless he was in a wheelchair. Cowardly scumbags!

Yet this simple concept is lost on many who still blame the gun for crime problems. That's like blaming the fork when you're in a feeding frenzy and stab your hand instead of the taters. A gun is just a tool.

All folks need to do is look at New York, whose 1911 Sullivan Act is the oldest and toughest in the country. When I was a cop and visited there, I had to leave my gun outside the city. Yet, guns are as common as rude, smelly, taxi drivers in towel turbans.

Go figure.

YOU'RE A WHAT?

He looked like the perfect applicant. Physically fit, intelligent, and eager to be a cop. And, he'd just graduated from Florida State. But, nobody's perfect. The problem was his application. In the box where you checked off race, he'd marked American Indian. Which he obviously wasn't. I looked at the application again, then back at him and said, "Son, if you're an American Indian I'm *Aunt Jemima*."

Chuckling at my remark--I said he was a smart lad--he said, "That's what I'm claiming and that's what counts." He went on. "I took a class in college on how to get a job and the EEOC rules are *you are what you claim to be*."

Doing the hiring at the SO, I was well aware of the EEOC, The Equal Employment Opportunity Commission. It was a federal agency that told you how many folks you had to have of each race. We weren't under a mandate as yet since we tried as best we could, but it was a tough nut. There was just the three of us: Sarah Creamer, Dave Johnson, and me. We were trying to hire over 100 folks a year, doing all the polygraphs, background investigations, interviews, and scheduling. And we gave everyone eligible a shot. But, it seemed the EEOC wanted us to hire people who were the right race, but otherwise unqualified. What the applicant had told us seemed to go against their intent. I told him that I was gonna make a call and I'd get back with him.

Called the office of the EEOC in Alexandria, Va. Had this conversation:

"Just had an applicant who is not an Indian but is claiming to be one for employment purposes," I said.

"Yes, and. . ."

"And is that legal?"

"Sure is. He can claim to be anything on the list. But it's only good for employment purposes. He can't claim he's an Indian and then go open up a casino. Different rules cover that."

I thanked her, hung up the phone and gave Dave Johnson, who was also keenly interested in this turn of events, a smile. "Why don't you go get Tonto," I said, "and give him a polygraph test. What he told us is the truth. And life is gonna be much easier around here."

So soon, after we'd made corrections to minor mistakes on new applications, we had guy's with names like Flynn Patrick O'Bradley who were mysteriously listed as an Eskimo. Or Denzil P. Fuddpucker claiming Pacific Islander heritage. Just for purposes of auditing, of course. And everyone was happy.

Ridiculous? Certainly. Nearly as asinine as the EEOC rules that prompted it. Your tax dollars at work.

I'M PEDDLIN' AS FAST AS I CAN
RANDY

Randy was a tall, good-looking kid that, when I met him, should've been a senior in high school. Instead, he was in the City Jail. For something stupid, drunk and disorderly, something like that. Back then they put juveniles in jail for minor infractions if they were incorrigible, repeat offenders. That was Randy. Yet, he was one of the most likable kids I ever met. Smart, multi-talented, and with a smile that made you feel good.

When Randy was in jail, I would teach him how to develop and print evidence photos in our little darkroom. It was actually an unused stairwell in the jail we blocked off and painted black. Randy was a quick learner and was soon developing and printing better than his teacher.

During these work sessions we'd have long conversations, mostly about his situation. It seemed such a waste, the way his life was going. He said, candidly, that he knew exactly what his problem was. When he got carousing with his buddies, pretty soon they were drunk, then trouble would soon follow. He was hanging out with the wrong crowd.

"Well then," I asked, "why don't you hang with the right crowd?"

"You don't get it." he said, "Because of my reputation, no one *decent* wants to be around me," he said. "That, or their parents won't let them near me."

Took me a while to swallow that one, but when I did it was like a punch in the gut. Advice, easy answers, aren't alway easy for the recipient. Or even possible. I do know he tried but it didn't work.

One night shortly after, I was called to the scene of a homicide. A young, enraged man had tried to crash through the jalousie windows of a house where his girlfriend lived. The father had shot him several times in the chest. I looked down at the face of Randy. He'd evidently been screaming with rage when the .357 slugs put him to rest. The rage I'd never seen before but had heard of and knew was in there.

When a child starts going bad, and travels so far, they come to a point where it's hard to turn around. You have to catch them early and make the necessary repairs. Sometimes

I'M PEDDLIN' AS FAST AS I CAN

a hitch in the military does it. Or a brush with the law. But the courts and juvenile system seldom work for hard case offenders.

LOU GIBBS

Today's political correctness has strangled common sense. There's nothing you can say that isn't taken as an insult by someone. You wonder how this insanity ever became so dominate, let alone even achieved a foothold. Then you remember some characters who, by their actions, planted, fertilized, and watered it. Such a character was Lou Gibbs.

Lou was the Chief of Corrections at the Collier County Jail. Loud and abrasive, I personally think he had a warped sense of humor rather than being a rabid bigot and misogynist. But, there he was and as far as Lou was concerned you could take him or leave him. Except, he was a Chief and had to be accommodated if you wanted to remain employed.

At the time, I was doing the hiring at the CCSO. Lou went through jail personnel like Tiger goes through mistresses. Once I took him two ladies who were applying to be his personal secretary. I told him both were excellent candidates and I'd like him to interview them and make a selection. Both were sitting outside his office, the door ajar. Lou thundered, "Bring 'em both in and bend 'em over the desk. Then I can pick one." I know they must have heard him.

Another time he called one of his rookie employees, an Oriental, to his office. "Go to the armory and get me a pair of left-handed handcuffs he said." This, of course, is an old joke pulled on novices. There is no such animal as left-handed cuffs.

Later, the Oriental jailer returned to Lou's office and admitted, sheepishly, that he couldn't locate the cuffs. Lou said to him, "Couldn't find 'em? You didn't have any damn trouble finding *Pearl Harbor*."

Lou finally quit and returned to Indiana. The next winter we received a photograph from him. Lou was lying naked in the snow, belly down. The caption read, How we measure the snow depth in Indiana.

I'M PEDDLIN' AS FAST AS I CAN

That was Lou. He's long gone now. And, I have to admit I liked him. A lot.

PS Someone reminded me that I was gonna have a big political correctness problem cause Japs and such aren't called Orientals now. Supposed to be called Asians. . .at least for today.

CLOSET CRITTERS

Peril comes in many forms for cops. Sometimes with disastrous and lasting effects. One night, Chester Keene and Ray Loosey found this out when answering a seemingly innocent call.

A lady had some kind of critter in her house. She'd seen the alien scurry in off the patio and then lost view of it. It wasn't a snake, it was something furry. About the size of a cat. And she was scared. Our blue knights were dispatched.

Arriving on the scene, Chester tried to calm the complainant, assuring her that everything was in good hands. They'd search the house and dispatch the hirsute intruder posthaste.

In just a few minutes Loosey did indeed find the culprit when he opened a closet door. And he was shocked. So was the householder, who was standing behind him. So alarmed she shoved Loosey into the closet and slammed the door. And the critter, also upset, did what those of his species do. Being a skunk, he sprayed Loosey down.

Now I know all of you, at some time or other, have whiffed the product of a skunk's displeasure. Maybe just driving down the road the distinctive odor has swept into your vehicle. It's a slap in the nose not soon dispelled. That in mind, consider being actually sprayed. Or being close up to some poor soul that was. Unbearable.

While Chester and the lady teared and choked, Loosey ran to the car and started to get in. Chester stopped him, telling him that if he got that stink on the interior, the car would be ruined, it'd never come out. What to do?

Chester was always an ingenious cop with a grand sense of humor. So, Loosey was put on the top of the patrol car, and told to lie down and hold on to the light bar. A second car

I'M PEDDLIN' AS FAST AS I CAN

followed to ward off traffic in case Loosey lost his grip and tumbled to the asphalt. In this fashion, he was hauled to the rear of the PD where the hose used to wash cars was put to use in an attempt to fumigate our smelly savior.

The hosing down kinda worked but Loosey was still rank. He wanted to go home and shed the horrid smelling costume and get in a good bath. And this was the only reasonable thing to do. But, on arriving at his house, his wife had other ideas. She wouldn't let Loosey in.

Eventually, the situation worked itself out. Loosey was sanitized, although there were those who said he had a distinctive air about him for several days. And for some time after, Critter in the House calls were answered by cops in Hazmat gear.

Handy Hint: Should you or your dog get zapped by a polecat, douse yourself with tomato juice. Seriously, it works.

BE CAREFUL WHAT ADVICE YOU GIVE

Cops give out a lotta advice. Better slow down. Don't do that again. Go home and sober up. Stuff like that. Sometimes it's heeded, most times just for a while, or not at all. But, sometimes a joke is taken for advice with disastrous results.

We had a black business woman who owned a juke/restaurant, The Green Top Social Palace, in McDonald's Quarters. Her name was Lillie Williams, but all referred to her as Miz Lillie and she was a force to be reckoned with.

Miz Lillie had been having trouble with a drunken customer, who we'll call S. Jay. She asked him to leave and he wouldn't. So she called the PD.

On arriving, Miz Lillie said S. Jay had left the premises, but she knew he would come back and cause more trouble. She didn't know what to do.

Our officer, Rich David, said joking, "Why don't you get out that pistol of yours and shoot him." Everyone knew that Lillie kept a hog-leg under the counter. The cop then closed out the incident and returned to patrol.

About thirty-minutes later Miz Lillie called the station. "S. Jay come back and I shot him." Officers hurried to the scene,

I'M PEDDLIN' AS FAST AS I CAN

one of them Mike Grimm. Mike said Lillie came up with that pistol and just started spraying lead. It was a miracle she hit the intended target. She shot her juke box, a pinball machine and scared the hell out of most of her customers. The ones who weren't hugging the floor were flying out of there like their asses were on fire. And, S. Jay had also been hit, a bullet in the leg.

When asked why she'd done it she said, "Cause Officer Rich *told* me to," she replied.

And I guess she was right.

PS *The Green Top Social Palace had many names. It was also called the Green Top Social Club or Place. But, Miz Lillie, herself, said it was supposed to be the Green Top Social Palace but the sign painter misspelled it to Place.*

THEY ALWAYS DO

In the early 80's I worked a short time as a Deputy in Tennessee. After about two days on the job, I gathered all my family and gave them the following instructions. "If a cop up here asks you to do anything, do it. Anything." There was good reason for this advice. These were the meanest, wildest, critters I'd ever encountered in law enforcement. All had blackjacks and other instruments of misery--that were just a memory in LE elsewhere--and they loved to use them. Especially if you didn't do just what they said. And the courts would back them up.

Most cops are against this. That's not to say that someone who attacks a police officer isn't due a demonstration of real police violence. But just beating up folks cause you can is usually a cowardly act.

Of course, their clientele were often hillbillies, or Deliverance folks as I called them. Maybe the cops in my part of Tennessee had found from dealing with them what worked and what didn't. They were different.

We had one community that didn't even recognize the existence of law enforcement. They wouldn't talk to you, look at you, or assist a cop in any way. And they had their own justice system. We would regularly get calls from delivery folks, or mail carriers that a body was lying beside the street, a victim of hillbilly justice.

On evening we received a call from the state prison. They had released a hillbilly from our county who had promised, as soon as he got back home, to kill his uncle. The uncle had testified against him in court.

We took the threat seriously. If a hillbilly says he's gonna go home and get his gun and kill you, you better arm yourself. They don't make idle threats. So we called the uncle and warned him, then headed to his house, about 40 miles away.

On the way there, we saw a car pulled over to the side of the road. On inspection, our quarry was passed out inside. Along with three other drunkards. Seems he'd caught a ride with them, and just becoming a free man, had way too much fun with liquid stupid. We gathered them all up, and headed for the jail.

Mine was a big thug about the size of Hulk Hogan. His arms were so huge I had to use two sets of cuffs, extending the length, to cuff his arms behind his back. On the way to the jail, he was strangely quiet. I usually tried to joke with or at least talk to folks, but he'd have none of it. It wasn't until we got to the jail, and I was locking him up, that he finally spoke. "I wanna thank you for not beatin' me with your blackjack," he said.

I was confused. "First off, I don't use a blackjack and second you didn't do anything to warrant an ass whuppin'. Why'd you think I'd beat you?"

He shrugged. "Cause they always do," he said.

And I have no doubt about it.

GOOD ADVICE?

Went to the doctor the other day and he said if I didn't lose some weight I was gonna die. I told him he caught me once, maybe twice, but that line wouldn't work any longer. He was confused. I explained that he told me years ago if I didn't quit smoking I was gonna die. So not wanting to die, I quit.

I'M PEDDLIN' AS FAST AS I CAN

Then, a couple years later, he said if I didn't get my cholesterol down I was gonna die. I told him I though quitting cigarettes would insure I wouldn't die. Nope, he says, cholesterol would whack you, too. So started working on that.

Now, he says I'm too fat, gonna die again. Thinking back, I'm beginning to suspect his advice. And honesty.

We once had a neighbor who looked like Gandhi. Had a towel wrapped around his head looked like a turban, emaciated body, baggy drawers. Went running in the neighborhood every afternoon. One day I was picking up the mail and he stopped at the mailbox, held on, gasping for air. I asked if he was okay and he said yeah but the running was miserable, made him feel like he was dying. So I asked why the hell he was doing it. He said he'd had a mild heart attack and the doctor said if he didn't start running he'd die. Sound familiar?

I told him he should get a second opinion and he said he had; exercise was where it was at if you didn't want to die. So away he goes, huffing and puffing, his face twisted in agony like when Denzil caught his *cahones* in the churn. But, he ran for about two more weeks. Then they found him beside the road, flies buzzing around his mouth, dead as his plan for eternal life.

And there was another guy, older, small in stature but well built. Used to run by the station every morning on his way to the beach. There, he'd swim outta sight, then swim back.

Had a conversation with him one day about sharks. How they were catching hammerheads and all types of baddies off the pier. (At the time you could fish for sharks off the pier and all the baiting caused them to migrate there for a meal)

Our athlete just laughed, said his doctor said swimming was the best exercise he could do and he was gonna keep it up. A few weeks later he turned up missing, after swimming out of sight. Every time I see Jaws I think of him. Or maybe his old heart just exploded like Gandhi's. Then I ponder on living seventy-some wonderful years or ninety-some miserable ones.

CURSE OF THE GYPSIES

Icy Winter winds blow much more South than freeze-dried snowbirds. Criminals, too, despise long underwear, butt-deep snow, and red dripping noses, and flock to Florida like woodpeckers to rotten mangos. This cunning gaggle includes everything from serial killers to bubble gum thieves. Among the sleaziest of these weasels, are the con artists—who'd steal their mother's last breath with a kiss. For these peddlers of deceit, no act is too reprehensible; no lie too shameful to perpetuate their scams. Their favorite targets? A group that can usually least afford the loss: senior citizens.

Even this trash has a hierarchy. At the bottom, neck-deep in criminal primordial sludge, just one rung above the child molesters, wife beaters, and sleazy telemarketers, lurk the Gypsies. In Naples, during the 60's and 70's the Gypsies spread an annual plague that cost residents thousands in cash and a boundless debt of grief. Their specialty was the home repair business.

At the time, most South Florida homes had a built-up roof system. These were favored because shingles had not reached a state of the art that allowed them to withstand the tropical sun. In addition, many of the roofs were either flat or had pitches not steep enough to drain a shingle roof. The built-up roof was composed of layers of tar and roofing material topped with gravel and a special thick, white paint that held the gravel in place and reflected the sun. Every few years the sun would take its toll on the roof requiring repainting. The Gypsies made a fortune coating these roofs with cheap white wash. They also re-coated asphalt driveways with a *special* substance that was largely used motor oil and gasoline. The roof jobs lasted until the first rain and the driveway coating eventually dissolved the pavement's asphalt.

They were slick sales-folks, promising a low price, then, when the job was complete, using guile or intimidation to extract an exorbitant price. They'd pick a middle-class neighborhood and cruise around until a worn roof or driveway was spotted. Then a pleasant young man would knock on the door and give his spiel. "We just did a job down the street, and have some material left over, enough to do your driveway. Since we're in the neighborhood, and don't want to throw away our extra coating, we can give you a great price."

The Gypsies also kept an eye out for houses where it appeared there was only one person at home. After spotting one, they'd engage the resident in conversation, at the front door, claiming to be lost and asking for elaborate directions, while other members of the clan entered the rear of the house stealing any valuables small and easily resold.

To compound the problem, due to their hit and run MO, never in town over a few days, they were nearly impossible to catch and harder still to prosecute. Once the calls started coming in—it took a few days for the shoddy workmanship to show up--they were long gone. In the rare instance they were caught they weren't deterred for long. Always flush with bond money—an absolute necessity since no bondsman in his right mind would touch them—they quickly made bail and disappeared like, well, thieves in the night.

Along with the Gypsies, and fermented in the same vat, were the Irish Travelers. Not real Gypsies, they used the same MO's, and was hard to tell the difference. Many were quartered in South Carolina. At home, they lived in large, well-maintained homes, in compounds and communes like the Hippies, Hare Krishna's, and Kennedy's. They drove expensive vehicles, preferring gaudy, top-end, pickup trucks. On their home ground, they were model citizens. Only when money was short, would they would hit the road, not returning until a sufficient number of marks had been fleeced, or the law got too hot on their trail.

At the time, there was very little coordination between law enforcement agencies. Today's computers and elaborate electronic police networks were still years in the future. Except to corral an elusive, high profile, homicidal maniac like a Ted Bundy, each agency did its own thing and was relatively unaware of what was going on in other jurisdictions. The Gypsies were well aware of the gaping holes in the net and preyed on communities with small local law enforcement agencies who had neither the time nor resources to perform an extended manhunt. This MO allowed them to operate with relative impunity.

This particular year we decided we were going to do a little pro-active enforcement on the Gypsies. I'd recently returned from an investigator's school at the University of Georgia where I'd met a detective out of South Carolina who, because of his homey drawl we'd dubbed Daryl of Dingleberry. Daryl's hobby was studying Gypsies and Irish Travelers. He'd become quite expert on their history, lore, and methods of operation. I gave him a call and asked for his help. He was more than willing, and for the next hour, he passed on helpful strategic hints.

One of his gems proved priceless. Daryl had said, "If you can get aholt of their eatin' utensils you can really tie a knot in their tails."

"How? Starve them to death?" I joked.

"Damn near, Son," he replied. "Gypsies, and they have to be genuine Old World Gypsies, not Irish Travelers, have a ritual they perform on their eatin' gear. Has to be sanctified a certain way and in a certain place. And if an outsider touches it, defiles it by their way of thinkin', they can't use it until it's sanctified again."

"So," I said, "that shouldn't be too much trouble for them. A little mumbo-jumbo here and there."

"Hell it ain't," Daryl said. "They have to go all the way back to their holy ground to perform the ceremony. Could be New York, New Jersey, could be Europe, who knows."

"Are you serious," I asked, at least a little dubious.

"Serious as a nest of crotch crickets," Daryl said. "Write it down, Son, it's the gospel I'm preachin' here."

I wrote it down.

Another of Daryl's suggestions was to enlist the aid of the news media. Making the public aware in advance of the coming plague could give us a slight edge. Who knows, one of them might actually read the stuff, or watch it on TV, and give us a buzz when one of these scumbags showed up at their door. We put our news release together, called the press

I'M PEDDLIN' AS FAST AS I CAN

and were greeted with less than enthusiastic yawns. "News isn't news until it's news." The local paper said they might use it on a slow news day. A few days later, it did show up, buried deep in the bowels of this prestigious organ, just below the garden club news. Yet, some people did read it and we received a few calls, always after the Gypsies were long gone.

We were nearing the end of the season, and the score was Gypsies 30-something, cops zero. They'd hammered us as usual. We'd almost given up hope of catching them when we were finally blessed with a break. The call came in as I was leaving the office for the day. Walking by the communications console, Dotty, the dispatcher waved me over. An elderly widow had answered her door and was greeted by a Gypsy asking for elaborate directions. She'd remembered reading about this scam in the newspaper—God love her—and slammed the door in the maggot's face. Returning to her kitchen, intent on giving us a buzz, she was shoved down by two men who burst from her bedroom and out the back door. Her wedding ring, which she had put on the sink while washing dishes, was missing. Two vehicles were noted hastily leaving the area: one, a bright red pickup truck, the other a second pickup truck with a slide-in camper.

Dotty was preparing to put out the BOLO when an incoming call crackled on the radio.

"I'm 10-50 on this pickup with a camper out here on 41 by Boat Haven," a uniformed officer reported. "When they spotted my marked car, they slowed down, started being *too* law abiding. I pulled 'em over to see to see why they got so righteous all of a sudden. I believe it's a mess of them Gypsies. The driver sounds like, he talks like Dracula, and the grandma looks like that old lady in the movies that hung out with the Wolfman."

Maria Ouspenskaya, I though, remembering the wonderful character actress who appeared in Universal's horror series.

"You want me to hold 'em?" I grabbed the microphone from Dotty, "Right by the marbles. I'm on the way."

I'M PEDDLIN' AS FAST AS I CAN

Heading south on 41, I found the uniform officer, a young hard charger, Byron Tomlinson, and his catch. Clustered around the pickup/camper was a linebacker type that glared at us from under black caterpillar eyebrows. I kept one eye on him. Next to him, the old crone in her full-length black skirt, flowered blouse under a spangled shawl, and huge hoop earrings looking just like Maria Ouspenskaya. Then there was the woman, in a tight t-shirt and jeans, looking nothing special until you got to the eyes. To call them bedroom eyes missed by a mile. These babies were waterbed, satin sheets, mirrors on the ceiling, tie me to the bedpost eyes. When she worked you with them, and she was, magic fingers massaged your body in the nicest places. I wondered how many potholed driveways and leaky roofs those eyes had cost male customers.

While the others in her clan remained silent, Mama Maria jabbered in some guttural tongue, occasionally screeching like a barn owl with laryngitis.

"You see the other pickup?" I asked Tomlinson.

"There was a red pickup in front of 'em. Loaded with five-gallon cans and ladders. They beat it the hell outta here headed toward Miami, when I put the siren on this one," he said nodding toward the truck. "I'd pulled these clowns over before the Gypsy call was broadcast. Didn't know we were lookin' for another pickup."

I checked with the station to see if there had been any other complaints about Gypsies. There had been none. But these people were the real article and I decided to play a little catch up.

I moved to the rear of the truck, opened the door to the camper, and stepped in. It was a jumble of piled clothing, scraps of food, newspapers and magazines; a real boar's nest on wheels. There was nothing that I could conceive would be stolen property. Then I found the mother lode. Wrapped neatly in a velvet silverware case was tableware for eight, their eating utensils. I picked them up and stepped out of the camper. The old crones eyes dilated to the size of her hoop earrings. She lurched for the silverware and was restrained by the uniform.

I'M PEDDLIN' AS FAST AS I CAN

I unrolled the case on the trunk of the marked car, took out each item, and handled it. I continued until each had been touched, or as Daryl had said, defiled.

Then the crone screamed something unintelligible at me, grabbed the hem of her long skirt, and whipped it over her head, exposing what could never again be referred to as her *private* parts. I didn't know whether to be embarrassed, enraged, or to burst out laughing. I certainly felt all those emotions, finally relying on the policeman's best defense, the wise crack.

"How often do you have to feed that thing," I said.

It would have been possible to arrest her for public indecency, but I wasn't sure the charge would hold up. This charge requires that some member of the public be offended by the act. Her family didn't seem embarrassed, indeed some cheered the act. Although there was traffic on U.S. 41, no one had stopped and offered public service as a witness. A police officer is a non-entity in these cases. Exposing yourself to a police officer is the same a flashing a lamp pole, according to the law.

I bundled up the silverware, tossed it in the rear of the camper. "Get out of here I told them. Don't come back. They contained mama, ushered her into the back of the camper then drove off. I congratulated Tomlinson on his good work.

Back at the station Dottie told me the sweet lady found her ring, under the kitchen counter. It had evidently been knocked off the counter when she was roughed up by the Gypsies. She'd scared them away before they could steal anything. Her portable TV had been unplugged, and moved next to the door. Several of her bureau drawers had been opened and rifled. She could find nothing missing.

The thing seemed to be wrapped up so I called Daryl, my mentor on Gypsy affairs, and related the story, adding "I found their silverware, handled it and they were mad as hell."

"Good, they're traditional. They'll have to go back to the homeland to sanctify new utensils. They do anything else, anything strange?

I'M PEDDLIN' AS FAST AS I CAN

Anything strange?"

"Yeah, the momma, I guess, the old hag, hiked her skirt and showed me *her* utensil."

My friend laughed loud and long, and then finally, "Son, you *really did* get to 'em. The old hag cursed you, put her evil eye on you . . . so to speak. It's the worst thing they can do to someone."

"Big deal. I don't believe in that crap. The Tooth Fairy or any politician either."

"Me neither. Besides, she probably wasn't much of a witch, didn't have much power. Depends on her power, you know. Chances of you runnin' into a full-blown Gypsy witch are pretty remote. Probably not more than two or three in the country, rest are back in Romania, that neck of the woods. Fella'd probably have to haul his ass over to Transylvania, the Carpathian Mountains, around in there to find a heavy-duty hex layer. Naw, I don't believe in that stuff. Those that do though, it's a different story. I read of cases where . . . well, you don't wanna hear that."

"Come on, "I said, "I could use a good laugh about now."

"You sure?"

"Lay it on me."

"Well this one fella, couple days after he got flashed by the Bulgarian beaver, he noticed this little red spot on the head of his penile protuberance. Just a little red pimple. But every day it gets bigger and angrier looking. Inna few days it's an open sore. He rubs on every medicine in the cabinet, nothin' works. Tries home remedies, you know, stump water, moldy moss poultices, still nothin'. It' keeps getting worse. Finally, he goes to the doctor, two or three even, still no relief, doctor's can't help, tried everything until it was too late."

"Too late?"

"Well there wasn't much use to keep on medicatin' since his carrot just sorta turned into a Brussels sprout. Kinda ate itself up, then healed over."

"You mean. . .?"

"Yeah, I do. *The Flying Nun* had more landin' gear. Then there's this guy, got hexed, his next kid's born with two..."

Naturally, I didn't believe him. He was having a good laugh at my expense. However, when I think back on it, some strange and terrible things did happen within a few weeks of the Gypsy encounter. First, I was driving to work on U.S. 41 and as I approached the intersection with Airport Road, I saw a car waiting to enter the highway. At the time, there was no traffic signal there. I knew the young woman and smiled at her. She smiled back, slammed the accelerator to the floor, and T-boned me dead center in the passengers door. Totaled both cars. She didn't have a scratch on her, nor did I. I signed the insurance release. The very next day I developed a blinding headache that the doctors couldn't relieve. It lasted, on and off, for ten years.

Later, I asked the young lady why she'd crashed into me. She had to have seen me. "Yes," she said, "I saw you plain as day, smiled back, if you remember, but, an uncontrollable urge came over me to run into you. I couldn't resist. It was like someone was inside my body, controlling me."

And then the worst curse befell me. Shortly thereafter, I was appointed *Chief of Police*.

I know the *Curse of the Gypsy* is ridiculous. Yet sometimes, when I'm alone, watching an old Universal horror flick on the late show and Maria Ouspenskaya appears...

Violation of Civil Rights Explanation

Back then if you were *civil* with the cops, you'd likely get your *rights*. If you weren't civil, you were gonna be *real* disappointed.

Politically Correct Disclaimer

I'm sure that there's a Gypsy or two out there who may read this and claim it's unfair, that I'm taking them all to the river in the same sack. Not true. This story relates my experiences with a few Gypsies. I'm sure there're some wonderful Gypsies out there. Hardworking family folks, a credit to their community, all that. It's just been my misfortune never to have met any of them yet.

10-7

Guilty, your Honor